Quotable

"And do thou (O Reader!)
Bring thy Lord to remembrance in your very soul,
With humility and in reverence,
Without loudness in words,
In the morning and evenings;
And be not thou of those who are unheedful."

– Qur'an 7:205

"Your neighbor's vision is as true for him as your own vision is true for you."

– Miguel de Unamuno. Spanish Intellectual. (d. 1936).

AUTHENTICITY AND ISLAMIC LIBERALISM

(Second Edition With 3 New Supplemental Essays)

Diwani calligraphy in the form of a pear with the phrase:
Alhumdu lillahi, Rabbi al alamin (Glory to God, Lord of the Worlds),
by Nasib Makarim of Lebanon.

Also by Jamal Khwaja

* Living The Qur'an In Our Times

* Quest for Islam

* Five Approaches to Philosophy

* The Call Of Modernity And Islam

* Essays on Cultural Pluralism

* The Vision Of An Unknown Indian Muslim

* Numerous articles and scholarly essays

To learn more about the author, visit

www.JamalKhwaja.com

Download free Digital Books, Lectures, Essays and more.

Authenticity and Islamic Liberalism

A Mature Vision Of Islamic Liberalism
Grounded In The Qur'an

(Second Edition With 3 New Supplemental Essays)

Jamal Khwaja
Professor of Philosophy
Aligarh Muslim University

Alhamd Publishers LLC
Los Angeles

Second Edition With 3 New Supplemental Essays
Copyright © by Jamal Khwaja 1987, 2015

All rights reserved. Copyright under Berne Copyright Convention, Universal Copyright Convention, and Pan American Copyright Convention. No part of this book may be reproduced, stored in a retrieval system, or transmitted in any form or by any means, electronic or mechanical or otherwise, including photocopying and recording, without prior written permission of the publisher, except for the inclusion of brief quotations in a review.

For permission to reproduce selections from this book contact the Publisher. Published and distributed worldwide by;

ALHAMD Publishers, LLC.
3131 Roberts Ave, Culver City, CA 90232, USA
www.AlhamdPublishers.com

Printed and bound in the United States of America
Book and Jacket Design by Sandeep Singh Sandhu.
Author Photo by Kenny Zepeda

More information about the Author and his works can be found at
www.JamalKhwaja.com
Look for FREE Downloads of Essays & Articles written by the Author.

ISBN-13: 978-1-935293-78-1 (Hard cover)
ISBN-13: 978-1-935293-68-2 (Soft cover)
ISBN-13: 978-1-935293-76-7 (E-Pub)
Publisher's SAN #: 857-0132

BISAC Subject Headings:
Religion/Islam/Koran & Sacred Writings (REL041000), and
Religion/Philosophy (REL051000)

In the name of God, the Beneficent, the Merciful.

In Memory of My Mother

Quotable

"Plato is dear to me, but dearer still is truth."

— *Aristotle. Greek Philosopher. Polymath (d. 322 BC).*

"An authentic life is the most personal form of worship. Everyday life has become my prayer."

— *Sarah Ban Breathnach. Best Selling American Author.*

Table of Contents

Author's Preface to the Second Edition xi

Author's Preface to the First Edition xiii

Chapter 1. How I See the Qur'an 1

Chapter 2. Authenticity and Faith in Revelation 29

Chapter 3. The Religious Revolution of the 18th Century & Islam 47

Chapter 4. Islamic Liberalism in India: A Brief Overview 59

Explanatory Notes 89

Supplemental Essay 1: Sharing of Religious Life Worlds 127

Supplemental Essay 2: Seven Letters to My RSS Friend 133

Supplemental Essay 3: Sir Syed, Iqbal and Azad 177

Appendix: Introducing Jamal Khwaja and His Works 191

Index 219

Quotable

"There's only one corner of the universe you can be certain of improving, and that's your own self."

– *Aldous Huxley. British writer, author (d. 1963).*

"Never for the sake of peace and quiet, deny your own experience or convictions."

– *Dag Hammarskjold. Swedish diplomat (d. 1961).*

Author's Preface to the Second Edition

The text of the original 1987 edition has not been altered, much as I would have liked to improve the work in several respects. However, I have added *Sharing of Religious Life Worlds and Seven Letters to My RSS Friend*, in the form of two appendices to my original work.

The paper on *Religious Life Worlds* is a transcript of a talk I gave at a seminar on *Religious Consciousness and Life Worlds*, 1987, at the *Indian Institute of Advanced Study*, Simla. I am full of gratitude to T.S. Rukmani for the trouble taken in recording and editing the talk and publishing it in the proceedings of the Seminar. But for his kindness and intellectual labor the contents would have perished. I have not made any change in the printed version except for one or two very minor corrections. The construction of the sentences is rather loose at some points, but the general sense and thrust of my talk has been clearly presented.

The *letters* were written in 2002 some time after the infamous killings of thousands of innocent Indian Muslims in Gujrat, India as a retaliation against the alleged putting on fire of a railway coach killing some fifty Hindu pilgrims returning from Ayodhya. I addressed the letters to Mr. H.D. Kainthla, a retired District and Sessions Judge of Himachal Pradesh, settled in Solan. The letters reveal my authentic response to the tragedy and my well-considered views on Indian history, recent politics, and tolerance.

I dare say the addition of the appendices in the second edition of this work would enhance its topical value and make it considerably more informative and interesting to the general reader.

Jamal Khwaja
Aligarh, July 2015

QUOTABLE

*"Be quick in the race for forgiveness from your Lord,
And for a Garden whose width is that (of the whole),
Of the heavens and of the earth,
Prepared for the righteous."*

– Qur'an 3:133

Author's Preface to the First Edition

The present work develops and brings into sharper focus some of the key themes of my previous book, *Quest for Islam*. The advances made by the human family in thought, culture and technology demand a fresh critical approach to the Qur'an—the ultimate authority and perennial source of guidance for the Muslim. Several far-sighted Muslim intellectuals and leaders in fact took a fresh look in India and elsewhere from the mid-nineteenth century onwards. This task must ever continue. Today it is imperative to apply the tools and techniques of functional linguistic analysis to the Qur'an for avoiding and removing several confusions, misunderstandings and fallacious ways of approaching a living religious and socio-cultural tradition. Only thus can one expect to identify and liberate the nuclear essence or ontogenetic message of the Qur'an from the historical Islam as a theological and socio-cultural system.

A modest beginning on the above lines was attempted in my *Quest for Islam*, 1977. But the dominant intellectual mood these days in several Muslim countries and Islamic states has been shaped by the requirements of Islamic power and group assertion rather than of open-minded inquiry and search for truth without fear or favor. If the honest search for truth, without the desire for gaining a ready audience be the real task of the philosopher, than I can claim that I have been trying to do my duty. The first chapter, *"How I See the Quran"*, is however, merely a preface of a work which requires a lifetime.

The concept of authenticity, which is perhaps the pivotal concept of contemporary existentialist thought and the basis of religious liberalism and cultural pluralism, has been analyzed in the second chapter. Unfortunately, classical religious thought has not given much attention to the possibility of the erosion of authenticity in the case of born or formal believers. While this predicament has never posed any serious problem for Hinduism and other religions of Indian origin, Muslims and Christians have had to pay a heavy price in terms of individual conflict, hypocrisy, repression, and even persecution at the hands of the establishment. Nobody genuinely concerned with man's spiritual or religious life should neglect this crucial concept, which is the neutral constitutive essence of religious faith, cutting across different religions.

The problem of the proper function or jurisdiction of religion is, again, a fundamental issue cutting across different religions and has been dealt with in the third chapter, which was originally published as a paper (without notes) in *Islam and the Modern Age*, February, 1983. This matter demands dispassionate analysis in the light of the history of ideas, but, unfortunately, it has become highly politicized in the Muslim world, which has recently won political independence and has acquired economic prosperity with a speed unprecedented in history. To my mind, the values of dispassionate analysis and objective reasoning in the light of reliable factual data have been retreating in the face of what claims to be a movement of Islamic renewal or resurgence. I dare say it is a temporary phase: one of those periodic slowdowns or reversals of the broad direction of man's halting and circuitous movement toward humanism, democracy, secularism, and religious liberalism. On a proper understanding of the nuclear core of religion; all religions (including Islam) are quite compatible with the above values.

The last chapter, after giving a brief definition of Islamic liberalism, attempts a synoptic survey of its career in the Indian environment from the thirteenth century up to date. The chapter ends with a reasoned affirmation of my historical faith and confidence that Islamic liberalism would prevail in the Islamic world in the 21st century.

Diacritical marks, and *Hijri*/double calendar computation have been deliberately avoided, as their function is technical rather than practical. The spelling of Arabic/Persian words, again, avoids technical transliteration and is in accord with the actual pronunciation of such words in the Indo-Islamic environment. I trust this effort at simplification would meet with the approval of the meticulous scholar no less than the general reader. A separate bibliography has not been given as full details of the books referred to have been given in the discussion notes. The translation of Qur'anic verses is from Pickthall's English version: *The Meaning of the Glorious Qur'an*.

Author's Preface to the First Edition

I thank my colleagues in the *Department of Philosophy*, Messrs. Naushad Husain, Tasadduq Husain, Zulfiqar Ahmad, Sanaullah for their help at all times. I am grateful to Prof. M.H. Razvi, of the Azad Library, for his unfailing courtesy and help. Prof. A.A. Siddiqui, Department of Economics, Mr. Ali Ashraf, veteran journalist, Dr. Harsh Narain, Visiting Professor in the *Department of Philosophy* read parts of the work and I am grateful for their advice and help. The veteran historian Prof. Mohibbul Hasan has ever encouraged me in my work. Prof. Taqi Amini and Prof. Mazhar Bilgrami of the *Faculty of Theology*, AMU, were most helpful whenever I approached them. The views expressed in this work are however, entirely mine. Thanks are also due to Mr. Shabbir Ghori of Aligarh.

I would also like to thank Mr. Ishtiaq Quraishi, Deputy Librarian and Mr. Aftab Ahmed of the *Maulana Azad Library* for their help. My very special thanks are due to Dr. Hari Dev Sharma of the *Nehru Museum and Library* for drawing my attention to the *Annual Register* and giving other relevant information. I also thank Prof. Ziaul Hasan Farooqi, Editor, *Islam and the Modern Age*, for permission to include my paper first published in the said journal.

Thanks are due to the University authorities for partly subsidizing this work and to Allied Publishers for the beautiful and prompt printing of the work.

Jamal Khwaja
Professor of Philosophy.
Aligarh Muslim University.
Aligarh. April 6, 1986.

Note: Suggested reading pattern for the book

The explanatory notes (pages 89 – 124) are meant to develop the theme and the line of the argument in the text. Each note contains some important information or insight. Reading each note along with the text should considerably add to the pleasure and the profit of reading the book.

Using two bookmarks, one in each section, would make the process effortless. This arrangement aims to serve the requirements of readers who are hard pressed for time as well as readers who can devote more time for pondering highly complex issues.

CHAPTER 1
HOW I SEE THE QUR'AN

Faith in the Divine revelation of the Qur'an is what distinguishes the Islamic faith from monotheism in general and constitutes its central core. For the Muslims the Qur'an is the supreme locus of the Divine Presence or the concrete mode of God's intervention in history and of contact with chosen human beings, among whom Muhammad ﷺ * is the apex as the recipient of God's last and final revelation.

One cannot be a Muslim unless one believes that the Qur'an was Divinely 'revealed' to the Prophet ﷺ *. But what exactly a believer commits himself to when he honestly holds the Qur'an to be the 'word of God' is far from clear to the vast majority of Muslims. In what follows I wish to explain my own approach to the Qur'an as the supreme mystery of Islam. Every Muslim must feel free to express any lurking doubts or difficulties (if any) in traditional views or beliefs instead of suppressing his reservations in this regard. The authentic Muslim must feel free to spell out, in all humility and after prayerful reflection, how the ultimate mystery of Islam appears to him according to his own inner lights. Without this inner freedom authentic faith would not be born. And authenticity is the lifeblood of faith (*iman*) without which any religious belief is merely a corpse.

I

The Islamic faith implies that the total contents of the Qur'an were revealed by God to Muhammad ﷺ who subsequently dictated them to

---
* "Peace be upon him" in Arabic

scribes who implicitly followed the directions given by the Prophet ﷺ. The Qur'anic text is thus held to be quite apart from the Prophet's ﷺ own words or reported sayings. The Qur'an was revealed in bits throughout the apostolic period of twenty-three years, the first thirteen of which were spent by the Prophet ﷺ in Mecca and the remaining in Medina. The process of revelation began in the cave of *Hira*, about two miles from Mecca, when the Prophet ﷺ was about forty and was repeated at irregular intervals (over which the Prophet ﷺ had no control whatsoever) until his passing away in Medina when he was about sixty-three.

The Qur'anic references to the nature or modes of Divine revelation are too abstract or vague to enable us to understand or conceptualize the Prophet's ﷺ extraordinary experience of revelation. But even if the Qur'anic references had been more specific this would not have helped unravel the mystery, since we ourselves have no experience of revelation. Indeed, we cannot conceptualize anything or any event without prior experience of it in some sense or the other. Thus we cannot conceptualize the nature of '*angels*' or the '*Holy Spirit*' (Gabriel) and his role in the revelatory process, as mentioned in the Qur'an.

> (42:51, 52)
>
> *And it was not (vouchsafed) to any mortal that Allah should speak to him unless (it be) by revelation, or from behind a veil, or (that) He sendeth a messenger to reveal what He will by His leave. Lo! He is Exalted, Wise.*
>
> *And thus have We inspired in thee (Muhammad) a Spirit of Our command. Thou knewest not what the Scripture was nor what the Faith...*

While we understand the expression 'X spoke to Y on the phone', and can easily distinguish this from the expression, 'X wired Y', or 'X sent a written note to Y', and so on, we just cannot claim to know the exact state of affairs described by the expression, 'God revealed to Moses', 'God revealed to the mother of Moses', and 'God revealed to the bee', etc., when we come across such expressions in the following verses:

(28:7)

And We inspired the mother of Moses, saying: Suckle him and, when thou fearest for him, then cast him into the river and fear not nor grieve ...

(16:68)

And thy Lord inspired the bee, saying: Choose thou habitations in the hills and in the trees and in that which they hatch;

Indeed, whenever, we talk of God or His actions we come across an opaque wall of *Noetic* ambiguity or vacuity (in religious language, a sense of mystery and bafflement). We should thus not demand or expect *Noetic* transparency when we use religious language. Beliefs that God *'exists'* or that God *'revealed'* the Qur'an are thus beliefs in a very different sense from beliefs like 'snakes exist' or 'Mohan revealed this secret to Sohan'. We know more or less exactly the situation in which the above sentences would be accepted as true even if we may not be able to give an exact analysis of their meaning, as desired by the British philosopher, Moore. Moreover, if someone were to deny such beliefs, we know how to establish them. In other words, we know both *what* they designate and *how* they are tested as true or false. But such is not the case where the word 'God' is used. We know neither *what* beliefs about God actually connote; nor how such beliefs could be made plausible, if not actually proved. [1]

What then are we to understand by the belief that 'God revealed the Qur'an to the Prophet ﷺ?' In the final analysis it means that **(a)** the Prophet ﷺ was not the author of the Qur'an in the sense in which Shakespeare was the author of *Hamlet*, though the Qur'anic verses were uttered and dictated by the Prophet ﷺ to some scribe; **(b)** the Qur'anic verses were not contrived or thought out by the Prophet ﷺ but 'came' to him or were crystallized in his consciousness fully formed or fashioned by some *'Other'*; and **(c)** this *Other* is nothing more and nothing less than the supreme Source of all that exists. This threefold analysis, however, says nothing about *how* the contents came to the Prophet ﷺ. Any belief or theory about how the contents came to him is not a part of the substantial belief *that* the contents were revealed, but an additional belief. Thus, for instance, the belief that Gabriel used to appear in human or angelic form to the Prophet ﷺ and made him recite and memorize the Qur'anic verses is not logically equivalent to the belief that God revealed the Qur'an, but rather a particular theory of revelation. Now the crucial point is that a Muslim may well believe that the Qur'an was revealed without accepting the above theory of revelation, or any other theory, for that matter. He may well hold that no theory of revelation could properly be asserted in the absence of any experience of revelation as such, and yet hold the Qur'an to be 'revealed' in the above threefold sense. He may take the revelation of the Qur'an as the supreme mystery of the Islamic faith, and not merely accept the Prophet's ﷺ own honest interpretation of his extraordinary experiences. [2]

A critic could possibly take the stand that even if the Prophet's ﷺ revelatory experience were genuine, he might have forgotten or missed some part of the revelatory content, or the scribe might have erred in recording it, or some written portion might have been lost and thus excluded from the final collection, or some spurious content might have been included in it through some mistake or oversight of the Prophet's ﷺ companions who collected the scattered verses/*surahs*. Well, the above type of doubts can *never* be historically settled. All a Muslim can say with historical certainty on the basis of evidence, as is generally deemed adequate in such matters, is that Muhammad ﷺ was a respected and highly truthful person who, at the age of forty, claimed to be the recipient of Divine messages (through revelatory episodes) which he claimed to remember and which were subsequently dictated by him to scribes who wrote them down on a piece of skin, bark or cloth, according to availability. The rest is all scholastic reconstruction or Muslim faith without any unanimity of belief.

The dominant view is that the Prophet ﷺ himself indicated to the scribes the sequence of the verses within a *surah* as well as the sequence of the separate *surahs* or chapters themselves. This implies that the Qur'an, in its standard written form (without, however, the Arabic vowels and the lexically equal division into thirty parts or '*paras*'), existed before the Prophet's ﷺ death. [3] According to another reliable view, it was the first *Caliph*, Abu Bakr, who, at the instance of his immediate successor, Umar, compiled and arranged the Qur'anic text in its standard form about two years after the Prophet's ﷺ

death. According to yet another view, the third *Caliph*, Uthman, about fifteen years after the Prophet's ﷺ death, first arranged the chapters in the standard form extant today. But the dominant view is that what Uthman did was to duplicate, on a relatively large scale, the earlier edition made by the first *Caliph*. According to the same view, Uthman recalled all the scattered verses/*surahs* in circulation and had them burnt to preserve the accuracy of the standard edition. In my opinion this is a historical issue to be settled through critical historical investigation, and should not be equated with the core content of the Muslim faith that the Qur'anic verses were Divinely 'revealed'.

It may be asked further whether the titles of *surahs*, the numbering of the verses, the Prophet's ﷺ directions (if any) to the scribes regarding the placement of the verses in different *surahs* were based on his own independent judgment (assuming that the present book form of the Qur'an had been finalized by the Prophet ﷺ himself), or were Divinely revealed or inspired. Whatever one's views on these questions may be these matters are distinct from faith in the revelation of the Qur'anic verses as such.

The Muslim faith implies that the Qur'an was revealed and has been preserved in its entirety, uncontaminated by error or interpolation.

(41:41, 42)
Lo! those who disbelieve in the Reminder when it cometh unto them (are guilty), for lo!, It is an unassailable scripture. Falsehood cannot come at it from before it or behind it. (It is) a revelation from the Wise, the Owner of Praise.

Faith in revelation in this sense, however, does not imply any additional belief or beliefs concerning the issue as to when and how the Qur'anic verses were collected, or numbered, or how they or the *surahs* were arranged, as we actually find them in standard editions of the Qur'an, for the past fourteen hundred years.

To sum up, neither the belief in the Prophet's ﷺ sincerity, nor the belief in his being unlettered, nor the belief in the hitherto unsurpassed literary excellence of the Qur'an, severally or jointly constitutes a proof (in the deductive or inductive sense) of the Islamic faith. [4] The justification of faith can be found only in the individual's authentic response to the Qur'an or, rather, those of its verses which may be said to possess a spiritual 'aura' or inner power to grip and illumine a receptive listener or reader of the Qur'an. At times even a non-receptive mind may come under the spell, as it were, of the Qur'an, as happened in the case of Umar when he heard for the first time some verses recited by his sister or her husband.

In the final analysis religious faith is an existential conviction, which may dawn suddenly or gradually, like love, rather than a belief, which could be inductively or deductively established or proved. Again, the religious response to the Universe is strikingly similar to, though not identical with or totally reducible to, the aesthetic response. Significantly, the Qur'an repeatedly exhorts man to reflect upon the beauty and wonder of nature and also of man's own inner self. The verses of the Qur'an and the phenomena of nature both are called *'ayat'* or signs which may evoke and reinforce faith in God for one who seeks truth with humility and sincerity. Consider the following Qur'anic verses:

> (3:190-191)
>
> *Lo! In the creation of the heavens and the earth and in the difference of night and day are tokens (of His sovereignty) for men of understanding, such as remember Allah, standing, sitting, and reclining and consider the creation of the heavens and the earth and say: Our Lord thou created not in vain, Glory be to thee: Preserve us from the doom of fire.*
>
> (30:22)
>
> *And of His signs is the creation of the heavens and the earth and the difference of your languages and colors. Lo! Herein indeed are portents for men of knowledge.*
>
> (30:23)
>
> *And of His signs is your slumber by night and by day, and your seeking of His bounty. Lo! Herein indeed are portents for folk who heed.*

(6:100)

He it is who sendeth down water from the sky, and therewith We bring forth buds of every kind; We bring forth the green blade from which We bring forth the thick clustered grain; and from the date-palm, from the pollen thereof, spring pendant bunches... Look upon the fruit thereof, when they bear fruit and upon its ripening. Lo! Herein verily are portents for a people who believe.

(41:53)

We shall show them Our portents on the horizons and within themselves until it will be manifest unto them that it is the truth. Doth not thy Lord suffice, since He is witness over all things?

It follows that all that could be said to an honest skeptic unmoved by the power and beauty of the Qur'an is exactly what can be said to one who remains unmoved by the beauty of a sunset, or the snow-clad peaks, or the slow movement of a symphony or concert "Please look or hear again with receptive humility; a fresh experience may lead to a new type of response or evoke in you a new chord. But please don't feel tense, guilty, inferior, or deficient in case your response remains different from mine."

The similarity between appreciation of the beauty of nature and faith in the Qur'an, however, does not amount to an identity. Indeed, the starry sky or the symphony does not issue forth any prescriptions or value judgments, which might possibly conflict with those of the observer. And this is precisely what may happen with the Qur'an. Even if one appreciates or feels overwhelmed by the beauty and power of the Qur'an one may honestly dissent from some of its prescriptive contents. [5] This predicament does not arise when one contemplates nature and experiences an inner and profound conviction that nature is not a blind accident. The following Qur'anic verses are deeply significant and intensely moving:

(44:38–39)

"And We created not the heavens and the earth, and all that is between them, in play. We created them not save with truth; but most of them know not."

(21: 16–17)

"We created not the heaven and the earth and all that is between them in play. If We had wished to find a pastime, We could have found it in Our presence—if We ever did."

(30:8)

"Have they not pondered upon themselves? Allah created not the heavens and the earth, and that which is between them save with truth and for a destined end. But truly many of mankind are disbelievers in the meeting with their Lord.

II

One will not be able fully to appreciate the Qur'an if one reads it as a systematic book comprising logically interconnected chapters divided into or built out of sections, as one finds in any well written work on, say, Theology, History, or Sociology.

The Qur'an is not a book in this sense. It is a collection of 114 'surahs', which are not 'chapters' in the usual sense but rather self-contained and complete compositions or units comprising 'ayats' (verses) which may or may not have been revealed in one single revelatory episode. Since *surahs* vary enormously in length (the longest *surah* comprising 286 verses, while the shortest a mere three), it is highly plausible and likely that the longer *surahs* were revealed piecemeal. [6] According to the orthodox view itself, the revelation of several fresh *surahs* started even before the completion of a previous *surah* or *surahs*, and later verses juxtaposed with earlier ones. Thus the unit of a set of ideas or theme is not even a *surah* but a set of verses. The division of the Qur'an into thirty parts of equal length (without any regard to the subject matter or the placement of the different *surahs*) is meant to facilitate its memorization or ritual recitation in fixed proportions.

The titles of the different *surahs* are also not titles in the conventional sense and one would be disappointed if one expects any close correlation between the title and the contents of a particular *surah*, Indeed the titles are rather mystifying or problematic, and it is almost impossible to be certain about the real significance or rationale of a particular title. One can certainly refer to a particular idea, word, or expression contained in the *surah* after which the title might have been given to a *surah*. But often this correlation or connection is highly tenuous or marginal relative to the dominant theme or themes of the *surah*. Thus, for instance, the second *surah* is titled 'The Cow' (*Al-Baqara*), or the fifty-seventh *surah* is titled 'The Iron' (*Hadid*), or the sixth which is titled 'The Cattle' (*Al-Anam*) and so on, but the main themes of these *surahs* are quite other than the cow, iron, or cattle. Indeed, in view of the tremendous repetition and juxtaposition of ideas and themes no title possibly could have done the conventional job of a title or heading. The titles are, therefore, proper names of *surahs* rather than clues to their content. It is, therefore, undesirable speculation or dogmatism to claim to grasp the real significance of the title.

Exactly the same applies, with much greater force, to the interpretations given to the mystic prefixes (*Muqataat*) to approximately thirty *surahs*. The prefixes, and perhaps also the titles, may be said to constitute the mystique of the Qur'an. If the titles are viewed as clues to decipher the spiritual or 'ontogenetic' power of a *surah*, one could select a particular *surah* for regular or repeated mystical recitation as one's favorite *surah*, depending upon one's inner needs, interests, or aspirations. This choice should, however, not be viewed as reliance on a '*mantra*' for realizing one's worldly aims or objectives. This would reduce the Qur'an to the level of a magical recipe book for worldly success.

Qur'anic themes have been repeated again and again and still again (depending upon their significance in the total economy of life) in different *surahs* and also in the same *surah*, even as themes are repeated in a musical composition. The *surahs* do have a basic theme and subsidiary or tertiary ones, but it would be going off the mark to claim (as is often done by learned Muslim commentators on the Qur'an) that there is a discernible logical sequence between the successive sections of a particular *surah*, as also between the successive *surahs*. It seems that there is no need to attribute any logical or systematic connection (in the conventional sense) to the actual order of the *surahs* or even to verses found in the longer *surahs*. Obviously, there should be some perceptible order in a set of successive verses in order to express a clear-cut theme; and order, in this sense, certainly is in the Qur'an. These themes are however, repeated very often. This again does not amount to any flaw, provided we do not view the Qur'an as a textbook, but rather as a spiritual symphony which is meant to warn, sustain, exhort and illumine man in the task of learning an integrated response to the mystery of the Universe.

Since there cannot be any one ideal order of reading the Qur'an, no *surah* or *surahs* (apart, of course, from *Al-Fatiha*, which has a unique status) should, in my opinion, be selected for ritual recitation on the basis of convention. A Muslim must learn to respond to the Qur'an authentically in his own individual manner as one responds to music, poetry, or the beauty of nature, Indeed, every true believer ought to discover the beauty and power of the Qur'an on the basis of his own inner prompting or spiritual instinct, as it were.

The Qur'an is certainly not a textbook of natural and social science, even as it is not a magic book of ritual recitation for attaining one's worldly desires and objectives. The Qur'an can be no substitute for the laborious learning process of observation, experiment, formulation of hypotheses and their verification in the field of inductive knowledge and of the rigorous grasp of logical connections in the field of deductive knowledge. The Qur'an makes no difference to, and leaves untouched, the pursuit of inductive and deductive truth, which falls in the domain of natural and social sciences. Nor does the Qur'an prove or claim to prove the basic beliefs which constitute the content of 'faith in the unseen'—the existence of God, revelation, life after death, and so on.

The Qur'an approaches such matters in an evocative rather than in a ratiocinative manner, and rightly so. The Qur'an exhorts man to look at nature and into himself and reflect again and again on the mystery of creation and holds out, to the sincere seeker, the promise of attainment of truth. This is quite different from deducing God's existence from a self-evident truth or set of truths. Indeed, the Qur'an dispels the illusion of the power of reason to prove or disprove the contents of 'faith in the unseen' (*iman bil ghaib*).

Apart from the importance of correctly grasping the Qur'anic approach to the above matters, discovering the right method of semantic interpretation of the Qur'anic text is the crux of the matter. Though classical Islamic scholars and divines have done valuable work in this field, much greater labors and more refined analytical techniques and tools are needed for dealing with this crucial issue. [7]

The Qur'anic verses belong to different types of discourse and perform different functions of language—informing, judging, exhorting, commanding, consoling, promising, eliciting, and so on and so forth. Qur'anic verses also differ in their 'functional genesis' or the purposive 'point' of their revelation. And the range of this difference may vary from the 'functional genesis' of the seven verses of the *surah Al-Fatiha* (regarded as the quintessence or 'mother of the Qur'an') to that of the verse which chides the Prophet ﷺ for forbidding to himself what God has permitted, or the verse teaching elementary manners to the rather crude and uncouth Beduin Arabs, for instance, announcing before entering into another's house. [8] The *Al-Fatiha* seems to have no functional genesis over and above its intrinsic value as a superb and matchless jewel which 'shines by its own light', possessing an unsurpassed interpretative, evocative and ontogenetic power. As compared to this, verses condemning one of the arch enemies of the Prophet, ﷺ or prescribing the procedure of swearing on oath, or describing the Arab calendar based on lunar reckoning, and numerous others, have a functional genesis which obviously has a contingent dimension. [9] It seems that careful and systematic reflection on this crucial point may help committed Muslim thinkers to distinguish verses which have an intrinsic significance from those having an instrumental function. This distinction would tend to promote and legitimize an open and truly dynamic interpretative approach to the Qur'an itself rather than to the *Shariah* alone.

The contingent and instrumental complexion of several Qur'anic verses implies that if the life situation of the Prophet ﷺ and his milieu had been other than what they actually were, at the time of the revelation, the verses in question might not have been revealed at all, and other verses, relevant and appropriate to a different situation, might have been revealed. [10] Likewise, if the grammar and syntax of the Arabic language had been different from what it actually is, the Qur'anic text would also have differed correspondingly. To go a step still further, if the Prophet ﷺ had been born in India or

China the language of the Qur'an would not have been Arabic. The point is that a merely literal adherence to the Qur'anic text without **(a)** a critical and sound method of semantic interpretation of the Qur'an, and **(b)** awareness of the Prophet's ﷺ milieu (the sociocultural conditions of Arabia immediately preceding and during his lifetime) is a simplistic and misleading approach harmful to the Muslims and, for that matter, to the entire human family.

The contention that adherence to the literal meaning without 'contextual exploration' is not enough should not be taken to mean or imply any indifference to the literal meaning of the Qur'anic text. Indeed, attention to the literal meaning is extremely important, and speculative interpretation of Qur'anic verses to suit one's own ideas is highly improper. [11] Likewise, one should not twist and stretch the plain meanings of words to explain away any doubts or difficulties which may arise for the reader of the Qur'an because of some reason or other. Some difficulties, however, arise due to a unique Qur'anic style of non-literal expression; in such cases insistence upon a literal interpretation would be a wrong principle. The application of common sense and attention to linguistic usage in Arabic or other languages will be found to remove these difficulties and quandaries without twisting or stretching the ordinary meanings of the words of the Qur'an. If, in spite of this, any perplexity remains it should be frankly acknowledged by the honest Muslim. Consider the following verses:

(2:6, 7)

As for the disbelievers, whether thou warn them or thou warn them not it is all one for them; they believe not. Allah hath sealed their hearing and their hearts and on their eyes is a covering. Theirs will be an awful doom.

(5:14)

And with those who say "Lo! We are Christians", We made a covenant but they forgot a part whereof they were admonished. Therefore, We have stirred up enmity and hatred among them till the Day of Resurrection, when Allah will inform them of their handiwork.

On their first reading and literal interpretation, these verses make God responsible for the hardened and intractable disbelief of the unbelievers and the mutual enmity of the Christians. But a little reflection makes it clear that this is not the case at all and that this impression is created only because of the style of expression employed by the Qur'an in such cases. The Qur'anic expression, *"We have stirred up enmity and hatred among them"*, or *"Allah hath sealed their hearing and their hearts"* is only an elliptical way of saying that "great mutual enmity and hatred have been produced among the Christians as a natural consequence of their deeds in conformity with well-established and social psychological laws which cannot be flouted by man at his sweet will". The same type of explanation applies to the expression concerning, *'God's sealing of the hearts'*.

The fact of the matter is that while, on the whole, the Qur'anic style is extremely simple and direct, going straight to the point, it becomes elliptical and perplexing in a few cases. And it is precisely in such cases that a literal interpretation sounds absurd. [12] Disagreements or difficulties also result from the allusive, vague, or metaphorical verses. In view of the above complications the intellectually honest Muslim simply must show tolerance and accept the principle of plural interpretations. The claim that only 'my' or the traditional interpretation is true has led in the past to suppression of free inquiry and even persecution. [13]

The following Qur'anic verse beautifully sums up the position:

(3:7)
He it is who hath revealed unto thee (Muhammad) wherein are clear revelations—they are the substance of the Book— and others (which are) allegorical. But those in whose heart is doubt pursue, forsooth, that which is allegorical seeking (to cause) dissension by seeking to explain it. None knoweth its explanation save Allah. And those who are of sound instruction say: We believe therein, the whole is from our Lord; but only men of understanding really heed.

III

The verses revealed in the Meccan period generally deal with the unity, majesty, omnipotence and mercy of God, life after death, the need for reflecting on the phenomena of nature and the inner life of the self, faith and righteous action, the record of nations in the past and their fate, tolerance, —in other words, the basic elements of faith (*iman*); the verses revealed in the Medinian period generally deal with rules and regulations of prayer, fasting and personal laws (chiefly marriage and inheritance) with a bare sprinkling of socioeconomic or political prescriptions. The exceptions to the above only go to show the interrelationship between the two themes in the corpus of the Qur'an.

The above distribution of themes is perfectly understandable and logical in the light of the sociology of knowledge, as the themes of revelation match the needs and demands of the situation. The diction and style of the Qur'an also match the theme. Medinian prescriptive verses are written in a crisp, matter-of-fact, and lucid prose, while the Meccan 'evocative' verses have been expressed in semi-rhymed poetic prose of the utmost simplicity and power that overwhelm the receptive reader, shaking him to the roots of his being, as it were. He is struck by their elemental spiritual force as one is struck by the fury of a storm in the forest or the ocean, or by the majesty of the calm sea at sunset or of snow-laden mountain peaks in bright sunshine. The full impact of such verses can be felt only in the original Arabic, translations being a very poor substitute. [14] Here are a few examples:

(2:17–19)

Their likeness is as the likeness of one who kindleth fire, and when it sheddeth its light around him Allah taketh away their light and leaveth them in darkness, where they cannot see, deaf, dumb and blind; and they return not.

Or like a rainstorm from the sky, wherein is darkness, thunder and the flash of lighting. They thrust their fingers in their ears by reason of the thunderclaps, for fear of death. Allah encompasseth the disbelievers (in His guidance).

(69:13–16)

And when the trumpet shall sound one blast. And the earth with the mountains shall be lifted up and crushed with one crash. Then on that day will the Event befall? And the heaven will split asunder, for that day it will be frail.

(69:38–52)

But nay I swear by all that ye see. And all that ye see not! That it is indeed the speech of an illustrious messenger. It is not poet's speech—little is it that ye believe! Nor diviner's speech—little is that ye remember! It is a revelation from the Lord of the Worlds. And if he had invented false sayings concerning Us, We assuredly had taken him by the right hand, And then severed his life-artery, And not one of you could have held Us off from him. And lo! It is a warrant unto those who ward off (evil). And lo! We know that some among you will deny (it) And lo! it is indeed an anguish for the disbelievers. And lo! it is absolute truth. So glorify the name of thy Tremendous Lord.

(70:6–14)

Lo! They behold it afar off While We behold it nigh: The day when the sky will become as molten copper, And the hills become as flakes of wool, And no familiar friend will ask a question of his friend though they will be given sight of them. The guilty man will long to be able to ransom himself from the punishment of that day at the price of his children. And his spouse and his brother. And his kin that harbored him and all that are in the earth, if then it might deliver him.

(78:40)

Lo! We warn you of a doom at hand, a day whereon a man will look on that which his own hands have sent before, and the disbeliever will cry: "Would that I were dust!".

(2:115)

Unto Allah belong the East and the West and whithersoever ye turn, there is Allah's countenance. Lo! Allah is All-embracing, All-knowing.

(2:255)

Allah! There is no God save Him, the Alive, the Eternal. Neither slumber nor sleep over taketh Him. Unto Him belongeth whatsoever is in the heavens and whatsoever is in the earth. Who is he that intercedeth with Him save by His leave? He knoweth that which is in front of them and that which is behind them, while they encompass nothing of His knowledge save what He will. His throne includeth the heavens and earth, and He is never weary of preserving them. He is the Sublime, the Tremendous.

(57:1-3)

All that is in the heavens and the earth glorifieth Allah. And He is the Mighty and the Wise. His is the sovereignty of the heavens and the earth; He quickeneth and He giveth death; and He is able to do all things. He is the First and the Last, and the Outward and the Inward: and He is Knower of all things.

(59:23-24)

He is Allah, than whom there is no other god, the Sovereign Lord, the Holy One, Peace, the Keeper of Faith, the Guardian, the Majestic, the Compeller, the Superb, glorified be Allah from all hat they ascribe as partner (Unto Him). He is Allah, the Creator, the Shaper out of naught, the Fashioner. His are the most beautiful names. All that is in the heavens and/ the earth glorifieth Him, and He is the Mighty, the Wiser.

(3:26-27)

Say: Oh Allah! Owner of Sovereignty! Thou givest sovereignty unto whom Thou wilt, and Thou with drawest sovereignty from whom Thou wilt. Thou exaltest whom Thou wilt and

Thou abasest whom Thou wilt. In Thy hand is the good. Lo! Thou art able to do all things. Thou causest the night to pass into the day, and Thou causest the day to pass into the night. And Thou bringest forth the living from the dead, and Thou bringest forth the dead from the living. And Thou givest sustenance to whom Thou choosest, without stint.

Such verses as the above serve to bring about a spiritual quickening of the 'heart' or the spiritual potentialities of the individual and to reinforce man's faith that there is a spiritual dimension of the cosmos and that religion is essentially the active recognition of this vital and crucial truth about the Universe. This function of the Qur'an may be called the 'ontogenetic' function, since it creates and reinforces an independent and irreducible dimension of human response, which enriches and enhances the inner quality of life or being. This function is not performed (directly) by the purely descriptive and legal or ethical verses. [15]

The 'ontogenetic' function, at its best and most effective form, is to be seen in the Prophet's ﷺ character and inmost being, which were shaped by the Qur'an. The experience of revelation also inwardly confirmed and reinforced his faith in the unseen, and every fresh revelatory episode provided a fresh confirmation. That is one reason why the Qur'an was revealed piecemeal rather than all at once or in a few extended episodes.

(25:32)

And those who disbelieve say: Why is the Qur'an not revealed unto him all at once? (It is revealed) thus that We may strengthen thy heart therewith; and We have arranged it in right order.

Keeping in view the above distinction in the Qur'anic themes of the Meccan and Medinian periods, it is, perhaps, advisable to study the Qur'an, neither in the present conventional order, nor in the strictly chronological order (as advocated by some Western scholars and commentators), but to focus one's attention, by and large, upon the Meccan verses prior to reading the Medinian ones. There cannot be any rigid plan of reading the Qur'an, just as there cannot be any one perfect or ideal plan of enjoying

Authenticity and Islamic Liberalism

the beauties of nature. One must discover for oneself the order proper for his own reading. This will be readily appreciated once we realize that the Qur'an is not a systematic book with interconnected chapters, but rather a Universe to which one should respond in his own authentic manner. I, for one, suggest that after finishing the first and second *surahs* one reads *surah* 57, *Al-Hadid* (The Iron), and after that the *surahs* composing the last part numbered thirty. This should be followed by the shorter *surahs* composing parts 25-29. The reader may then turn to the longer *surahs* composing parts 3-5. This much reading would cover exactly one-third of the contents of the Qur'an. The remaining two-thirds of the Qur'an can be studied in any order whatsoever.

In my view, the reading of the above-mentioned third of the Qur'an would cover all the themes it contains, and even at this stage the reader will come across plentiful variations on the same basic themes. This, however, does not mean that the remaining part is merely repetitive. Indeed gems of rare beauty and insight remain scattered and embedded throughout the Qur'an. Moreover, no topic is exhaustively dealt with in any one single place. One is thus most likely to misjudge the full import of a verse if one does not consult all the relevant but scattered verses. One is also more likely to misjudge unless one understands the historical situation or the context (*shane-nuzul*) of the revelation.

IV

Next in number to the evocative verses of the Qur'an praising the glory, power and mercy of God, stand the exhortative verses prompting the believer to be good and do the right—to speak the truth and testify to what is true, to be just and kind, to have faith in God and act righteously, to keep up prayer and pay the wealth-tax, to strive and spend liberally in the way of God, to assist and help the needy and the poor and the wayfarer and the orphan and the widow, to be patient in adversity, to control one's passions, to be modest and chaste, to be kind to women and children, to beware of the temptations of Satan, to be kind and respectful to one's parents, to reflect on the wonders of nature, to glorify and thank God, and so on. Next come the historical or biographical verses, which relate the stories of the messengers and warner's sent by God in earlier times. The number of such verses is very large indeed, but they all serve to warn, exhort and comfort rather than give much factual or historical information. The parabolic verses of the Qur'an are very few in number, but they also serve to exhort and morally educate.

The exhortative verses are couched in general terms, and this is why they possess a timeless and universal relevance and appeal, which they would have lost if they had partaken of casuistry. Moreover, the spelling out of details would have blurred the crucial distinction between intrinsic values and instrumental rules for realizing them in an ever-changing human situation.

Space does not permit an elaboration of the spirit of the numerous exhortative verses comprising almost one-fifth of the Qur'anic text. The stress of these verses is undoubtedly on faith and righteous action (*iman wa amal e salih*), and, after this, on keeping up obligatory prayers and paying the wealth-tax for the benefit of the poor and the needy. [16] Of the four following verses the first two have been repeated time and again:

(18:107)

Lo! those who believe and do good works theirs are the Gardens of Paradise for welcome.

(32:19)

But as for those who believe and do good works, for them are the Gardens of Retreat—a welcome (in reward) for what they used to do.

(103:2, 3)

Lo! Man is in a state of loss, Save those who believe and do good works ....

(107:1–3)

Hast thou observed him who belieth religion? That is he who repelleth the orphan. And urgeth not the feeding of the needy.

Authenticity and Islamic Liberalism

Faith without action is lame; right action without being rooted in some faith is blind. Ad hoc right actions are liable to be displaced by wrong deeds at the slightest blowing of the wind of impulse in the wrong direction. The Qur'an, therefore, stresses faith flowering in righteous action or righteous action rooted in faith. Now the field of righteous action includes man's obligations to God (*ibadat*) and obligations to society (*moamilat*). The former obligations fall in the transcendental 'I-Thou' sphere, while the latter in the social 'you-me-they' sphere. The major area of righteous action belongs to the social sphere.

Social behavior (*moamilat*) involves man-to-man transactions, while praying and fasting involve the man-God relationship. Now, the mistake of the popular value system lies precisely in abstracting a part from the whole and treating the part as the whole. Says the Qur'an:

(2:177)

It is not righteousness that ye turn your faces to the East and the West, but righteous is he who believeth in Allah and the Last Day and the angels and the Scripture and the Prophets; and giveth his wealth for love of Him to kinsfolk and to orphans and the needy and the wayfarer and to those who ask, and to set slaves free; and observeth proper worship and payeth the poor-due. And those who keep their treaty when they make one, and the patient in tribulation and adversity and time of stress. Such are they who are sincere. Such are the God-fearing.

Turning to the popular Muslim conception of the supreme vices, the cardinal vice, according to the plain texts of the Qur'an, is certainly not consuming alcohol/pork and fornication, but hypocrisy and backbiting. This is what the Qur'an says about alcohol:

(2:219)

They question thee about strong drink and games of chance. Say: In both is great sin, and (some) utility for men; but the sin of them is greater than their usefulness.

(5:90, 91)

O ye who believe! Strong drink and games of chance and idols and divining arrows are only an infamy of Satan's handiwork. Leave it aside in order that ye may succeed. Satan seeketh only to cast among you enmity and hatred by means of strong drink and games of chance, and to turn you from remembrance of Allah and from (His) worship. Will ye then have done.

Now consider what the Qur'an says about backbiting:

(49:12)

O ye who believe! Shun much suspicion; for lo! Some suspicion is a crime. And spy not, neither backbite one another. Would one of you love to eat the flesh of his dead brother? ...

Do not the wordings of the above Qur'anic verses make it manifest that the degree of evil inherent in backbiting and hypocrisy is infinitely greater than that of consuming alcohol? But backbiting is an extremely common social phenomenon, and hardly appears to be as serious an evil as the Qur'anic text makes out. A little reflection, however, amply confirms the Qur'anic view, since backbiting and hypocrisy are essentially cases of fear of truth, and it is this fear that is the seed of *all* evil. [17]

Likewise, the belief fairly common among both Muslims and non-Muslims that the Qur'an prohibits Muslims to befriend non-Muslims has arisen due to confusing a conditional Qur'anic advice not to befriend or trust the aggressive and unethical opponents of the Prophet ﷺ with a permanent ban on friendly relations with non-Muslims. The Qur'anic verses concerned are as follows:

(3:28)

Let not the believers take disbelievers for their friends in preference to believers. Whoso doeth that hath no connection with Allah unless (it be) that ye but guard yourselves against them, taking (as it were) security.

(4:144)

O ye who believe! Choose not disbelievers for (your) friends in place of believers. Would ye give Allah a clear warrant against you?

(5:51)

O ye who believe! Take not the Jews and the Christians for friends. They are friends one to another. He among you who taketh them for friends is (one) of them. Lo! Allah guideth not wrongdoing folk.

Now the above verses, when read in isolation and without full knowledge of the historical situation or the background of their revelation, do lend themselves to the interpretation that has actually been placed upon them that the Qur'an bans friendly relations and mutual trust between Muslims and non-Muslims. But if the verses are read carefully to determine their exact import, and if *all* the relevant verses (which are scattered in different places in the Qur'an) are examined in the historical context of their revelation, it becomes pretty clear that the anti-humanist interpretation of the Qur'anic verses in question in not justified. Indeed, it can be said with full intellectual honesty that the Qur'anic texts encourage interreligious tolerance and universal kindness, holding that religious or cultural plurality is part of God's plan and that God could have obliterated all differences, had He so wished. Consider the following verses of the Qur'an:

(60:7–9)

It may be that Allah will ordain love between you and those of them with whom ye are at enmity. Allah is Mighty, and Allah is Forgiving, Merciful. Allah forbiddeth you not those who warred not against you on account of religion and drove you not out from your homes, that ye should show them kindness and deal justly with them. Lo! Allah loveth the just dealers. Allah forbiddeth you only those who warred against you on account of religion and have driven you out from your homes and helped to drive you out, that ye make friends of them. Whosoever maketh friends of them—(all) such are the wrongdoers.

(3:113–115)
They are not all alike. Of the people of the Scripture there is a staunch community who recite the revelations of Allah in the right season, falling prostrate (before Him). They believe in Allah and the Last Day, and enjoin right conduct and forbid indecency, and vie one with another in good works. They are of the righteous. And whatever good they do they will not be denied the meed thereof. Allah is aware of those who ward off (evil).

(5:69)
Lo! Those who believe and those who are Jews, and Sabaeans, and Christians—whosoever believeth in Allah and the Last Day and doeth right—there shall no fear come upon them neither shall they grieve.

(49:13)
O mankind, Lo! We have created you male and female and have made you nations and tribes that ye may know one and another. Lo! The noblest of you, in the sight of Allah, is the best in conduct. Lo! Allah is Knower, Aware.

(10:100)
And if thy Lord willed all who are in the earth would have believed together. Wouldst thou (Muhammad) compel men until they believe?

(5:48)

For each We have appointed a Divine Law and a traced out way. Had Allah willed He could have made you one community. But that He may try you by that which He hath given you (He hath made you as ye are) so vie one with another in good works. Unto Allah ye will all return, and He will then inform you of that wherein ye differ.

Let us now turn to the prescriptive or directive verses of the Qur'an. These verses deal with **(a)** transcendental '*I-Thou*' matters—prayers, fasting, essential rites, method of ablution, **(b)** matters of personal law—rules of inheritance, marriage, dowry, divorce, prohibited degrees, food and drink, **(c)** matters of social law—crime and punishment, adultery, perjury, rules of evidence, and finally **(d)** political and economic matters—prohibition of usury, rules of peace and war, etc.

All the prescriptive verses put together number approximately 170 out of a total approximately 6,250 verses of the Qur'an, and the majority of these prescriptive verses deal with the transcendental sphere and personal laws. These prescriptive verses also do not go into concrete details, with a few exceptions which are worth mentioning—rules of ablution (in the transcendental sphere); rule of inheritance, prohibited degrees, divorce, adultery (in the sphere of personal laws); perjury and rules of evidence (in the sphere of social laws) and perhaps one or two other matters. The general or 'open' character of even the prescriptive or directive verses of the Qur'an, with the few exceptions noted above, quite understandably led to the view that the Qur'anic prescriptions are inadequate, as a source of guidance to the believers, unless they are supplemented by the sayings and the example of the Prophet ﷺ. In other words, it led to the bracketing of the 'Book' and the 'example' (*al-Kitab wal sunnah*) on an almost equal footing as the supreme source of guidance for the Muslim community in all matters. However, if we look at the matter with an open mind instead of blindly adhering to the traditional approach we shall come to realize that the proper role of the sayings and the example of the Prophet ﷺ lies in the transcendental sphere rather than in the political, economic, social and cultural. In all the latter spheres 'creative fidelity' to the spirit of the Qur'an is the only valid response of the Muslim in an ever-changing world. [18]

The bracketing of the Qur'an and the *sunnah* and holding Islam to be a complete code of conduct for every aspect of human life (a view which I call the 'totalistic' approach to Islam) has been the chief cause of injecting regimentation and rigidity in Muslim societies. This approach is being vigorously propagated in many parts of the Islamic world today, though the emphasis is on a dynamic (in place of the long accepted static or closed) approach to *Shariah*. It is hardly realized by the champions of this well-organized, well-financed and somewhat militant movement that the 'totalistic' approach was the common feature of all religions until the 18th century and is, by no means, a peculiar feature of Islam.

The totalistic approach to Christianity was greatly weakened in Western Europe due to the broad cultural impact of the rapid growth of the natural and social sciences from mid 18th century onwards. But Islamic religious thought has yet to appreciate this crucial change in the religious thinking of some of the most intelligent, and morally developed Christian thinkers and also lay scholars of the history of ideas without any Christian missionary interest. [19]

I long to see the day when the Muslim mind would realize, on the basis of a mature orthogenetic movement of religious thought, rather than in the spirit of imitating the West, that the primary function of the Qur'an and of religion, as such, is inspirational and humanistic rather than legal and authoritarian in the totalistic sense. Unless this is realized the intelligent, well-informed, authentic Muslim cannot appreciate the power and beauty of the Qur'an, and creatively nourish the cultural heritage of Islam in the spirit of a ceaseless quest for value.

V

This concluding section discusses the problem of a possible conscientious objection to any portion of the Qur'an, which a Muslim accepts as an infallible scripture. At first sight it seems that believing the word of God to be infallible leaves the Muslim with no freedom to exercise his independent reasoning and with no option but to surrender before the Scripture. But the matter is not so simple as this. The word of God has first to be understood by the believer before he can properly evaluate or act upon it. And proper understanding of all discourse requires knowing not merely the literal meanings of atomic words in isolation from their situational context, but the concrete usage of the words and expressions of a natural language as also the various uses or logical grammar of human language in general. In other words, understanding of any language system requires semantic interpretation, be it the word of man or Divine communication. The interpretation of the language of the Qur'an is thus a precondition for purposeful action by the believer rather than the favorite but dispensable preoccupation of the learned. And no human interpreter can claim finality or infallibility.

The infallibility of Divine revelation does not imply the infallibility of its human interpretations, no matter how learned or spiritually elevated a person might be, since the faith that the Qur'an was revealed to the Prophet ﷺ does not imply that its interpretation was also revealed, even when the interpretation was made by or accepted by the Prophet ﷺ himself. Just as faith in the Divine revelation of the Qur'an does not imply any particular theory of revelation, similarly, faith in its infallibility does not imply that any particular interpretation of the text is sacrosanct and immutable. Indeed, theories of revelation and the interpretation of revealed Qur'anic texts both require a conceptual framework which is bound to change as human knowledge and insight grow and man's analytical tools improve. The interpretation of the Qur'an must, therefore, be viewed as a continuous creative process or task.

The infallibility of the Qur'an, thus, does not rule out the possibility of plural interpretations of the text in the light of man's growing knowledge and insight, provided the interpretation is not forced and does not violate any clear and categorical Qur'anic injunction.

The above approach to the Qur'an does not imply any disrespect toward the Prophet or denigration of his unique status among God's numerous messengers in the course of history. The above view certainly does not reduce the status of the Prophet ﷺ to that of a mere 'postman' who delivers but does not interpret God's communications. [20] This approach does not compromise the supreme spiritual status and ethical excellence of the Prophet ﷺ and the value of his authentic precepts and example; it merely holds that infallibility belongs to God alone. Indeed, the Qur'an itself refers to the occasional mistakes or errors of the Prophet ﷺ. Also it is well-established that on quite a few occasions *Caliph* Umar disagreed with the Prophet ﷺ

who modified his own judgment after discussion. The reader may refer to the following Qur'anic verses:

(66:1)

O Prophet! Why bannest thou that which Allah had made lawful for thee, seeking to please thy wives? And Allah is Forgiving, Merciful.

(80:5–10)

As for him who thinketh himself independent, Unto him thou payest regard.. But as for him who cometh unto thee with earnest purpose And hath fear, From him thou art distracted.

The crucial distinction made above between the infallibility of revelation and the fallibility of its human interpretations should enable Muslims to solve any possible conflict between faith and reason. But a conflict may well arise in an honest believer between his authentic conscience and a Qur'anic text which cannot possibly have more than one interpretation. The issue of the Qur'anic punishment for theft and adultery or the issue of the unequal status of women witnesses as compared with men may be mentioned in this context. The relevant Qur'anic verses are as follows:

(5:38)

As for the thief, both male and female, cut off their hands. It is the reward of their own deeds, an exemplary punishment from Allah. Allah is Mighty, Wise.

(24:2)

The adulterer and the adulteress scourge ye each one of them (with) a hundred stripes and let not pity for the twain withhold you from obedience to Allah, if ye believe in Allah

> *and the Last Day. And let a party of believers witness their punishment.*

(2:282)

> *... And call to witness, from among your men two witnesses, And if two men be not (at hand) then a man and two women, of such as ye approve as witnesses, so that if the one erreth (through forgetfulness) the other will remember ....*

In case an honest Muslim believer has a conscientious objection to the above contents of the Qur'an, several responses are possible: **(a)** one may rationalize (in the Freudian pejorative sense) in favor of the Qur'anic text; **(b)** one may suppress one's judgment and suffer from internal uneasiness; **(c)** one may joyfully surrender one's autonomy to the postulated higher inscrutable wisdom of revelation; **(d)** one may suspend one's judgment hoping that further self-reflection or Divine grace would resolve the conflict; **(e)** one may suspend one's judgment and reconcile himself to a perpetual tension or polarity between the text and his reason in relation to the issue concerned: and **(f)** one may hold that no God's revelation to any 'revelatee' can, in principle, claim to be infallible in the absolute or infinite sense which is applicable to God and to God alone. In other words, spatio-temporal traces or limitations (which are inseparable from all revelatory situations or processes) lead to 'nuclear' rather than 'molecular' infallibility.[21] Thus the Qur'anic perfection is that of a seed that grows leading to new dimensions and levels of perfection, and not the static perfection of an inert prefabricated structure which is incompatible with any movement or inner growth.

Of all the above responses open to the believer only the first two are clearly objectionable and undesirable; all others are legitimate possibilities out of which the believer should make his own authentic existential choice.[22] To my mind, an integrated total response (harmoniously blending the functioning of perception, reason and faith in their appropriate spheres) to the essential mystery of the Universe is possible. However, no one style or mode of an integrated response can claim exclusive validity.

Chapter 2
Authenticity and Faith in Revelation

The word 'authenticity' has become a prestigious word in contemporary academic and literary circles like the words 'democracy', 'evolutionary', 'dialectical', 'justice', 'equality', 'revolutionary', 'scientific', and 'verification', etc. However a good deal of confusion or ambiguity surrounds it in the thinking of many people. The purpose of this paper is to analyze the central meaning of this word as used in contemporary or recent existentialist literature and to raise some basic questions as to how a person could claim to combine faith in revelation (with special reference to Islam) with authenticity in the existentialist sense.

I

The word 'authentic' in its ordinary usage means exact and literal correspondence or agreement of an entity 'e' with some other original entity 'E' which is sought to be copied, represented or referred to by 'e'. In this sense a copy of an original deed is authentic if the copy is exactly the same as the original, a printed book is authentic if its contents exactly reproduce those of the original manuscript, a quotation is authentic if it is identical with the original remark, and so on and so forth. This use is slightly changed when we speak of an authentic painting, for, in this case, we mean the original work itself rather than its copy, no matter how excellent the reproduction may be. Again, the use of 'authentic' in the expression 'authentic translation' is different, since what corresponds here is the meaning of the two texts and not the observable physical letters or words. In the case of 'authentic confession' or 'authentic declaration', the correspondence is between an external entity and an intention or inner psychological condition not open to inspection by the observer. In the case of 'authentic news/report', the correspondence is between statements and facts. 'Authentic will' means the will or testament is not a forgery in part or full, so that the contents of the will, as a document, correspond with the contents of the testator's will in the psychological or semantic sense. This use is partly similar to 'authentic declaration', but not the same, since an unauthentic declaration or confession cannot be said to have been 'forged'. Again an authentic signature' means that the signature was actually made by the person concerned, but it may or may not correspond with his usual signature. Often it does correspond, but at times the signature may be authentic and yet fail to correspond with the usual signature because of some reason or other.

Turning to the sphere of religion, 'authentic faith/religious belief' means that the faith of a person springs from his 'heart' without any doubt, pretense, hypocrisy or motive of worldly reward (as distinct from spiritual salvation). In other words, the profession of faith corresponds with a genuine belief, attitude or response without any pose, desire to impress, deceive, gain any advantage exclusively linked with the profession of belief, and so on.

Authentic faith leads to either willing or spontaneous action in accordance with the requirements of the faith without cajoling, coercing, or luring the agent into the desired action. Authenticity is a matter of degrees and the highest degree of authenticity leads to spontaneous action, while a relatively lower degree of authenticity leads to willing action by the agent. The total absence of appropriate action, or action performed out of fear of worldly punishment or the lure of worldly reward signifies the lack of authentic faith behind the verbalization of a creed. In other words, faith is active commitment, or an inner state of 'being' ever turning into 'doing' by virtue of an inner motivational *nisus* or necessity quite independent of fear or hope of gain.

An authentic Muslim/Christian/Hindu is a person, who inwardly accepts, for its own sake, the system of beliefs, values, obligations and behavior patterns deemed to be the central core of the religion, and acts accordingly. If, however, the person inwardly dissents from some feature of the system but freely, that is, without any extraneous motive of fear or reward, opts to defer to the system (because of the overwhelming depth appeal of the system as a whole) and also molds his actions accordingly, he too may be said to be an authentic believer. If, however, such a person remains in a state of inner doubt, tension and indecision or ignores the conflict between his inner responses and some feature of the system, or tries to rationalize the stipulated 'higher wisdom' of the system by arguments which he (in his heart of hearts) rejects, he would cease to be an authentic believer. [23]

II

We thus find that there is no one use or standard meaning of the word 'authenticity' but a whole spectrum or gamut of uses. Now what does an existentialist writer mean when he says, "X is an authentic person"? Is this sentence literally equivalent to the sentence, "X is a sincere person"? The answer is 'no', since authenticity includes sincerity in its meaning, but is not reducible to it. Thus a sincere woman may think she loves her husband, and yet her sincere love may lack authenticity, in the existentialist sense, since the sincere wife's love may not be rooted in the depth of her being but may be merely a disguised form of loyalty or friendly concern for her husband, expected by society from a good wife. In other words, a sincere person may not be authentic, since to be authentic is to be sincere to one's inner depth rather than to some 'other', whether person, book or creed. An authentic person is one whose self-awareness not only extends to his surface thoughts or feelings but penetrates into his existential depth, so that the faintest and most nebulous or inarticulate stirrings, attitudes, desires, aspirations, evaluations—in short, the multifarious human responses, just as they arise in man's almost inaccessible depths—get registered to some degree by the authentic person.

The concept of authenticity thus presupposes the concept of human 'depth' or, in other words, a model of human personality, which partly resembles but also differs from Freud's division of man's psyche into the '*id*', 'ego', and 'super-ego'. For Freud, the '*id*' is the system or totality of spontaneous drives, which are faintly reflected and partly distorted as they reach the level of consciousness or the 'ego'. The 'ego' may be likened to an air bubble that arises on the surface of water whose depth is infinitely greater than the bubble. The 'super-ego', according to Freud, is the internalized censor and is superimposed on the '*id*' and the '*ego*' as a result of cultural conditioning without having any existential roots in the '*id*' as such. Thus the conscious '*ego*' is sandwiched, as it were, between the totally non-rational and amoral instinctive drives or the '*libido*', in the broader sense, and the system of ethical values or ideals, which however, do not have any a priori or internal source in man's basic depth or constitution.

Freud's conception of the '*id*' is non-moral and non-rational, if not positively evil, and his conception of the '*super-ego*' is basically sociological and non-transcendental so that all human rational and ethical systems rest upon the shifting sands of impulse without any solid existential foundation, as it were. The conception of many existentialist writers, on the other hand, holds that the deepest layer of the human being is the locus of the Divine spark, the point of contact between humanity and man's potential or latent Divinity. In terms of Indian thought also the *Atman* and the *Brahman* intersect and overlap each other in man's depths.

The ultimate depth or Divine spark in man lies covered or encrusted with his thoughts, feelings or volitions, layer upon layer, reducing the effulgence of the spark to a hardly perceptible dim light. The normal waking stream of consciousness thus acts as a barrier between man's depth and his *ego*, which becomes alienated from its depth. Such an *ego* may be compared to a boat, which has lost its moorings and starts drifting with the currents of water or air. Man has the capacity to journey into the depths of his being. As the diver dives into the depths of the ocean, man can journey into the depths of his being, seeking communion with his vibrant center—the God within man. However, there can be no certainty, in the logical or objective sense, that he has indeed touched his ultimate depth. Indeed, to plumb one's own depth is more difficult than to identify with the naked eye an object a billion times smaller than a pinhead, embedded in a dark deep well of muddy water. Tentativeness of approach and a receptive frame of mind are, thus, essential for protecting man against the danger of spiritual arrogance or conceit, which lead him to fanaticism.

Authenticity is inseparable from subjectivity. An authentic person is one who lives the life of inwardness and subjectivity, but this subjectivity is not to be confused with the subjectivity of impulse which creates conflict and discord, or the subjectivity of taste which does not involve man's deeper ethical levels, and does not affect his total conduct of life. A '*kingdom of authentic persons*', therefore would not lead to conflict or chaos, as may be feared by some. Indeed, if the subjective depth of every person really touches the shores of Divinity, or if the Divine spark is present in all of us, the subjectivity of the authentic person will not be an exercise in arbitrary impulse or caprice, but would bind together autonomous persons respecting one another as co-sharers of the Divine spark. The practical or institutional expression of this mutual respect is democracy as a way of life. [24]

'Authentic being', in the existentialist sense, is thus not reducible to religious authenticity, since authenticity, in the existentialist sense, means rootedness in one's depth, irrespective of its content, without demanding an original normative entity 'E' with which one's beliefs or actions ought to correspond. Christian or Islamic authenticity, on the other hand, involves an already given norm or antecedent faith. An authentic Christian must, by definition, be committed to Christian values, while an authentic being in the existentialist sense, is committed to inner freedom alone. A person who values merely the authenticity of a Christian or that of a Hindu will not be able to appreciate the authenticity of an atheist or Dialectical Materialist. But one who values authenticity or authentic being, as such, will respect and admire an authentic person irrespective of where his authenticity may have led him.

This, however, does not mean that a person who gives supreme value to authentic being cannot himself have an authentic faith in a particular religion. In other words, there is no essential incompatibility between authentic being and authentic faith in a particular value system. Man's freedom to choose remains abstract and his concrete being remains indeterminate until he commits himself in a specific way. The moment he does so his hitherto 'open' freedom becomes bounded or acquires specific contours. But this does not mean any loss of freedom as such. Being a committed Muslim or Hindu, in the higher authentic sense, is a specific form of authenticity having a particular content, just as a rose is a particular species of flower, and not something other than a flower.

A person may intensely love roses or Bach's music, but he may also appreciate other flowers or forms of music. Likewise, one may well combine a supreme concern for authenticity, in the existentialist sense, with authentic faith in a specific religious creed *provided* no portion of the creed or the value-cum-prescriptive system given by the legitimate 'Authority' raises any inner tension or conflict within the religious believer. This would be the case when all judgments or commands of the 'Authority' evoke in the believer

Authenticity and Islamic Liberalism

an *'existential echo'*. [25] Though such a person may find it difficult to act in accordance with any particular command or commands of the 'Authority' he has no difficulty in accepting their validity or legitimacy. Thus, for instance, he may find it extremely difficult to speak the truth or to love his neighbor as he loves himself, or to sacrifice his own personal interests for the greater social good, and so on, and yet he accepts their legitimacy. However, if some command or commands evoke a negative *'existential echo'* in the believer, mere external obedience to it/them would not satisfy a Muslim who cares for both authenticity and Islam. What should he do in such a case?

Obviously, the first thing the person should resort to is a careful reflection, after reading and discussion, on the issues involved and a reconsideration of the reasons for his dissent from the Authority. The individual may also pray to God for guidance. If, despite all these efforts, his dissent remains he will find himself in a dilemma.

Let us take a hypothetical illustration. Suppose 'A' is a member of a society which holds that a woman who has been raped is a curse to all and should be put to death in the best interests of society. Let us further suppose that the society enforces this rule and brooks no dissent in this matter. Now suppose 'A' is in general agreement with the group mores which he loyally follows, but he cannot help feeling that this particular rule is improper or unjust. In other words, 'A' has a conscientious objection to the rule, without being culturally conditioned by extra-group mores. Even if 'A' may have been influenced by knowledge of the mores of other groups this does not amount to his being determined by others rather than by this own group. 'A' may have been carried away by alien group mores, but this need not necessarily be so. Indeed, in the illustration at hand, 'A' continues to accept and practice his group mores, which he has no difficulty in internalizing, but for this particular matter. His dissent is thus orthogenetic, and inwardly different from the culturally conditioned objection by a member belonging to an out-group with different mores. To deny the very possibility that 'A' could ever make such an authentic or free choice would be unwarranted.

Let us now turn to the case of a Muslim who finds that some Qur'anic injunction or some provision of the *Shariah*, which has the approval of the Prophet ﷺ, does not evoke his free assent, say, the stoning unto death as a penalty for adultery. The Muslim, after careful reflection, may be convinced that though adultery is socially harmful and reprehensible, the degree of its evil is far less than that of rape or murder; thus while the latter two do merit capital punishment, adultery does not. However, even if it be accepted for argument's sake that he concedes the validity of capital punishment for adultery, the peculiar mode of death through stoning may appear to him to be morally wrong. Since, however, the Qur'an does not prescribe this particular punishment (though the *Shariah* does) no difficulty arises in respect of the Qur'an. If, however, it be admitted that this particular penalty was approved of by the Prophet ﷺ, this would amount to a conscientious objection against something approved of by the Prophet ﷺ. But then the same problem *may* arise with respect to some actual Qur'anic injunction, say, the permissibility or desirability of the husband chastising his wife by beating her, or the penalty of flogging, or the denial of equal rights to women in some matters, and so on.

What is a Muslim to do in such a case? Let us suppose he has discussed the matter with competent and sincere co-religionist's who are unable to remove his conscientious objection, he has thought over the problem in all its aspects, he has shed tears of humility in the silence of the night while seeking Divine grace and guidance. But the more he reflects on the problem and seeks to understand God's inscrutable wisdom, the more his inner conviction grows about the moral impropriety of a particular rule or injunction. Had he been a mere deist without believing in the Divine revelation of the Qur'an, he would not have been bothered by any conflict between his authentic judgment and the Qur'an. But the traditional conception of perfection or infallibility of the Qur'an does not permit such indifference.

If a Muslim who values authenticity (as has been analyzed above) raises this problem in a discussion with a traditional divine, the most likely answer will be as follows: "*Man is an insignificant creature, while God, the source of truth and wisdom, revealed in the perfect Qur'an. The Muslim must submit his essentially fallible private judgment or reason to the infallible wisdom of the Qur'an.*" Indeed, this advice is actually followed by innumerable Muslims. Such Muslims are further told that their disagreement with the Authority is an indication that their faith is as yet immature and contaminated by un-Islamic influences and subjective attitudes. The advice goes on to say that if a Muslim persists in his submission to the Qur'an his doubts and difficulties would be removed through Divine grace in the course of time, and he would attain the state of perfect satisfaction (*nafs-e-mutmainnah*). Reasonable as this view sounds, it does not take into account the difficulty that may arise if the inner doubts and difficulties of the Muslim persist, despite the passage of a fairly long time. To repeat the same advice, time and again, would be a failure to come to grips with reality. A Muslim following the above advice for an indefinite period would be condemned to inauthentic existence, marked by perpetual tension between his authentic responses and the demand for submission to the Authority, making his life extremely difficult. In one sense of authenticity he can function as an authentic Muslim, provided he molds his conduct according to the pattern approved by the Authority and provided, further, that the surrender is made willingly and with full awareness of the conflict between one's authentic responses and the command of the Authority. But such surrender will fail to lead to authentic being, in the higher existentialist sense, that is, the sense of inner responsible freedom of choice and a willing acceptance of the consequences of such a choice. Consequently, if one gives the highest value to inner freedom or spiritual autonomy, irrespective of where man's authentic freedom (as distinct from the surface freedom of impulse or license) leads him, one cannot follow the counsel of surrendering one's judgment to the Authority.

A striking illustration is provided by one's approach to the institution of marriage. A married person may be quite content if he has achieved understanding or adjustment with his spouse, without any passionate love gushing forth from the depths of his being. Another married person may feel dissatisfied with a marriage of the above pragmatic type, and his fascination for the romantic concept may be so strong that he feels profoundly uneasy about a union, which satisfies needs but not ideals. Now neither of the above approaches to marriage could be said to be true or false. The person who prefers the romantic approach to marriage cannot claim the pragmatic approach to be false, though he may encourage or invite others to accept his own preference as a 'higher' and not merely an arbitrary choice. Likewise, a person who gives supreme value to authentic being would be justified in rejecting the infallibility of the Qur'an (as traditionally understood), if despite his best efforts, he fails to overcome his conscientious objection to some portion of it.

The question arises: Is no other option open to him to combine his supreme concern for authentic being and his faith in the infallibility of the Qur'an? It seems to me one could combine the two, if one were to hold that Qur'anic infallibility belongs to the *telos* or the basic objectives adumbrated by the Authority rather than any specific or instrumental rules formulated by the Authority or established by traditional interpretations. The believer who values authentic being, in the existentialist sense, would then be free to follow his conscience if he has a conscientious objection to any specific prescription, without giving up his basic faith in Qur'anic infallibility (in the above suggested sense) as a Divine revelation. In brief, if infallibility is interpreted as 'value-centric' rather than as 'rule-centric', no problem would arise for the committed Muslim who gives supreme value to authenticity in the existentialist sense. Another way of saying the same thing is to distinguish between 'nuclear' and 'molecular' infallibility of the Qur'an, holding that infallibility is a characteristic of or belongs to the 'Qur'anic nucleus' rather than the 'Qur'anic molecule'.

III

By the expression 'Qur'anic molecule' I mean a complete intelligible sentence of the Qur'an, while by 'Qur'anic nucleus' I mean the intentional thrust/*telos* or final objective intrinsic value(s), or more familiarly, the spirit of the Qur'an. This spirit is discernible only through full knowledge of the situational context of the revelation and sustained reflection on the 'directive message' underlying the words rather than the literal meaning of the letter of the Qur'an. The Qur'an is not a systematic book divided into chapters, sections, paragraphs, sentences, or a long didactic poem composed according to subject matter. Nor is the Qur'an arranged in the chronological order of revelation; the sequence of the Qur'anic verses (some of which may be said to be linguistic molecules, while others sub-molecules); was determined by the Prophet ﷺ himself. A proper understanding of numerous verses admittedly presupposes knowledge of the situational context of their revelation, while a balanced insight into the Qur'an, as a source of Islamic theology, law and morality, requires the collation and interpretation of widely scattered verses related to the subject matter.

No verse, as an abstract linguistic molecule or, isolated from other relevant verses, could possibly claim infallible truth in the literal sense, or claim to exhaust the spirit of the Qur'an. The spirit or *telos* of the Qur'an is not a fixed literal meaning out there in the Qur'anic 'linguistic space', but is the nucleus of an ever-growing, yet ever-incomplete, 'directive message' which never yields itself to full disclosure to our finite minds and to full realization in the human situation. This directive message must be understood or interpreted in the light of the continual growth in human knowledge and awareness leading to new dimensions in old values and in the vision of the good life.

This 'dimensional growth' is inspired and shaped no less by the 'ontogenetic' or spiritual power of the Qur'anic *telos* than by ever-growing human knowledge and self-understanding. However, while the human *telos* continues to change or mature, the eternal letter of the Qur'an remains static. This inevitably results in the alienation of the believer's emerging value system from the letter of the Qur'an. If, and when, such alienation takes place the letter of the Qur'an fails to evoke an 'existential echo' in the believer even after he goes through a painstaking inquiry and sustained prayerful reflection on the issues involved in a sincere effort to overcome his spiritual alienation from the letter of the Qur'an. The only way to overcome this alienation without abandoning the ideal and prospects of dimensional growth is to define Islamic piety and faith in terms of 'creative fidelity' to the nuclear *telos* or spirit rather than in terms of mechanical adherence to the letter of the Qur'an. To say that the Qur'an is infallible in the nuclear sense means that its spirit represents the proper direction of ceaseless dimensional growth, whether or not, any particular molecular expression, that is, the letter of the law, is literally or permanently applicable to the human situation.

The above suggested interpretative discretion and freedom may conceivably be misused, but its denial to the believer on the ground of this risk would amount to extinguishing all dimensional progress of man apart from sheer arithmetical approximation or further linear movement toward a static ideal articulated in the past. Indeed, rigid adherence to the letter of any value system (religious or secular) either retards dimensional growth or turns the believer into an inauthentic being or rebel, as the case may be. The concept of 'creative fidelity', on the other hand, enables believers to be true to their own self as well as to the scripture and the faith. Let us now turn to some concrete illustrations in support of this claim.

Let us consider the letter and the spirit of the Qur'an concerning slavery. The Qur'anic molecule does not censure the institution of slavery as an unmitigated evil like, say, female infanticide, and does not prohibit its practice, but merely prescribes kindness toward the slave. [26] The intentional thrust or spirit of the Qur'an, however, prescribes universal kindness, justice and social welfare by means of liberal spending in the way of God and encouraging voluntary emancipation of slaves as an act of charity and penance. Now, if justice and social welfare clearly demand equality of status and equality of opportunity, the spirit of the Qur'an would require us not merely to be kind toward slaves but to abolish slavery as an institution, while the letter of the law would not. Indeed, a person holding the Qur'an to be infallible and perfect in the conventional sense could well oppose the abolition of slavery on the ground that had God desired to abolish slavery, root and branch, the Qur'an (or the Prophet ﷺ) would have expressly done so. He may further, take the stand that any attempt to improve upon Qur'anic injunctions amounts to claiming that man is wiser than God. And indeed, this was the actual stand of the Muslim establishment until very recently. [27]

The Qur'anic permission for vicarious retaliation for murder offers another illustration. Vicarious retaliation was an ancient pre-Islamic Arab custom prevalent in other societies as well. The Qur'anic molecule nowhere abolished it, but merely moderated it by stressing that retaliation should not exceed the original injury. The Qur'an did not introduce the idea that murder is a crime against the state, which alone has the right (in the legal sense) to punish the wrong-doer, and that nobody related to the victim may justifiably indulge in vicarious punishment in the form of like injury to the wrong-doer himself. Even if it be held that the Qur'anic principle of retaliation for murder—"*the freeman for the freeman, and the slave for the slave, and the female for the female*" applies only when the wrong-doer belongs to an alien tribe or society and cannot be traced, the permission for vicarious punishment '*according to the legal and biological status of the victim*' clashes with the modern concept of equality before the law and of individual accountability. Though reprisals do take place even now, they do not enjoy the sanction of law or international norms. Acceptance of the latter implies going beyond the Qur'anic molecule or the letter of the Qur'an. [28]

Another pertinent example of the difference between the letter and the spirit of the Qur'an is the question of women's rights. No scripture or legal system grants greater rights or a higher status to women than does the Qur'an, though the letter of the Qur'an does not prescribe complete equality of men and women in several matters. Nevertheless, the intentional thrust or spirit of the Qur'an lies in this very direction. Consequently, if numerous authentic believers yearn for complete equality of status and of opportunity for all human beings, irrespective of their sex, why should not the believer choose to follow the spirit rather than the letter of the Qur'an?

In other words, the believer need not have religious qualms in moving in the direction of social justice as pointed out by the Qur'an. [29]

The distinction between intrinsic values and instrumental rules also tends to fructify and legitimize the distinction between the spirit and the letter of the Qur'an and the desirability of following its spirit rather than its letter. If instrumental rules are clearly means and not ends, and if advances in knowledge create more effective means of reaching our objectives than was possible earlier, should not the clearly instrumental rules of the Qur'an be suitably modified to make them maximally effective? And such modification would imply giving up the notion of molecular infallibility of the Qur'an. As an illustration, let us consider the Qur'anic prescription to the believers to procure horses as a war preparation. It would readily be conceded that to follow this command, in the literal sense, is not practicable in the age of tanks and airplanes. Now if the pursuit of basic objectives is rightly given precedence over literal compliance in this case, should not the primacy of basic values over instrumental rules be conceded in other cases as well? [30]

Whether or not the second *Caliph*, Umar, made a distinction between nuclear and molecular infallibility, or between intrinsic values and instrumental rules, his reported actions give the impression that he did so. For instance, by refusing to have the hands of a thief cut off (on the ground that this penalty was unjust under famine conditions) he seems to have given rather more importance to the spirit of the Qur'an than to its letter, if we take into consideration the fact that the Qur'an categorically enjoins this punishment to the thief without any reference to the prevailing social and economic conditions. [31] Umar's example implies that his conception of the infallibility of the Qur'an and of being a good Muslim did not preclude the exercise of his own discretion. On several occasions he differed from the Prophet ﷺ during his lifetime as well as after his death. Had Umar accepted either the Qur'an or the Prophet ﷺ to be infallible in the molecular sense, he could not have suspended a clear Qur'anic command or differed from the Prophet ﷺ. [32]

Nuclear infallibility should not be confused with what may be called 'selective infallibility', that is, holding some portions of the Qur'an as infallible while others as not. This approach sounds incongruous with faith in the Qur'an as the word of God revealed to His messenger. This conception introduces an artificial division within the Qur'an, destroying its unity, sanctity and authority, while the concept of nuclear infallibility does not.

Authenticity and Faith in Revelation

Nuclear infallibility is the highest possible level of perfection for any entity less than God—Prophet, angel or word of God. None can be equated with God, the absolute Being, Who alone could be said to be infallible or perfect in the absolute sense. The revelatory situation is essentially finite; therefore the perfection of revelation and the 'revelatee' is essentially relative, even if the source of the revelation be infinite and infallible in the absolute sense.

A Qur'an, which is believed to be infallible in the above-suggested nuclear sense, should not be deemed to be inferior to a Qur'an regarded as infallible in the molecular sense. The concept of nuclear infallibility does not compromise the sanctity of the Qur'an or impair its essential 'ontogenetic' and inspirational function. Qur'anic infallibility, in this reconstructed sense, would still impose limits on the Muslim as is done by the ordinary conception. But these limits would be set, not by the Qur'anic molecule, that is, the literal sense of its contents but rather by the 'spirit' of the Qur'an as one understands it. This understanding will inevitably vary from individual to individual and age to age. To me, this is pre-eminently desirable, so that nobody could claim he alone possesses the only one infallibly true and binding interpretation of the spirit or of the letter of the Qur'an and that anyone who rejected it was guilty of heresy or apostasy.

It seems the authentic Muslim should habitually explore and sound his existential depths and, on principle, eschew surrendering to or mechanically obeying the command of an external authority, as is traditionally recommended and practiced. It cannot be over-emphasized that eternal vigilance is the price of authenticity and creativity. However, after having explored one's authentic being one may (as a committed Muslim) surrender one's own free judgment to the letter or spirit of the Qur'an, as the case may be. We resent restrictions on our freedom, but we are also afraid of our own freedom, as brilliantly pointed out by Eric Fromm several decades ago. [33] Fear of freedom is partly the fear of facing one's existential abyss—that which lies in the depths of one's being and has an awesome and irresistible power before which our cherished values and pious intentions often begin to melt like wax before fire.

The fear of one's existential depths and the apprehension that man's freedom must necessarily push him into the pit of chaos and disaster is rooted in a low opinion of man's nature and also of one's own self rather than in a mature realistic insight into one's own and human limitations and frailties in general. While a mature understanding of human nature and an insightful humility with regard to one's own strong and weak points are pre-eminently desirable, a compulsively low image of man or one's own self results in what Fromm has called the neurotic 'fear of freedom'.

Once, however, we realize that man's deeper self is not a raging sea of passions and irrational drives (though they do have lodgment in man's depths) but that man's ultimate depth touches the shore of Divinity, man's fear of his subjective depth is transmuted into a longing to reach out into the ecstasy of Divine communion.

Man's self-image, as an isolated Divine ray trembling on the dark surface created by the ignorance of man's Divine origin, is his ontological promise that man's inner freedom would not necessarily degenerate into license or sheer impulse. Though human lapses and failures are certainly endemic and countless the risk of tragic accidents on the road should not hold man back from his journey into inner space, fortified by the conviction that there is a Divine spark in the depths of his being. This is a fateful choice each must make for himself alone, though he could well recommend his choice to others.

The escape from freedom pushes man into the arms of an external authority as a compensation for his intense feeling of his own worthlessness and propensity to evil in the absence of a strong external authority. Surrender before such an authority not only disciplines the person; but gives him a sense of power and ego-expansion through identifying himself with the Authority. Such a person lives at the mass level, ridding himself of the burden of self-direction, which flows from authentic freedom and the courage to accept the consequences of exercising this freedom. He prefers the stability and security of cultural conditioning provided by the Authority to the risks involved in authentic being.

The lack of authenticity or self-communication with the depths of one's being leads one to self-alienation—the drifting away of the conscious ego from its creative center and source of inner joy. The self-alienated ego then seeks to compensate for this joyless state of being by trying to dominate the inner life of others.

The desire for power is a natural human condition. When, however, the desire becomes a craving for controlling the minds and hearts of others (whether the ideas and values be religious or secular) the permissible level of the natural human drive for power shoots up abnormally to produce the pathological condition of fanaticism. And fanaticism is an evil, no matter what its content might be. True concern for the welfare of others lies in working for their inner freedom and growth rather than in steering them in a predetermined direction.

Fear of others leads to lack of communication with others or social alienation, while fear of one's own inner freedom leads to lack of communication with one's deepest self or self-alienation—a condition in which men live, think and act in conformity with external norms and expectations. Such men profess beliefs and values, religious or secular, without the joy of commitment and the satisfaction of sincere action, and then they run after compensatory substitutes like sensual pleasure, organizational power, prestige and similar goals.

The self-integrated and authentic person, on the other hand, (no matter what religion he may profess) communicates with his own deepest center and also that of others for whom he feels a sense of human kinship and ontological harmony overriding all difference of caste, color or creed. Such a person is self-integrated, socially integrated and cosmically integrated, radiating spiritual peace and cosmic love as a flower gives fragrance to all without questioning their caste, color or creed. His beliefs and values are not apparel, which he can discard to suit his own convenience or that of others, out of fear or favor, but a part of his bones, as it were.

At the same time the authentic person who cherishes equally his own inner freedom and that of others is fully aware that other persons may be committed to other beliefs and values. Such persons must be respected for a sincere commitment to their beliefs and values, though different from one's own. The authentic person is also aware or easily becomes aware, if he looks at the matter with intellectual curiosity, that his religious beliefs cannot be proved like propositions of mathematics or science; he, therefore, rejects what may be called 'religious rationalism' in favor of religious existentialism. The bliss of an inner certitude or conviction courses in his spiritual arteries, as it were, and he is content if others also enjoy this bliss, no matter what religion or creed they profess. Being a free man of God rather than the prisoner of any dogma, instilled into the vocabulary of his spiritual mother-tongue, his religious response is that of a person overwhelmed by a sense of mystery together with the unshakable conviction that the mysterious is also supremely good, making life worth living and giving our authentic ideals and aspirations the promise of their fulfillment. And this is the essence of religious faith.

Religious faith, like true love, wells forth from the depths of one's being as water gushes forth from a perennial spring. The function of faith is to provide anchorage and stability to man's basic attitudes toward the human situation. This is also the function of a philosophical worldview, which however, should be critically acquired by the adult, while religious faith is normally imbibed in the lap of the family circle. The function of a worldview can be performed only by philosophy or religion, and no other cultural activity can take their place. Science describes and explains in terms of verifiable hypotheses, poetry pleases and great poetry edifies and illumines man, technology serves our needs, morality' evaluates and regulates our inner acts, law regulates our outer social relations, but none can claim to give a basic meaning of the Universe and a direction to life as a whole. This is the residual basic function of religious faith or a philosophical world view which itself is 'philosophical faith', as pointed out by the German philosopher, Karl Jasper's. [34] Both kinds of faith integrate man's thinking, feeling and willing into a total existential response of a conscious self confronting the mystery of the cosmos comprising the phenomena of birth, growth, death, suffering, struggle, guilt, love, beauty, joy, fear, tragedy, and so on. Even an atheist (provided he does not turn into a nihilist rejecting the pursuit of all values, including truth, goodness and beauty) who pursues the good (unknowingly) pursues God as the cosmic Ground or Source of all value, even though he does not relate himself to this Source as a 'Holy Thou'. Whether or not the individual who pursues truth, goodness and beauty chooses to establish an *'I-Thou'* relationship with the Source of all value, our respect for the individual must not be linked with this very crucial personal decision, but must depend only upon the person's active concern for truth, goodness and beauty.

It is a fairly common belief that a deeply religious person who really has faith in the truth of his religion must hold other religious beliefs to be false and wish all others to be converted to the one and only true religion for their own good. This approach makes the peaceful conversion of others part of one's religious duties. The underlying assumption of this approach is that the entire human family is destined to accept the one true religion sooner or later but it is the duty of the true religious believer to expedite the consummation of the Divine Plan.

The above approach fails to see that since religious convictions just cannot be proved or disproved by logical or scientific reasoning they, *ipso facto*, cannot be altered by ordinary persuasion, in proportion, as the convictions are really genuine. Indeed, the greater the degree of existential certainty of a sincere believer the less open would he be to the rationalistic pretensions of those who have the illusion that their religious beliefs are rationally demonstrable. If, and when, the crucial insight dawns on the true believer that religious truths are existential convictions rather than demonstrable certainties the desire to convert others tends to wither away, or to yield to the desire that all human beings should rise to the level of authentic being instead of remaining at the level of mere cultural conditioning. When, for instance, one realizes that neither the Semitic 'linear' concept of life after death, nor the Aryan 'cyclical' concept could be proved true in the exclusive sense, while both actually serve a common basic function (metaphysical and ethical), one tends to become more concerned with doing good deeds himself and also motivating others toward goodness rather than in converting the 'cyclical' concept of afterlife into the linear, or vice versa.

Religious convictions, in the final analysis, are nearer to aesthetic evaluations rather than factual or logical truthclaims of the type 'p' or 'not-p'. While we cannot accept contrary or contradictory truthclaims in the latter case, why should one object to plural religious convictions so long as they do not violate our authentic conscience? One may well have deep religious convictions without the additional belief that the religious convictions of others are false or that they ought to be substituted by one's own in the entire human family. Tolerance, permissiveness and genuine respect for religious convictions, other than our own, are thus, quite compatible with deep religious faith.

CHAPTER 3

THE RELIGIOUS REVOLUTION OF THE 18TH CENTURY AND ISLAM

In this chapter I shall seek to answer (1) how the rise and development of the natural and social sciences in the modern era have gradually transformed the medieval conception of the nature and function of religion in human society; (2) how this change has gradually led to the emergence of religious existentialism, cultural pluralism and 'permissiveness' in Western society; and (3) the imperative need that Muslims should grasp the historical logic of the above developments for autonomously applying them to the great Islamic tradition instead of merely revising the *Shariah* here and there as part of a program of adjustment to the modern age.

I

The remarkable progress of the natural and the social sciences during the modern age has enormously increased the range of man's free choice in dealing with nature and society both. For instance, man can now control his population growth and, hopefully, even the sex of his progeny, conquer disease and poverty, make deserts bloom or colonize the moon. Likewise, man can now abolish monarchy, dis-establish the church, nationalize the means of production, equalize the sexes, discontinue free elections and last but not least (if he so chooses) banish God from his ideal society. The novel feature of the human situation in the contemporary period is that he can banish religion without giving up morality, philosophy, art, literature, in brief, the various elements of the good life. This degree of freedom was just not possible a few centuries earlier, since all the above aspects of the good life formed an integral part of religion, which functioned as a total map of the good life. Moreover, individual liberty was very restricted, and no one could freely criticize the mores of his group with impunity. Today he may do so fully, in theory, and largely, in practice, in all democratic societies. Today a man can claim to pursue morality without God or religion as is done in communist society, or by secular humanists like Mill, Russell, Dewey, and others.

This process had started with the European Renaissance in the 15th century, gained effective momentum due to the scientific revolution in the 18th century and has been reaching for full maturity and fruition in the 20th century. Even though the vast bulk of the Muslim world has not yet felt the full impact of this revolutionary change in the human situation, all thinking minds must face the question: Should religion be or not be? If the answer be 'yes' then what religion? Again if 'Islam' be the answer of a born Muslim then what version or interpretation of Islam should prevail, since every religion has not one, but several versions, each claiming exclusive truth.

Ever since the time of Sir Syed Ahmed, the founder of the *Aligarh Movement*, one has been hearing about the need for reinterpreting Islam or discovering its essential spirit as distinct from its varying sociocultural expressions and legal schools. However, the work that has been done in this field has lamentably failed to attack the problem of reinterpreting Islam in the light of the sociocultural history of the human family as a whole. Muslim religious thinkers and theologians have viewed the task of reinterpreting Islam essentially as the liberalizing of the *Shariah* regarding rather trivial mailers—the permissibility of music, photography, the microphone for congregational prayers, contraception, interest on bank deposits, timings of the prayers, and duration of fasts in certain geographical regions, and so on and so forth. Perhaps, the greatest advance made in this genre of Islamic reinterpretation is to stretch the classical Islamic concept of 'consensus of the Muslim community' to mean the legislative authority of an elected assembly of Muslims. But none, not even Iqbal, makes any attempt to redefine the nature and function of religion in the modern age in the light of sociocultural history, despite the suggestive title, '*The Principle of Movement in the Structure of Islam*' of one of his lectures on Islam. [35]

The Religious Revolution of the 18th Century and Islam

Substantial military, administrative, fiscal, educational and political reforms (including the convening of an elected Parliament, which however, could not function at all) had been made in Ottoman Turkey as long back as the end of the 18th century. [36] But neither those reforms nor the much more drastic and radical innovations made by Kamal Ataturk in our own times were rooted in a systematic thought system as their theoretical rationale or basis, as Western democracy is based on the thought system of Locke, Kant, Voltaire and others, or Communism on that of Marx and Engels. [37] Perhaps, Sir Syed still excels all others in this regard. But his efforts were not backed by full knowledge of the methodology of the natural and social sciences, and a full grasp over modern philosophy. His religious rationalism, therefore, convinces neither the critical mind of contemporary man nor those who consciously or unconsciously think in the medieval framework of ideas.

Sociocultural history shows that all religions performed a fourfold function right until the end of the 18th century: **(a)** provision of a basic world view or thought system to serve as a conceptual anchor and justification for a stable attitude to the Universe as a whole; **(b)** provision of a value system comprising a set of intrinsic moral values and instrumental rules for realizing them; **(c)** prescription of a set of symbolic practices and rituals calculated to stabilize and reinforce the thought and value systems and also to create a sense of group cohesiveness or emotional integration; and **(d)** provision of a legal system for regulating the external conduct or social relations of human beings in different spheres of activity. Religion was thus a complete map of the good life and religious piety meant that the true believer follow the map in all its details without questioning its validity or desiring its improvement in any respect. The map included every activity from personal hygiene to inheritance, marriage and divorce, commerce and war. As a result, the focus of religious piety tended to shift from religious inwardness to conformity with the prescribed rules dealing with the minutiae of life, that is, from the inner quality of being to the details of living. Pietism and mysticism (which are found in every religious tradition) were attempts to restore inwardness to religion.

Apart from the above tension between the inner and the outer aspects of religion there was another crucial tension between the supreme priest and the king as to who was superior. This is the conflict between the church and the state and has permeated all societies at all times in some form or other. It has not yet been resolved and never can be fully resolved, though different societies have tried to do so in different ways. The Christian Reformation in the 16th century and some other factors divided Western Christianity into Catholics and Protestants, who differed on the status and powers of the Pope vis-a-vis the king. But in actual practice it was the king who emerged as the symbol and locus of sovereignty, that is, supreme power and authority over the territorial state. In short, the civil power of the king triumphed over the ecclesiastical power of the priest.

What has been said above about the fourfold function of religion applies equally to all religions up to the mid 18th century. Thus, the belief held by numerous Muslim theologians, scholars and others that Islam alone is a complete code of conduct or a total guide to life in all aspects, while Hinduism and Christianity are merely a set of rituals and rather innocuous ceremonies, without any concrete guidance in the enterprise of living, is totally wrong. The great wealth of Hindu or Christian casuistry exposes this fallacy. But it is important to probe why this wrong impression has been created.

It seems that in the case of Hinduism the impression has been created by its looseness or internal diversity, while in the case of Christianity by ignoring its grand, 'totalist tradition', right up to the 18th century (which is as imposing and complex a structure as the Islamic *Shariah* itself) and viewing Christianity after its transformation in the 18th century under the impact of the scientific and industrial revolutions. [38]

This change was not merely the *de facto* adjustment of Christian practices but a profound alteration in the liberal Christian's conception of the nature and function of religion. From the viewpoint of those who favored this change, it was certainly not a degeneration or decay of Christianity but, on the contrary, its inner growth or maturation. The process of the gradual transformation of Christianity and the impact of science on human society have been well-explained by modern Western historians and philosophers like Butterfield, Briffault, Whitehead, Russell, Bernal and others. [39] But unfortunately, Muslim intellectuals rather uncritically equate the above change with a change for the worse. This applies, particularly, to Muslim theologians including the most eminent and reputed among them. Unfortunately, they have totally ignored the crucial importance and relevance of modern history for the proper understanding of the human situation. This state of affairs is all the more unfortunate in view of the great contribution made by Muslim historians during the period of Muslim cultural creativity. [40]

II

How exactly did the development of science initiate the process of transforming Christianity from a totalist religion into an existentialist response to the 'mystery of Being'. The developments in the 18th century were the cumulative result of the slow but steady accretion of exact quantitative description and descriptive explanation of natural phenomena, especially the mechanical motion of material bodies according to mathematical formulas. The contribution made by Copernicus in the field of astronomy, by Descartes, Leibniz and Newton in the field of mechanics, Galelio, Kepler and Maxwell in the field of physics, and similar other piecemeal advances in factual knowledge empirically confirmed and psychologically assured educated persons that all natural events obeyed exact laws ascertainable by the scientific method, without any reference to Divine will or to any other supernatural agency. [41] The concept of natural law thus displaced Divine will, purpose, or fiat in the working of nature and also greatly weakened the belief in miracles. The great increase in industrial productivity, which was brought about by the application of science, enabled man to satisfy his economic needs without depending upon Divine help. Likewise, progress in pharmacology and medicine assured man that biological phenomena could also be controlled. This eventually led to the extension of the concept of natural causation to the biological and social spheres.

By the time Adam Smith wrote his classical and seminal work, *The Wealth of Nations*, Western intellectuals had become interested in ascertaining social causes of social phenomena like increase in wealth and property or the causes of the rise and decline of nations. [42] In other words, the concepts of social science and social engineering had emerged. Limited and modest as this beginning was, it enhanced the status and prestige of secular knowledge, as compared with theology, and of science as compared with metaphysics. Indeed, theology and metaphysics came to be known as woolly disciplines leading to futile and never-ending disputation as against the exact and highly useful branches of science. This was the germ of philosophical positivism of the 19th century and of *scientism* of the 20th century. [43]

The full flowering of the social sciences came about in the 19th century. Hitherto history had been more or less the narration of the fortunes and misfortunes of kings written by their friends or foes, as the case may be. In the course of a few decade's history emerged as a critical study of man's total experience in the past and thus became the all-embracing study of social space-time. Philology, comparative religion, anthropology; all became important streams of social sciences, whose most general discipline was obviously sociology. This phenomenal increase in factual knowledge of social phenomena led to the general acceptance of the historical or genetic method as the crucial tool for the study of social phenomena and discovering their full nature and function. The genetic approach, first formulated and extensively applied in Germany in the 19th century, may well be called the historical revolution comparable in importance with the scientific revolution of the 18th century. [44]

The progress of the social sciences mentioned above was further augmented due to the fruits of technology. The facilities of speedier travel promoted the rise of cultural geography and accelerated growth in philology bringing about much more accurate knowledge of distant lands and languages. The direct acquaintance with diverse languages and cultures and a vastly expanded historical vision liberated some of the best Western intellectuals from the traditional and natural ethnocentricity of man. The finest symbol of this cultural catholicity is, perhaps, Goethe, and, to a lesser extent, Hegel. [45]

The concept of evolution as an all-pervasive feature of the Universe or the view that becoming is inseparable from being was put forward by Hegel and later by Herbert Spencer. [46] This concept of evolution is obviously closely related to the genetic or historical method. Thus, in the third quarter of the great 19th century Marx, applied the historical method (after immensely enriching it with the help of his version of historical materialism) to the evolution of human society, from its earliest beginnings to the present, after passing through several clearly demarcated stages like primitive Communism, Tribalism, Mercantilism, Feudalism, and Capitalism, etc. Slightly earlier Darwin had applied the evolutionary method to the emergence of biological species (including man himself) instead of their creation in the traditional sense. Thus, if Marxism can be called Social Darwinism, we could as well term Darwinism as Biological Marxism. The point is that the belief that all structures (be they material, biological, or social) evolve in time through different stages, in accordance with ascertainable laws and are, therefore, subject to human control is a tremendous advance upon the pre-modern thought system. Indeed, Darwin's theory of organic evolution is perhaps the greatest single advance in human thought that has profoundly transformed man's classical religious perspective and philosophical world view. It is a great misfortune that the Muslim mind has not yet come to terms with this crucial postulate, as it were, of the modern mind. [47]

III

Another important landmark in the cultural history of the West is the emergence of Pragmatism in America and analytical Philosophy in Britain in the last quarter of the 19th century and the beginning of the 20th. This was also due to the impact of the scientific method and the scientific temper of the West, which had by now acquired global military and economic control. The leading names are William James, Moore and Russell whose contributions gradually led to the emergence of the method of linguistic analysis. The analytical genius of Wittgenstein has also greatly contributed to our present insights into the nature and function of language, including religious language. [48] This approach has led to the basic insight that language has several types of uses or functions: descriptive, explanatory, metaphorical, evaluative, prescriptive, and evocative, etc. and that confusing those different uses or reducing them all to the plain descriptive use, is one of the main causes of controversy. Many philosophical disputes arise due to such confusions and are dissolved through linguistic analysis, which removes the very need for formulating rival philosophical theories, say, Idealism vs. Materialism, Monism vs. Dualism, Empiricism vs. Rationalism, etc. The other equally significant finding is that no religious judgment can be proved to be true or false; so the rationalistic religious approach of the Christian Deists in the 18th century and the protagonists of Liberal Christianity in the 19th cannot claim to demonstrate the truth of religion. [49] Thus, for instance, not only the dogma of Christ but even the existence of God cannot be proved. Linguistic analysis may, but does not necessarily, lead to skepticism, or *scientism,* which breeds plain indifference to religion. In actual practice linguistic analysis has rather supported the existentialist approach to religion. [50]

Scientism means that scientific knowledge acquired with the help of the scientific method is the only valid model of true cognitive awareness. Consequently, all knowledge-claims must first satisfy the criterion or test of scientific truth in order to claim the full status of knowledge. If they cannot do so they are not knowledge but opinion, feeling, emotion, intuition, as the case may be. This contention by itself is perhaps innocuous. But the moment this contention also implies (whether implicitly or explicitly) that the status of feeling or intuition is lower than reason or direct knowledge acquired through perception or reason, *scientism* becomes definitely misleading. Indeed, any approach, which implies, directly or indirectly, that the religious, aesthetic and ethical types of awareness are less valuable or significant than the logical or scientific is an unbalanced and unacceptable approach. The logic of each type of basic human response is different, and no one single logic or criterion of truth can or should be applied to the totality of human response as if it were the only single valid logic.

The theistic existentialist approach of Kierkegaard and the atheistic existentialism of Nietzsche in the 19th century have also immensely contributed to the clarification of the nature and function of the religious response or faith—in other words, the clarification of the nature and function of the 'objective' type of judgments of mathematics, logic and science, and the 'subjective' type of judgments of metaphysics, ethics, aesthetics and religion, together with the most eloquent and passionate stand that subjective truth was not lower in status or significance but just different from objective truth. [51] According to the existentialist approach, religion is not a set of objective beliefs (scientific or metaphysical) but a deeply inward response to the mystery of Being, a response which is more akin but certainly not identical with an aesthetic response at its best. This implies that religious faith is neither logically nor scientifically demonstrable though this is not an admission that religion is nothing but a poetic response or a mere source of consolation. Religious truth is the most vital form of subjectivity and the deepest and highest level of existential response to the mystery of the cosmos. To call it subjective by no means implies that it is subjective in the sense in which my preference for coffee hot, and your preference for coffee cold, is subjective. It is subjective in the sense in which deep personal love or commitment to fundamental moral values are subjective, and also in the sense that no logical or scientific demonstration can be given in its favor. This is why existentialism strengthens religious pluralism and active tolerance, including tolerance of atheism, if it be rooted in humility and a genuine search for truth.

The classical rationalistic theists like Aquinas, Descartes, Locke, the Christian Deists of the 18th century, and others like Sir Syed thought that they could rationally prove at least the existence of God. [52] To this extent, if no further, they thought the atheist could be proved to be wrong. But, in the manner of Kant, religious existentialists do not make even this claim, frankly acknowledging that religion is not centered on proof but my personal commitment, inwardness, depth of feeling, without demanding uniformity of belief. In this sense and some others Iqbal's approach is existentialist, but he does not accept existentialism in the full sense.

The growing awareness that the common man in a communist society is more or less as decent or moral as his counterpart in other societies, despite the banishment of God and religion from human affairs has stimulated critical reflection upon the nature and function of religion and consciously or unconsciously strengthened the attitude of tolerance and religious permissiveness. Indeed, many perceptive students of human affairs are increasingly inclined to look upon Communism as a new religion in the functional, though not in the structural, sense.

Last, but not least, the spiritual measures found in Persian and Urdu *Sufi* poetry, especially the former, and the central message of Buddhism and Hinduism that salvation depends upon one's good deeds rather than one's creed have also greatly influenced the religious sensibility of contemporary times in the direction of religious pluralism and permissiveness. Philosophers and poets like Aurobindo, Radhakrishnan, Tagore, and other authors like Gandhi, Nehru, Azad, and others have all contributed in this matter. [53]

In conclusion, just as the scientific revolution of the 18th century, led to a new conception of nature, and the historical revolution of the 19th century to a new conception of history and of its significance, the existentialist revolution, coming to full maturity by mid 20th century is leading us to a new conception of the nature and function of religion.

IV

An integrated 'analytical-cum-existentialist-cum-historic' approach to religion shows that the thought system of any religion is not a theoretical proposition of the objective verifiable type but essentially a basic subjective response to the mystery of Being or Becoming. The truth of the thought system is thus not scientific but existential. The believer must seek the confirmation of the truth in the depth of his authentic response and not in objective reasoning or verification. Likewise, the validity or truth of the value system of any religion is to be sought in the inner imperatives of one's soul, and not in external commands. The existentialist approach exhorts the individual to transcend a morality whose source and sanction are external rather than internal. Moreover, it gives prime importance to intrinsic moral values rather than to instrumental rules, which must inevitably change in a fluid human situation and must inevitably be left to the discretion of the autonomous moral agent, responsible to the God within. As regards the symbolic rites of any religion the existentialist approach views them as the grammar and syntax of a particular spiritual language, there being no harm whatsoever if different languages have different grammars. However, if one wishes to speak a particular language one will have to accept its grammar in order to speak it correctly and in a manner intelligible to others. Lastly, since the legal system of any religion is, obviously, an instrument or regulatory device for enforcing the moral values of a society in outer conduct and social relations, provisions of the legal system must reflect the content of our moral values and the laws must be framed through the democratic process.

In short, religious existentialism locates the essence of religion in true subjective experience of the 'Numinous' (as the term is used by Rudolph Otto) by an inwardly free or authentic person, rather than in his mere literal adherence to the classical fourfold content of a particular religion. This may be called the spiritual or religious revolution of the 20th century. [54] In the long run the significance of this revolution may become comparable with the scientific revolution of the 18th century and the historical revolution of the 19th though it would be rather wishful to make this claim right now.

Religion, in the above sense of a response to the mystery of the cosmos and an integrated world view, is indispensable. Like morality, art, and power structures, religion in the above sense always has been and always will be. But religion, in the totalist sense, can hardly survive in the long run. Its function has gone, though the elan of the idea of totalist religion is still rather powerful in Muslim societies. This idea is waiting to be transferred under the continuing impact of science, the ever-growing awareness of the mystical dimension of all world religions and the powerful currents of cultural pluralism and international humanism in human society, as a whole, despite the peculiar form of Islamic resurgence which has gripped the rulers of Iran, Pakistan and some other regions, but, hopefully, not their people as a whole.

The existentialist conception of religion is maturation and not the degeneration of religion. [55] Existential Christianity or religious existentialism, in general, is not an ineffectual apology of Western thinkers for their having acquiesced in the death of religion in the modern world. Those who think on these lines do not see the function of religion in the light of the total cultural history of man. But one who attempts to do so is most likely to agree with the existentialist approach. He will also appreciate that the so-called retreat of religion in the age of science is, from the existentialist point of view, not a forced surrender of its lawful territory but an insightful and free abdication of its de facto over-extended or totalist authority. Though very understandable in the infancy of mankind, such a totalist authority is not called for today. When religious faith functions in its proper sphere without encroaching upon other spheres, religion comes truly of age. And the same is true of science.

CHAPTER 4
ISLAMIC LIBERALISM IN INDIA: A BRIEF OVERVIEW

This chapter supplements the main argument of the preceding pages. It briefly traces the genesis of Islamic liberalism in India through the ages and also discusses its prospects in India and Pakistan. The object is to bring Islamic liberalism into focus at a time when it appears to be in permanent retreat in the face of an ever-advancing movement of Islamic revivalism or fundamentalism (by whatever name it may be called) in the Muslim world as a whole. [56]

I

Islamic liberalism is a much wider term than Islamic modernism, since liberalism and fundamentalism, as basic religious attitudes, are as old as religion itself and cut across different religions. Generally speaking, mystics and poets of all religions tend toward liberalism, while theologians and jurists tend toward fundamentalism.

Islamic liberalism does not imply any rigid religious, political or economic system of ideas, but is, primarily, an approach and attitude toward the nature and function of religion as such, as also the Islamic articles of faith. Islamic liberalism is thus compatible with a wide spectrum of views on politics or economics. [57] A person who may rightly be called a liberal Muslim in one epoch may well be deemed to be non-liberal in another. There

Authenticity and Islamic Liberalism

is a scale of liberalism and there are also types of liberalism, as a religious response, depending upon one's intellectual and cultural orientation. However, we shall have to give a minimum core content to Islamic liberalism for the purpose of a fruitful discourse. [58] Difficult as it is to give an absolutely non-controversial formula or definition, I have used the expression 'Islamic liberalism' as implying three basic beliefs:

(a) The acceptance of a monotheistic world view and the special status of Prophet Muhammad ﷺ as the recipient of the Qur'an, which has a special status in the universal and perennial process of Divine revelation for guiding the ceaseless spiritual and moral growth of mankind.

(b) The acceptance of a system of symbolic acts and practices fixed by the Prophet ﷺ, concerning man's *I-Thou* relationship with God and a few absolutely unequivocal directive principles, basic commands, and intrinsic values given in the Qur'an, but not necessarily or primarily any detailed policy or fixed rules governing every sphere of human activity. This implies a separation between the church and the state.

(c) The acceptance of religious faith, as such (including Islam) as an individual's existential response, grounded in the depths of his being, to the inscrutable mystery of the Universe, and not as a logical or rational certainty. This further implies a sense of humility and fellowship with all sincere believers (be they Muslim or not) and sincere respect for the genuine faith of others rather than any sense of superiority to non-Muslims.

Islamic liberalism thus rejects the view that any epoch in Islamic history, as the golden past, is the perfect and final norm of what and how things should be done for all times and that any attempt at improvement violates the sanctity of the Prophet's ﷺ example. Islamic liberalism holds that the finality of revelation or the special status/perfection of the Prophet ﷺ does not preclude our striving for the ceaseless growth of the ideal or norm itself as held by the Prophet ﷺ or his pious companions.

Islamic liberalism also rejects the approach of contemporary revivalist movements according to which Islam affirms the organic unity of the church and the state and is a complete guide to the total conduct of life.

Islamic Liberalism in India: A Brief Overview

Islamic liberalism holds the primary function of religion to be spiritual 'ontogenesis' or growth through an integrated system of discipline based upon broad directive principles of the Qur'an without reducing religion to legalist or institutional engineering. According to Islamic liberalism, this latter task should be left to the cumulative collective wisdom channelized through the democratic process in Muslim as well as plural societies, as the case may be. In brief, Islamic liberalism encourages the pursuit of secular wisdom and continual progress through the exercise of responsible freedom by the Muslim in the major area of human activity, in cooperation with the larger human family.

Islamic liberalism rejects the view that all other religions are aberrations from the one and only straight path and should, therefore, be displaced by persuasion, if not by force. Islamic liberalism accepts the approach of cultural pluralism that there are several paths leading to the same goal even as different languages serve a common purpose, while religious absolutism holds that there is only one correct grammar of symbols and rites leading to salvation. [59]

Islamic liberalism thus rejects the concept of exclusive salvation; that all non-Muslims (no matter what their character and conduct) ultimately would go to hell, while all Muslims (no matter what their character and conduct) alone would go to heaven after due expiation for the evil done by them in this life. Islamic liberalism holds that good and evil, virtue and vice cut across religious labels, and so does salvation, since God is the *'Lord of the worlds'* rather than of the Muslims alone. [60]

As already described in the preceding chapter, liberalism in modern Christianity developed under the impact of the industrial and secular revolutions in Western Europe in the 18th century. Until this time all religions (rather than Islam exclusively) had the basically 'totalist character' of providing an integrated code of conduct for all spheres of life. The revolution in Protestant Christianity in the 18th century transformed this totalist character, or rather started the process of transforming it, into an existential interpretation of the mystery of the Universe, particularly of the appearance in history of Jesus, the Christ. Modern liberal Christianity is the cultural product of and constituted by this transformed conception of the essential function of religion.

Authenticity and Islamic Liberalism

Among the other major religions of the human family Hinduism has been most receptive to this new conception of the essential function and jurisdiction of religion in the total economy of human life (under the impact of Christian Modernism), thanks to the vision and perspicuity of Hindu reformers; Rammohun Roy, Vivekananda, Gandhi and others. As we all know, contemporary Hinduism, as expounded by Radhakrishnan or Aurobindo, is a far cry from the Hinduism of the Manusmriti which regulates every detail of human life, while the current of Islamic liberalism, initiated in India by Sir Syed and some of his contemporaries, is getting lost in the sands of contemporary fundamentalism. There are, however, good sociological reasons for holding that the present trends would be reversed and that the Muslim world would gradually return to liberalism, as a mature orthogenetic response to an ever-changing human situation, rather than as an imitation of the Christian or Hindu religious responses to recent situational challenges. [61]

The orthogenetic movement of Islamic liberalism would however, take a pretty long time, at least a century if not more, from now to become a dominant cultural force, in view of the established fact that religious response, at its best, must arise from the depths of the human psyche. Traditional patterns of religious response linger on for centuries, and ancient sentiments, memories and aspirations cast their shadows and hold captive the believer's will to believe on traditional lines.

The inherent difficulty of making an easy and smooth transition toward a liberal reinterpretation of a hallowed thought and value system is further complicated by the endemic clash of political and economic interests of men and the resultant fear and hatred at both macro and micro levels of society. Nations clash with nations, and groups within them clash among themselves just like mortal enemies, as if, the survival of one were impossible without the total subjugation of the other. This unfortunate feature of the human situation generates abysmal fear, hatred and insecurity in the human family, rendering a free, rational and creative response to the human situation practically impossible. Clinging to his past, praying and hoping for miraculous help out of Divine mercy, the believer readily abjures rational striving to solve his problems.

Much more tragic than man's cultural inertia and resistance to new insights and inner growth is the conscious or unconscious effort of powerful and wealthy nations to use weaker sections of the human family as

Islamic Liberalism in India: A Brief Overview

a means, rather than as ends, in themselves. It is futile blaming the great powers for their desire to cling to their power and privileges through aggressive nationalism, since the evil of egoism, embedded in man's depths, is only the other side of the Divine spark in humanity. Egoism, both individual and collective, is the root of man's struggle for survival and power, and both individuals and groups would disintegrate without some measure of the egoistic striving for preserving, if not expanding, one's own level of well-being even at the expense of others. Nevertheless, moral and spiritual geniuses do arise from time to time and transcend the limitations of their own society and culture and, with charity for all and malice toward none, strive for the well-being of the entire human family. Such souls are often heard and obeyed, albeit, very marginally and haltingly. And a reluctant humanity moves, slowly and circuitously, now advancing, now retreating, now finding the way, now losing it, toward a relatively less imperfect human condition, in some part of the great human family, for at least some duration which keeps alive human hopes for a better scheme of things, on a bigger scale, in the long run. Such is the human story as seen in history's mirror, with the eye of hope but without the spectacles of illusion.

II

After a supposedly romantic reception given to Islam in the Malabar Coast of South India, which had very ancient trade relations with Arabia, Muslims became a militant force in Sind in 712, where they remained confined for the next almost 500 years. [62] Mohammad Ghori's ascent to the throne of Delhi in 1193 marks the beginning of a pervasive Muslim presence in North India, and the beginning of the long-drawn-out process of cultural interaction between Muslims and Hindus.

Coexistence and emotional distance between the ruling urban elite and the peasant masses marked the early period in Sind and elsewhere. The Sultans and the top nobility were, on the whole, tolerant of religious differences and their code of conduct toward their Hindu subjects (who vastly outnumbered the Muslims) was shaped by the requirements of statesmanship rather than the strict *Shariah*. The Muslim ruling class was least interested in propagating their Islamic faith. [63] This led to a continual tension between the Sultans and the scholar jurists or the *ulema* who held that the king should actively propagate Islam and be subordinate to the *Shariah*. A tug of war also existed between the sovereign and the nobles who wanted more power or influence than the Sultan thought safe or prudent in his own interests. [64]

Barring a few exceptional cases there was no persecution or forced conversion, though the Muslim elite naturally did occupy a privileged position in the realm and this must have prompted some Muslims to behave arrogantly and some non-Muslims to get converted to the creed of the ruling group. The view of Qazi Mughisuddin, the most learned divine in the reign of Allauddin Khiliji (d. 1316), concerning the proper method of collecting '*jizya*' from non-Muslims, or the execution of the liberal Hindu saint, Buddhan Brahman, during the reign of Sikandar Lodi (d. 1517) do not go to disprove the general practice of tolerance in the realm. It is significant that Allauddin rejected the advice of theologians who thought on the lines of the learned Qazi. Indeed, Muslim rule could not, conceivably, have lasted so long if reciprocal tolerance and respect had been generally absent in Indian society. The tolerance shown by the Hindus was not due to any lack of spine as some Hindu fanatics are apt to allege (out of a desperate attempt) to rouse sectarian militancy in their passive coreligionist's against the Muslim 'aliens' for having corrupted and destroyed '*Bharati Sanskriti*'. The tolerance shown by the Hindu masses as well as the classes sprang from their realistic appreciation of the then military and technological superiority of the Muslims who, indeed, led the medieval world in almost all fields of human endeavor, even as other members of the human family had done so in the ancient period, and the Western wing does today. The Hindu concept of '*isht-devata*' (free choice of deity), which had been the established basis of the intersectarian tolerance of all religions of Indian origin, was (in actual practice) extended and applied to the Muslim rulers and nobility and later to the masses, most of whom were converts from Hinduism as such. Though exceptions prevailed in a land of such vastness and variety as India the extension generally given to the above concept of '*isht-devata*' gave spiritual legitimacy to the *de facto* tolerance shown by the Hindus.

Turning to the part played by the Muslims in the long-drawn-out process of emotional and cultural integration, the Muslim rulers and cultured classes were quite susceptible to the fabulous charms of Hindustan; its fauna and flora, music and dance, myths and fables, divergent seasons and festivals, and, last but not least, the unsurpassed spontaneous grace of its womenfolk. The predilection of the cultured classes for the artistic and sensual elements of the culture of their adopted homeland was made the butt of attack by puritancial theologians and jurists who took pride in the

Islamic Liberalism in India: A Brief Overview

fact that the religion of Islam was singularly free from the admixture of myth, fantasy, music and sculpture found in the styles of Hindu and Christian piety. But all their exhortations failed to prevent the cultured Muslim classes from appreciating the rich art and culture of Hindustan. Likewise, no denunciation of interest or usury stood in the way of the Muslim landed gentry from borrowing money from Hindu moneylenders or traders. Nor did the ill conceived exhortations of some theologians to the rulers and the nobility to avoid trusting and befriending non-Muslims and giving them high positions in state services prevent the closest political and military cooperation and alliances on purely secular lines. Thus, both Muslims and Hindus freely employed each other for military, professional, commercial and domestic purposes, though there was a total ban on inter-dining and intermarriage. This, however, did not stand in the way of a sharing of the common joys and sorrows of life, and mutual trust and loyalty definitely cut across religious lines. [65]

In the above process of emotional integration of the diverse ethnic and religious elements of Indian society the most crucial role was played by the *Sufi* saints, especially those who wrote poetry or were drawn to poetry and music. With a few exceptions, the *Sufi* approach to Islam was far more flexible and liberal in contrast with the approach of the theologians. The *Sufi* saints held universal love and human kindness (irrespective of caste, color or creed) to be equally important as formal Islamic worship. This universal tolerance and kindness and their exemplary character attracted the Hindu masses and prepared the soil for their peaceful mass conversion, especially among the economically weaker and culturally backward sections of an essentially rigid caste-ridden society. The better-placed and educated Hindus also developed a sympathetic understanding of Islamic concepts and values through their contacts with the *Sufis* and association with friendly Muslim quarters in the enterprise of daily life. Moinuddin Chishti, Baba Farid (d. 1265), and Nizamuddin Auliya (d. 1325) symbolized the emerging Catholicism. Baba Farid wrote poetry in Punjabi and appreciated Hindu piety and spirituality. No wonder, Guru Nanak included this poetry in the Granth Sahab.

Early coexistence thus ripened into co-discovery of the great wealth of the ancient Hindu and medieval Islamic cultural streams. This made the enlightened sections, among both Hindus and Muslims, aware of the basic similarities between the two religions behind the differences in doctrine or idiom. Nanak (d. 1539), and Kabir (d. 1518) symbolize this approach. At the same time secular contacts and needs led, in the course of time, to the growth of the common language of Hindavi or Persianized Hindi (now known as Urdu) which first became a literary vehicle in the Bahmani Kingdom of South India and latter flowered in Delhi, Agra and Lucknow. The poets Amir Khusro (d. 1325), and Malik Muhammad Jaisi (d. 1542) and the Sultans, Quli Qutab Shah of Deccan (d. 1612) and Zainul Abidin of Kashmir (d. 1470) represent this emerging cultural synthesis. A fusion of cultural values thus gradually took place in literature, music, architecture, painting, gardening, manners and dress, and last, but not least, in religion itself. Indeed, what is Sikhism if not the fusion of Hinduism and Islam in the Indian environment? But, as we all know, the ban on intermarriage remained as absolute as ever. Perhaps, the fact that Hinduism itself prohibited intercaste marriage prevented the rise of a movement against the ban on Hindu-Muslim marriage. In any case, the ban on inter-dining and intermarriage could not prevent the practice and the ethic of genuine mutual understanding and friendly cooperation in all matters; domestic, civic and political, subject, of course, to individual alignments in the conflict of interests and the struggle for power; features which are inherent in the human situation, irrespective of time and place. [66]

The movement of religious liberalism reached its peak with Akbar (d. 1605). Instead of viewing it as a cultural mutation or sudden reversal it would be more accurate to regard Akbar's religious approach as a 'utopian culmination' of a long-drawn-out process whose logic had clearly been grasped by the genius of Al-Beruni (d. app. 1040) in his monumental work on India. [67]

Akbar's robust common sense, intellectual curiosity, a sense of fairplay and intuitive wisdom led him from the idea of mere tolerance of diverse faiths to the higher idea of the unity of spirit and purpose behind different forms of religion. This is why he did not object to his Hindu wife retaining her own faith, and even provided a temple for her within the palace. Akbar's genuine commitment to liberalism is also reflected in his befriending and trusting numerous Hindus in every walk of life and at the highest levels, civil and military! Non-Muslim religious scholars were also made eligible for state grants for the first time.

Rather unfortunately, however, (possibly due to his lack of formal education and the ambitions of some of his advisers to elevate their own ranks as high priests of a new dispensation) Akbar was led toward founding

Islamic Liberalism in India: A Brief Overview

a new religion in place of being content with a mere liberal interpretation of Islam. [68] Though neither force nor bribery was used in propagating the royal religion (which could win only two dozen or so adherents), this step shocked Muslim opinion. This 'spiritual adventurism' and perhaps some actual or alleged excesses committed by Akbar or with his acquiescence led to a mounting opposition from Muslim fundamentalism and puritanism, represented by Shaikh Ahmad Sarhandi (d. 1624). This slowed down the momentum of the liberal movement and its inner growth and consolidation in court circles and Muslim society after Akbar.

The debate and the conflict between liberal humanist values and a rigid legalist totalist approach to religion lasted throughout the 17th century. Saints like Sarmad (d. 1661), Mian Mir (d. 1635), Mohibullah Shah (d. 1648) and the scholar prince Dara Shikoh (d. 1659) championed the cause of liberalism, while Aurangzeb (d. 1707) supported Islamic legalism and totalism, dominating the scene for approximately sixty years.

Aurangzeb was not a bigot or anti-Hindu, as has come to be believed in many quarters, due to an understandable confusion between his politics and his religious convictions. Indeed, his valor, learning and moral integrity continued to command the respect, not only of the Muslims, but also of the vast majority of the Hindus till the very end. Yet, there can be no doubt, whatsoever, that Aurangzeb not merely checked and reversed the syncretist 'spiritual adventurism' of Akbar or Dara Shikoh, but that Aurangzeb's approach to Islam prevented the orthogenetic flowering and evolution of Islamic liberalism in the Indian environment. [69]

After the death of Aurangzeb in the beginning of the 18th century Indian society was plunged into sociopolitical turmoil, civil wars, foreign invasions and intellectual stagnation. While the West went on advancing in political liberalism, science and technology on the foundations securely laid by Bacon, Descartes, Spinoza, Newton, Leibniz, Adam Smith and others, political decay and cultural stagnation set in throughout our country. South India fared better for a time under Hyder Ali and Tipu Sultan in Mysore and the Nizam in Hyderabad, but this did not last long.

In the turmoil of the 18th century arose Shah Waliullah of Delhi (d. 1763), the greatest Muslim theologian of the age, and virtually, the first translator of the Qur'an (into Persian). Waliullah stood for a liberal and permissive approach to differences within the *Sunni* Muslim sects and *Sufi* schools of thought. Intellectually highly gifted, as he was, as a theologian and social critic Waliullah, was not a critical philosopher and historian analyzing man's moral, religious and mystical experience as was, in fact, being done by his Western contemporaries; Voltaire and Kant, who stood on the shoulders of their predecessors. Waliullah's magnum opus, written in Arabic, contains several reports (without any critical scrutiny) of the sayings and doings of the Prophet ﷺ of Islam, and his theological approach was not free from elements of intolerance and ethnocentricity, also found in Shaikh Ahmad Sarhindi of the previous century.

Other notable Muslim liberals of the 18th century; the poets, Sauda (d. 1780), Khwaja Mir Dard (d. 1785), Mir Taqi Mir (d. 1810), Mazhar Jane Janan (d. 1781), Bedil (d. 1720), and the liberal theologian of Firangi Mahal, Lucknow, Nizamuddin (d. 1748) (who formulated the syllabus for higher secular studies still in vogue in Islamic seminaries in India) had a more humanist and tolerant approach. But their tolerance and liberalism were rooted more in *Sufi* ways of thought than in the secular and scientific temper that was steadily emerging in the West due to advances in Mathematics and natural science as also the rise of democratic values of respect for individual freedom and rights of man due to advances in the social sciences. The remarkable 18th century which saw in the West the birth of the liberal religious revolution and the American and French revolutions, saw in India only the birth of the Asiatic Society of Bengal, and that too on British initiative.

In general, the 18th century in India is a long tunnel of stagnant darkness; civil strife, the collapse of moral integrity, and a total loss of national dignity and direction for the sake of a disgusting short-term search for power or wealth. Yet, religious liberalism, in a broad sense, prevailed in Indian society, since the endemic struggles for short-term power ran on secular or regional, rather than religious or communal lines. Thus, not religious kinship, but political ambition or military strategy, devoid of all ethical considerations, decided the choice of one's allies or opponents, collaboration or confrontation, loyalty or betrayal, in both individual and collective life. This applies, without exception, to the Mughals, Rajputs, Mahrattas, Jats, Afghans, Rohillas and European adventurers in North India and to the henchmen of Tipu Sultan and the Nizam in the South. In fact, Hindu Mahrattas and Rajputs showed greater respect and kindness, than the Muslim Rohillas and Afghans, to the nominal Mughal suzerains confined to the

Red Fort in Delhi. Likewise, Hindu generals displayed greater loyalty than several of their Muslim counterparts to the dynamic, secular, but unlucky Tipu Sultan of Mysore. [70]

III

The exposure of the Hindu elite of Bengal to Western thought from mid 18th century onwards acted almost like dynamite blowing up the centuries-old crust of stagnant concepts and values, and the symbol of this awakening is, of course, Ram Mohun Roy (d. 1833). The long interaction with Islam had weakened the grip of an ethnocentric and chauvinistic mentality, increasing the receptivity of the Hindu mind to the new ideas and values represented by the rising British power. High class urban Hindus, in fairly large numbers, were attracted to the scientific and spiritual humanism of the West rather than to official Christianity, and the *Brahmo Samaj* movement emerged in 1828 as an attempt to reinterpret the ancient Hindu tradition. Later on Vivekananda and Dayananda, and after them, Tagore and Gandhi reverently pruned the tradition as 'insiders', giving their own conception of the essential core of the 'eternal religion' (*sanatana dharma*). They criticized the tradition and yet claimed to belong to it. More importantly, Hindu society, in general, did not reject this claim, though many quarters tenaciously fought back the reformers in losing battles.

The Muslim response during the same period was quite different. Muslims had recently lost their political supremacy in the late 18th century to the British whose religion and culture were felt as anathema. Moreover, the emerging way of life did not hold any promise of future betterment of worldly prospects for the Muslims for whom court or military service had been the traditional avenues of advancement. Disillusionment, frustration and despair of the future conspired to generate among the Muslims of North India a tenacious sectarian militancy under the leadership of Saiyid Ahmad Barelvi (d. 1831). Inspired by the school of Waliullah, he led a crusade even against the liberal and tolerant Sikh ruler of Punjab, Ranjit Singh (d. 1827). Likewise, Shariatullah of Bengal (d. 1840) launched the *Faraizi* movement in eastern India seeking to purify Muslim society of corrupt and un-Islamic elements. The Muslims thus had to wait till the third quarter of the century when Sir Syed (d. 1898), helped by a galaxy of brilliant associates, [71] created a wind of change and opened a new window to the contemporary human situation, enabling the Indian Muslim to think afresh about the central meaning of Islam in an ever-changing world. Some other distinguished Islamic liberals of the same period also worked on similar lines: Salar Jung I of Hyderabad (d. 1882), Badruddin Tayabji (d. 1906), Khuda Bakhsh (d. 1931). Abdul Latif (d. 1893), Chiragh Ali (d. 1895), and Amir Ali (d. 1928). The founder of Ahmadi Islam, Mirza Ghulam Ahmad (d. 1908) also contributed (albeit, in his own unique way) to the task of thinking afresh.

Amir Ali's work, *The Spirit of Islam*, was the most widely read classic of Islamic liberalism of the period, while Chiragh Ali's work, *Proposed Political, Legal, and Social Reforms in the Ottoman Empire*, 1883, is the most radical and consistent essay in Islamic Liberalism. While Amir Ali's approach is apologetic rather than philosophical, Chiragh Ali's was far too ahead of his time to strike a responsive chord in the then situation. However, none among the liberals possessed the charismatic personality of Sir Syed who influenced the Indian Muslim mind and Muslim politics more than anybody else.

As a forward looking person, deeply impressed with the achievements of Western science and technology and the spirit of Victorian liberalism, Sir Syed first established a Scientific Society to promote the study of science among Urdu speaking people and, later in 1877, the *M.A.O. College*, Aligarh. He wished the college to be a place for '*free inquiry, large-hearted tolerance and pure morality*'. Believing that the Qur'an was the 'word of God' he wished to interpret it in the light of human reason which together with revelation (confined to the prophets) was God's gift to man. Denying miracles, Sir Syed held that the interpretation of the 'word of God' must harmonize with science, which described the 'work of God', that is, nature governed by uniform laws, which are essentially Divine commands.

Holding that the Islamic law (*Shariah*) was not an integral part of the immutable essentials of faith (*deen*), Sir Syed declared that the *Shariah* should be changed to suit the ever-changing conditions. He rejected the traditional division of society into the 'land of Islam' (*darul Islam*) and the 'land of war' (*darul harb*) and the related concept of 'holy war' (*jihad*) as an integral part of the essentials of faith. Putting forward the concept of '*darul aman*' (areas under non-Muslim rulers where Muslims lived in peace and had full rights to practise the essentials of faith) Sir Syed pleaded for full cooperation with the British rulers whose character and scientific achievements he admired.

Islamic Liberalism in India: A Brief Overview

Sir Syed stressed the spirit and the essentials of Islam rather than following the details of the legal corpus or established ritual and custom. He held that Muslims should join the national mainstream of secular progress, not as atomic 'community-blind' individuals, but on a corporate basis, as members of the Muslim community within the Indian nation. This task implied coming to terms with modern education and the British. And this was perhaps the farthest limit of Sir Syed's political and social vision beyond which his lights became as blurred as those of the Deoband school under the leadership of Muhammad Qasim (d. 1880) who, drawing inspiration from Waliullah, was dead against British rule and Western education and values. [72]

Sir Syed's grasp of modern thought and his self-proclaimed rationalism were, however, so unsophisticated that he honestly held that the existence of God and the prophecy of Muhammad ﷺ were rationally demonstrable. Liberal as he was in the religious sense, Sir Syed was not fully aware of the conceptual foundations of Victorian liberalism; Cartesian doubt, scientific method, spiritual autonomy, respect for the individual, equality of man, sovereignty of the national will, parliamentary democracy and rule by majority and separation between the church and the state. Sir Syed's religious liberalism was, thus, nothing more than a simple Islamic monotheism, freed from the gloss of traditional Muslim theology and law (*Shariah*) combined with the spirit of universal tolerance and a sense of special kinship with Christianity and Judaism. This approach was admirably calculated to enable the Muslims to cooperate with, and to prosper (along with other communities of India) under the protection of permanent British rule or paramountcy, while retaining a good Islamic conscience. But what this approach lacked was a social and political philosophy, which could yield long-term political goals for Muslims and other Indians. In other words, Sir Syed's religious liberalism was geared to short-term goals and the ideal of '*the loyal Indian Mohammadan*', but not to the long-term needs and problems of the Muslim community and the country, as a whole, after the passing phase of British rule came to an end.

While the earlier Hindu liberalism of the *Brahmo Samaj* had really captured the religious and political imagination of the educated urban Bengal, the Islamic liberalism of Sir Syed remained almost a closed book for those very Muslims who eagerly obtained degrees from the M.A.O. College as passports for entry into government service. Thus did the process of superficial Westernization continue among the upper and professional classes of

Muslims without their modernization or exposure to Victorian liberalism, or even to Sir Syed's own version of Islamic liberalism, unlike the relatively steadier growth of the liberal secular outlook in several enlightened Hindu quarters in cosmopolitan Calcutta, Bombay and Madras in the wake of English education, *Brahmo* and other kindred movements.

One should, however, not be too harsh on the failure of the Muslims to respond in the way the Hindus did. The idea of secular democracy favored the interests of the Hindus (because of their overwhelming majority) while it created grave apprehensions and fears among the Muslims in view of the long-standing caste and communal divisions of Indian society. Muslims naturally felt apprehensive of being reduced to a 'perpetual minority', at the mercy of the majority, in a political set-up which was formally and, in theory, secular, but which, in practice, might become almost totally sectarian on the principle of one man, one vote. In other words, while the ideal of democracy coalesced with and promoted the interests of the majority community, the ideal clashed with the practical interests of the minority. The now well-established sociological principle of 'the situational evocation of ideas and attitudes' was brought into play, obstructing the growth of secular liberalism among the Muslims while promoting it among educated Hindus.

The fears and apprehensions of the Muslims eventually led to what some modern historians have called 'Muslim separatism' in India. Separatism may or may not be conjoined with liberalism. After Sir Syed's death the leader, of Muslim separatism; the Agha Khan (d. 1957), Syed Husain Bilgrami (d. 1926), a distinguished civil servant of Hyderabad, and some other founder members of the Muslim League (most of whose members were liberal in a restricted sense); succeeded, in 1906, in getting the active support of the then Viceroy, Lord Minto, for the demand of separate Muslim electorates. This was the nuclear idea, which eventually developed into the idea of a separate Muslim state. The Muslim divines of Deoband, steeped in Islamic fundamentalism, on the other hand, gradually turned into staunch allies of the liberal Indian National Congress which (paradoxically) had been founded by the British civil servant, A.O. Hume (d. 912). Such are the fascinating mazes and mutations of history.[73]

IV

Lacking any long-term political vision of independent India, Sir Syed went on making *ad hoc* political moves in the context of the developing

Islamic Liberalism in India: A Brief Overview

political situation for preserving rather short-term Muslim interests as he conceived them to be. This approach failed after his death, in 1898, to satisfy the younger educated generation due to the political psychological fallout of the conflict between Ottoman Turkey and Greek Slav nationalism in the Balkans from the first quarter of the 19th century onwards. [74]

The liberation of Greece in 1829 was followed by the wresting of independence from Turkey by a string of Balkan states with the passage of time. This conflict was purely ethnic and political, but it gradually acquired religious overtones for Indian Muslims, more especially after Turkey's entry into the First World War against Britain. The decline of Turkey's political and military strength had jeopardized the custody of the Muslim holy places (Mecca and Medina, traditionally under Turkish control) and greatly agitated the Indian Muslims. Sir Syed's liberal stance of separating religion from politics, his unqualified and absolute support to the British government and his calculated aloofness from the aspirations of the liberals of the Indian National Congress, founded in 1885, thus gradually lost its relevance, giving way to a rather confused patchwork synthesis of pan-Islamism and nationalism.

Shibli [75] (d. 1914), brilliant historian and man of letters, Abul Kalam Azad (d. 1958) in his early phase, and Mohammad Ali (d. 1931) showed the new way. and numerous Muslims came under the spell of the pan-Islamic movement which predates the Congress struggle for independence. Both the movements, however, reached their peak when they coalesced under the joint leadership of Gandhi and Mohammad Ali during 1920-1923. Deeply committed as were Mohammad Ali, Azad and other prominent *Khilafat* leaders to the cause of Indian freedom and Hindu-Muslim unity, they abandoned Sir Syed's religious liberalism in favor of a totalist approach against which Sir Syed had so courageously struggled under the auspices of the *Aligarh movement*. [76] In other words, the *Khilafat* movement was not just a political reversal of Sir Syed's undeniably over-zealous commitment to the British crown, but also a sort of religious regression from Sir Syed's version of Islamic liberalism and a return to a modified totalist approach to Islam. The cooperation offered by the *Khilafat* leaders to the Congress and the massive participation of Muslims in the freedom struggle, under Gandhiji's leadership, was not rooted in a clear-cut Islamic liberalism (wedded to separation between the church and the state) but rather in a most confused totalist or fundamentalist conception of Islam (wedded to the idea of an organic unity of religion and politics in Islam). Even Azad (who in his later mature phase was to become the pillar of Islamic liberalism) at this juncture thought on totalist lines holding that the institution of *Khilafat* was an integral part of the Islamic faith and that defending and helping the *Caliph* was the religious duty of the Muslims. He also stood for a separate and distinct political identity for the Muslim community (cooperating with the Hindu community) in a state conceived as a federation of distinct communities, rather than as a sovereign territorial state composed of individual citizens having equal rights. Mohammad Ali's speeches and writings also reflect the same position. His declared stand on what he would do in the event of Afghanistan attacking India in the name of Islam, and his subsequent opposition to the application of the Sharda Act (banning child marriage) to Muslims sprang from his essentially totalist, as against Sir Syed's liberal, approach to Islam.

Electrifying and tremendous as was the effect of the *Khilafat* movement, in terms of mass political awakening and the growth of nationalism, it indirectly led to the considerable weakening of Islamic liberalism and the idea of separation between the church and the state. The *ulema* from Deoband and other Muslim theological centers rubbed shoulders with Congress liberals (both Hindus and Muslim) in a united struggle for India's liberation from British rule, little realizing how utterly different were their visions of a free India and also of the proper role of religion in the modern age and in a plural Indian society.

That the totalist approach to Islam and its corollary of pan-Islamism were unrealistic in the modern era was shown by the decision of the Turkish National Assembly, under the supreme leadership of Mustafa Kamal (d. 1938), to divest the then *Caliph* of all political powers and functions in 1923, and the final abolition of the institution as such in 1924. [77] It is significant that Jinnah, who was later to emerge as the architect of Pakistan, had, on principle, remained aloof from the *Khilafat* movement in its heyday. [78]

The *Jamia Millia Islamia* (National Muslim University) founded in Aligarh in 1920 under the patronage of the veteran Deoband divine and freedom fighter, Mahmudul Hasan (d. 1921), and with the active blessings of Gandhiji, was the cultural expression of the political partnership between the *Khilafat* and the Congress movements, and of pan-Islamism and Indian nationalism. At this stage the thinking of the *Jamia's* first Vice-Chancellor, Mohammad Ali, was perhaps, relatively closer to Islamic liberalism, as defined in this essay, than the views of Azad, contained in his book *Ma-*

Islamic Liberalism in India: A Brief Overview

salae Khilafat wa Jazirae Arab, Lahore, 1920, on the issue of *Khilafat*. Yet, with the exception of Hakim Ajmal Khan (d. 1928), M.A. Ansari (d. 1936), A.M. Khwaja (d. 1962), Syed Mahmud (d. 1971), and one or two others, the *Khilafat* leaders and supporters, in general (including Mohammad Ali himself), lacked a philosophical basis or rationale for reconciling the full demands and implications of nationalism with those of institutional Islam which the *Khilafat* leaders (quite unlike the then secular liberal Jinnah) made the emotional rallying point for the Muslim masses. What inspired their emphasis on communal harmony and national unity was not territorial nationalism, but their (correct) political perception that effective help to the *Khilafat* cause needed a united front of Hindus and Muslims, just as Gandhiji knew that it was a precondition for Indian independence. It is, therefore, hardly surprising that the abolition of *Khilafat* in 1924 led to a slump in the political honeymoon of Hindu and Muslim political activists during the early twenties.

A.M. Khwaja who had somehow managed to keep the infant *Jamia* alive, in spite of the waning away of the early enthusiasm, and despite tremendous financial odds, shifted the *Jamia*, in 1925, to Delhi, where Zakir Husain took over charge the following year. [79]

Zakir Husain (d. 1969) and the young liberal intellectuals who gathered around him at the *Jamia*: Abid Husain (d. 1978) and M. Mujib, together with some older liberals, such as Aslam Jairajpuri and Shafiqur Rahman Kidwai, had very clear notions of the relationship between religion and politics and were committed to Islamic liberalism. But Zakir Husain's efforts at the *Jamia* in Delhi centered on providing sound primary and secondary education in a broadly liberal Islamic and patriotic atmosphere rather than on higher studies or research on Islamic liberalism. Substantial as was the *Jamia's* contribution to adult literacy and children's literature in Urdu, it could not make any effective impact upon the Indian Muslim mind. In the final analysis, the resources of the *Jamia* were too limited for the magnitude and complexity of the task. Much later, in the fifties and the sixties, however, Abid Husain and Mujeeb did valuable work in this direction.

In the thirties and the forties a number of distinguished Muslim intellectuals, in different fields and in different parts of India, enriched the content of Islamic liberalism. [80] These liberals looked at Islam, in varying degrees, from an historical perspective and clearly de-linked political and economic questions from the sphere of religion. They, however, lacked the moral courage to spell out their views and to develop them to their logical conclusion. Rejecting the pre-sociological pseudo-rationalism of Sir Syed, these neo-liberals moved toward a more pronounced, though as yet unnamed, religious existentialism stressing man's authentic '*I-Thou*' relationship with God, rather than the organic unity of the church and the state, as the central meaning of Islam.

Some neo-liberals also gave a new turn to Urdu literature from the thirties onwards. Their poetry, short stories, novels, and other works helped to generate a liberal atmosphere congenial to the growth of religious liberalism. [81] Some among the neo-liberals came under the spell of Marxism which undoubtedly marks the beginning of a new era in man's history.

Though Marxist intellectuals among Indian Muslims are understandably few in number, they have helped in the growth of Islamic liberalism by forcing discussion upon basic religious and cultural issues. Marxist writers have helped to awaken Muslims from their '*dogmatic slumbers*', as it were. [82] However, educated Muslims, generally, prefer the gentle breeze of liberal reform to the stormy winds of revolution. Since Marxism is a particular version of the historical and sociological approach to society, no honest observer of the human condition should ignore the indirect but powerful role of Marxist writers in the complex process of the evolution of liberal ideas and values. While many disillusioned liberals might, one day, turn to the 'panacea' supplied by Moscow or Peking, many more who stand disillusioned with the results achieved so far are likely to turn away from it and return to the original liberal fold.

As pointed out earlier, Sir Syed's Islamic liberalism had lost its relevance and directive power by the first quarter of the present century, since Sir Syed's approach, being devoid of a consistent long-term political vision, led to a sort of isolation of Muslims of India from the mainstream of Indian nationalism as also from pan-Islamism. The *Khilafat* leaders claimed to have supplied this vision. But, as we have seen, their political vision took no account whatsoever of the growing power of territorial nationalism in the Islamic world itself and elsewhere and the emerging religious modernism, under the impact of science, on human society in general.

This inadequacy is explicable since the *Khilafat* leaders, generally speaking, could not lay claim to any thorough familiarity with modern Western thought. But the case of Mohammad Ali, and, more especially, of Iqbal was different.

Well-versed in both Islamic and Western thought, Iqbal was the most gifted and qualified Muslim luminary of the age to nourish and foster Sir Syed's nascent Islamic liberalism in the light of modern thought. And, indeed, he did attempt to do this in his famous work, *The Reconstruction of Religious Thought in Islam*. Unlike Sir Syed's confused rationalism, Iqbal put forward a systematic theory of knowledge, which does justice to the claims of reason as well as intuition or feeling, holding that it is wrong to dismiss feeling as mere subjective emotion devoid of any epistemic status. His rejection of the proofs of God's existence and his avowedly existentialist approach to religious faith is a definite advance upon Sir Syed's religious rationalism. This existentialism could well have flowered into full-fledged Islamic liberalism, as defined in this essay, if Iqbal could have wielded greater historical and sociological perspicacity. But, instead, Iqbal reversed Sir Syed's religious liberalism in regard to the crucial issue of the proper jurisdiction of religion.

Though Iqbal could be called an Islamic liberal, in a broad sense, his liberalism remained ambivalent and halting because he neglected the sociology of religion. Despite a fairly wide range of his central argument in his attempted reconstruction of religious thought, Iqbal nowhere raised the crucial problem of the function of religion in the contemporary human situation. By and large, Iqbal accepted the totalist approach to Islam. Rejecting the more or less unconscious thrust of Sir Syed's thinking in the direction of a pragmatic separation between the church and the state, Iqbal once again, forcefully and categorically, affirmed the doctrine of the organic unity of the church and the state as the differentia of Islam, and held that without such unity religion loses all social relevance and becomes mere ritualism. This meant dismissing without much ado Sir Syed's pioneering efforts to find religious legitimacy for 'functional secularism', that is, a secular approach for Muslims living in a plural society, in regard to political, economic, social and cultural matters.

Though Iqbal's concept of organic unity of the church and the state in Islam together with the stipulation of an 'open' or dynamic approach to *Shariah*, may work well (up to a point) in a predominantly Muslim society, it cannot possibly fully satisfy the legitimate needs and interests of Muslims living in a plural society. Such Muslims would always tend to look down upon themselves and actually would be looked upon by others as second class or 'candidate Muslims' in relation to the 'full' Muslims who live in an Islamic society where the church and the state are one. In other words, Iqbal's version of Islamic liberalism cannot possibly have a universal appeal for Muslims. Even the predicament of Pakistan today, in the name of the program of Islamization (thanks to the ever-growing impact of Maududi's ideas after Jinnah's death) is, to a great extent, the legacy of the philosopher-poet. [83]

Azad presents an interesting contrast with Iqbal in regard to the issue of the proper function and jurisdiction of religion. Azad started out in his early *Al-Hilal* and *Al-Balagh* phase with a totalist approach to Islam, but moved away from it after the Turkish revolution under Mustafa Kamal.

The collapse of the institution of *Khilafat* made Azad aware of the difficulties inherent in the very concept as such in the present human situation and turned his early Islamic fundamentalism toward the liberal principle of separation between the church and the state. It seems the change, or rather the evolution, in Azad's thinking was greatly facilitated by his studies in the history and philosophy of religion as a preparation for his monumental commentary on the Qur'an. Gradually Azad veered round to the modern view of human society as a federation of plural functional associations— religious, political, economic and cultural— for satisfying human needs in different spheres without one sphere encroaching upon the other. It must be noted that this evolution of Azad's ideas was due to the maturation of a deeply religious and fully integrated personality, rather than a political compromise or strategy to further his political ambitions, as was unfortunately and uncharitably, alleged by Azad's detractors. The same remarks apply to some other public figures notable for their patriotism and secularism on the one hand, and sincere commitment to Islam, on the other. [84]

V

The Pakistan demand originally adumbrated by Iqbal in 1930 and officially adopted by the Muslim League in 1940 was a political demand of Muslim liberals, of some hue or other, who were dissatisfied with their

Islamic Liberalism in India: A Brief Overview

Hindu counterparts in the Congress rather than a religious demand rooted in Islamic fundamentalism. The leaders of the Muslim League, most notably Jinnah; the political architect of Pakistan, were definitely disposed toward Islamic liberalism rather than the totalist approach which was mildly and, somewhat ambivalently, held by Iqbal, who is looked upon by many as the spiritual architect of Pakistan. That there was a measure of contradiction between the approaches of the political and spiritual fathers of Pakistan was not given much significance before its establishment. And this is understandable.

The Pakistan concept was, in essence, an ideology of the modern educated urban Muslim who felt himself disadvantaged or discriminated against by the majority community. The demand, however, also harmonized with the traditional totalist approach to Islam, which remained more or less dormant in the Muslim psyche, despite Sir Syed's pioneering approach of Islamic liberalism. The idea of a state of Muslims, run by Muslims, and for Muslims, in accordance with the Qur'an and the *sunnah*, thus deeply stirred the religious imagination of the educated urban Muslim even (rather especially) in the minority provinces which, however were to be outside the proposed Pakistan.

Paradoxically, the Deoband and other Muslim divines, on the whole, did not support the demand which (again paradoxically) drew support from the Indian Communists on the principle of self-determination of nationalities within India. The Deoband and other Muslim divines vigorously opposed the political thesis that Hindus and Muslims were two nations; the thesis Jinnah put forward as the basis for the partition of the country. They also rejected the religious thesis emanating from a rather small dissident group of Deoband and other *ulema*, that the practice of Islam, in its entirety, demanded living as a citizen of an Islamic state as Pakistan was proposed to be. Though a lot of confusion prevailed in different quarters the general elections of 1946 (based on a limited franchise and separate Muslim electorates) gave an overwhelming Muslim mandate in favor of Pakistan. However, it is significant that more than thirty per cent of the Muslim votes were cast against the Muslim League or, in other words, against the concept of Pakistan. The overwhelming victory of the League was in terms of the number of seats won in the legislatures (due to the one man, one vote system) and not in terms of the number of Muslims who stood for partition. [85]

Authenticity and Islamic Liberalism

The emergence of independent Pakistan and several other Muslim states after the Second World War has strengthened the appeal of pan-Islamist ideas of Jamaluddin Afghani and the totalist approach of Islam, which, as pointed out earlier, was common to all religions until the mid 18th century. It was precisely this totalist approach, which had been courageously rejected by Sir Syed.

The totalist approach to Islam, has been most consistently championed by Maududi (d. 1979) in his voluminous writings in powerful Urdu prose. His dedicated life, the enchanting philosophical poetry of Iqbal (who also supports the totalist approach) and the emergence of several sovereign Muslim states in the comity of nations have brought the totalist conception into the focus of Muslim thinking in far-flung Muslim societies. A powerful struggle between competing approaches or interpretations of Islam is going on in Iran, Egypt, Turkey, Pakistan and also elsewhere with varying degrees of intensity. Though it is too early to predict the outcome of this struggle in the near future, it is evident that the totalist approach amounts to a reversal of the general direction of the history of religions which are gradually outgrowing the totalist conception that religion and politics, the church and the state, are one and inseparable. [86]

It is true that the contemporary Islamic totalist approach favors an open or dynamic *Shariah*, and thus does not attract the charge of rigid blind conformity to the past. In this sense, therefore, it does represent a considerable advance upon medieval traditionalism. Nevertheless, the totalist approach does have implications and ramifications that obstruct the ceaseless growth of our ideas and our value system. In the final analysis, effective ceaseless growth requires, not merely *ad hoc* adjustments in the religious law, but the authentic and creative reinterpretation of basic values and their distinction from instrumental rules. Equally importantly, proper growth requires demarcating the valid jurisdictions of faith and reason, religion and science, spirituality and morality. Merely an open approach to the *Shariah* (though useful up to a point) is not enough, until one realizes the proper function or the jurisdiction of religion in the total economy of human life. And one shall not be able to do so until one studies the history of religions as a part of universal cultural history. Unfortunately, Muslim theologians and jurists, despite their prodigious religious learning and (in some cases) great integrity of character, totally neglect history and the social sciences in their official as well as private studies. As a result they just cannot look upon

Islamic Liberalism in India: A Brief Overview

Islam as a developing process in social space-time. Moreover, the approach of the *ulema*, in general, especially the scholarly protagonists of the Islamic Resurgence movement, becomes polemical or defensive instead of being analytical or exploratory.

The approach of the *Tablighi Jamat*; the missionary movement initiated by Ilyas and Muhammad Yusuf of Delhi in the early forties and which has gradually become a worldwide movement in our times; is, on the other hand, utopian and simplistic. This approach emphasizes simple Islamic piety without attempting any solution of the complex problems of life, on the naive assumption that if we pray to God and are kind to our neighbors all our problems would automatically be solved by Divine mercy. This approach appeals, primarily, to those who are consciously or unconsciously seeking an emotional refuge from the complex demands of the human situation. The social psychological genesis of this movement is, thus, basically, similar to the rapid rise of *Sufi* orders in the Islamic world in the 13th century after the destruction of the once mighty Abbasid Caliphate. [87]

VI

The social psychological impact of partition upon Indian Muslims was traumatic. The creation of Pakistan did not, and possibly could not; help those Indian Muslims who did not migrate to the proposed homeland. And, obviously, the vast majority have not. Indeed, it must have begun to dawn on them (belatedly) that Pakistan was calculated to cater to the interests only of Muslims living in the seceding regions rather than of the Indian Muslims as a whole. Some on this side might even be wondering now, was not their advocacy of Pakistan, after all, political suicide, under the spell of the magnetic personality of Jinnah in the shadow of Hindu chauvinism in some quarters?

Under the above conditions the protagonists of partition stood totally bewildered and demoralized, and the task of giving moral support and political direction to the Indian Muslims devolved upon the liberal nationalist Muslims who had consistently stood for the unity of the country and a secular approach to politics. The pillar and symbol of the approach in post-independent India is, of course, Abul Kalam Azad. However, many other distinguished *Khilafat* and Congress veterans who had been repudiated by

Authenticity and Islamic Liberalism

the urban Muslim electorate (under the spell of Pakistan) naturally came to the fore and responded to the need of their community in their hour of trial and the crisis of self-confidence. The changed political and social conditions were conducive to the acceptance of Islamic liberalism and its corollary of separation between the church and the state and a secular approach to politics. The historical vision and far-sighted statesmanship of Nehru who guided the nation for almost two formative and critical decades and the selfless service rendered by such dedicated souls as Azad, Syed Mahmud, A.M. Khwaja, Zakir Husain, and Rafi Ahmad Kidwai (d. 1954) led to the policy of liberal financial aid to the Aligarh Muslim University which, only a few years previously, had served as the 'arsenal' for the fight for Pakistan.

Under the inspiring stewardship of Zakir Husain, who was later to become the President of India, and B.H. Zaidi, the University turned a fresh leaf in the direction of Islamic liberalism. The liberal approach and writings of the liberals mentioned above and of still younger liberals is helping, in varying degrees, the development and gradual consolidation of the liberal approach to Islam. Indeed this approach is very much a continuing process.

The founding of the *Islam and the Modern Age Society* in Delhi in the sixties under the patronage of Zakir Husain; the liberal approach of the journal bearing the same name; the spirit of free inquiry and unhindered discussion gradually gaining ground in the *Jamia Millia* and the Aligarh University; the ever-growing educational, professional and political opportunities for Muslim women unhindered by the purdah system; all augur well for the future of Islamic liberalism. Reputed centers of traditional Islamic learning and culture such as *Nadwa* and *Deoband* are also giving a fresh look to their old syllabi and methods of teaching, displaying receptivity to new ideas. [88]

Turning to the political scene, the emergence of Bangla Deshi nationalism in the seventies has made the Indian Muslim realize that religion cannot be regarded as the sole bond for uniting people, and that language and culture do play a crucial role in human affairs. [89] The gradual realization that the root cause of communal violence is not mutual hatred or antagonism, but rather complex social conditions, administrative failures, and the machinations of unscrupulous politicians for promoting short-term-gains has led to mutual Hindu-Muslim cooperation on a secular and liberal basis. Moreover, the realization that repeated organized violence (though most harmful and tragic) fails to destroy Muslim prosperity, in the long run, or to disrupt the

Islamic Liberalism in India: A Brief Overview

deeper mutual understanding and harmony of our people has helped all concerned to judge matters in a proper perspective.

The electoral power wielded by Muslims, as Indian citizens, with equal rights and responsibilities, the high offices of state that have been freely accessible to them, both in theory and practice, the prosperity flowing from the incredibly rapid developmental process in West-Asia, apart from local opportunities in small and medium industry and commerce, the steady educational and cultural advance cannot but steer Muslims, in the long run, toward Islamic liberalism, despite some negative factors that hold them back or lead them in other directions. [90]

VII

It is important to ask why Islamic liberalism has not made much headway in India despite the sincere efforts of Sir Syed in the 19th century and of Azad in the 20th. A brief reference to the 18th century would be helpful, to begin with.

The extreme social and political turbulence of North India after Aurangzeb; a spate of civil wars, invasions from Afghanistan and Persia, and the eventual loss of Bengal to the British, forced Muslims into a protective shell. More importantly, there was no sociocultural base for the emergence of Islamic liberalism, in the Western sense, as no scientific, industrial and secular revolutions had occurred in the previous decades. The percentage of literacy was extremely low, while printing was totally unknown. The process of change in India started in the third quarter of the last century, but the pace of change was rather slow. Though science, medicine and, to some extent, engineering had been introduced in Indian universities and colleges established by the British by the closing decades of the 19th century, no industrial advance took place until after the end of the First World War. Even until the Second World War the extent and range of industrial production in India was extremely limited. It was only after independence that the industrial revolution really came of age in our society. Henceforth the pace of change is likely to be faster, thus paving the way for Islamic liberalism as a mature religious response in the age of science and technology. But at least a century would be needed to complete the process. After all it took England more than two centuries to establish religious tolerance (in the contemporary sense) in the universities of Oxford and Cambridge after the Glorious Revolution of 1688. [91] It is important to identify other factors responsible for the slow pace of change in our society. One crucial factor is the fear of the consequence of dissent from the religious establishment. Notwithstanding the clear Qur'anic verse that there is no compulsion in religion, the Muslim tradition condemns to death a born Muslim who renounces Islam. Though this penalty has been a dead one in India, thanks to the British dispensation, the fear of the consequence of dissent continues to linger on in the depth psyche of the Muslim. In any case he knows that the establishment, *suo moto*, may declare any Muslim to be guilty of heresy if not of apostasy, and make his life unbearably miserable or insecure. [92] To give a recent instance, Muslims opposed (on religious grounds) to vasectomy, as a method of family planning, threatened to boycott co-religionists who underwent the operation. Under these conditions it is easy to castigate liberal Muslim intellectuals or public men living in a democratic society for lacking the moral courage to declare in public what they think in private. But the moral courage needed is not easy for even a Sir Syed or an Iqbal in view of the painful realities of our situation. [93]

Paradoxical as it may appear, many liberals who are forced to silence their inner voice due to the fear of the consequence of dissent are pushed into communism. This weakens the growth of a liberal movement despite the presence of liberal ideas in numerous individuals who are scarcely suspected of being liberal and who perhaps hardly realize this truth about themselves. Though liberal and secular ideas have become a part of our political way of life, our religious thought system has not become correspondingly liberal. For numerous Muslims, therefore, liberalism remains a mere political strategy in a secular and pluralistic society rather than an authentic religious response, as it certainly was, in the case of Sir Syed and Azad.

Well-educated Muslims as also the masses are in conscious or unconscious search for an Islamic interpretation that could give spiritual legitimacy or depth approval to their de facto political liberalism and secularism. This legitimacy will gradually come about if, and when, Muslim intellectuals help in developing liberal Islamic thought, which subsequently reaches the common man in the form of popular Urdu and Hindi literature on Islamic liberalism. It was precisely the paucity of such literature in the years following Sir Syed's pioneering efforts in this respect that has hindered the growth of Islamic liberalism as an authentic religious expression. Without the base provided by a suitable and consistent Islamic thought system the mere

Islamic Liberalism in India: A Brief Overview

advocacy of a de facto liberal humanist position would always be dubbed either as blind imitation of the West, because of its material progress and political dominance, or as sheer political expediency dictated by the unhappy minority status of Muslims in several parts of the world.

The movement for Islamic liberalism should not fight shy of identifying any irrational or unacceptable views that may be found in the tradition, no matter how respected their source. The plea that past is past and that criticism of venerable figures might lead to unpleasant controversy will never really help Muslims. [94] Indeed, if Muslim intellectuals shy away from the task of self-criticism of their tradition, others may take it up with undesirable results.

It is often objected that the liberal interpreters of Islam have no proper credentials to do so as they do not know Arabic or do not know it sufficiently well. This objection is meant to be purely methodological or academic, but, in reality, it signifies an inner resistance to new ideas and to independent thinking. If one were writing on Muslim theology, Qur'anic exegesis, or Arabic literature, surely a thorough knowledge of Arabic would be necessary just as a knowledge of Sanskrit or Greek would be essential for a historian of Indian or Greek thought. However, when the objective is to re-interpret the basic concepts and values of Islam in the light of modern thought, the primary methodological prerequisite is not thorough grounding in Arabic language and literature (though by itself highly enviable, indeed, for all Muslims) but rather an 'insider's insight' into Islamic concepts and values, and a genuine concern for their ceaseless growth in the light of man's ever-growing knowledge in an ever-changing human situation. [95]

To close this essay on a note of sociological anticipation, the prospects of Islamic liberalism are very favorable in democratic India because a plural society is more conducive to the inner acceptance of humanism and secularism than a homogeneous society. Nowhere else do Muslims have the opportunity to freely reinterpret basic Islamic concepts and values, as a genuine spiritual response claiming religious legitimacy, and not as a mere political adjustment, or strategy in a predominantly non-Muslim environment. Exclusively or predominantly Muslim societies, probably, would not follow a common road to Islamic liberalism or agree to the thesis of the separation between the church and the state. Countries such as Turkey and Indonesia where the secular revolution has already taken place are likely to preserve the separation between the church and the state and develop the politico-economic patterns of their own choice, while Pakistan and Iran and some others may insist upon a formal or structural link between the church and the state as the *sine qua non* of Islam, and yet (in the long run) restructure their polity and laws, as if, they had accepted Islamic liberalism.

It seems, no matter whether secularism be accepted or not, Muslim societies or states will not be able to resist some basic features of the *'zeitgeist'* or spirit of the age; liberty of the individual, human fraternity, dignity of labor, equality of the sexes, the welfare state, technology, and so on and so forth. However, the actual Islamic approach to the above-mentioned features of the *'zeitgeist'* has not been uniform (as is indeed quite natural and understandable). Muslim countries, which do not retain the unity of the church and the state would have to face tremendous opposition from the religious establishment. The organic unity between the church and the state naturally gives substantial leverage to the religious establishment to veto any proposed change in the traditional system, or, conversely, to exercise pressure, in the name of Islamization, for purging the alleged un-Islamic features that may have entered into the Islamic body politic in the course of time.

In other words, while Iqbal's version of Islamic liberalism, that is, a dynamic approach to the *Shariah* in the framework of an organic unity between the church and the state may work in a homogeneous Muslim society it would not work smoothly. Moreover, it would not work at all in heterogeneous plural societies, whether Muslims be the majority or the minority, as the case may be. Where Muslims preponderate, as in Malaysia, the non-Muslims would not feel very comfortable at having to live under the umbrella of the *Shariah* or to have a somewhat second class status; where the Muslims are in the minority, as in Thailand, Philippines, and other places, they will not feel comfortable at being citizens of a state which is 'alien', in the religious sense, making them feel rootless and homeless right inside their own homeland. To overcome this state of religious alienation and bring about an organic unity between the church and the state would mean mass conversion of their fellow-citizens to Islam or secession and continuing conflict or tension on communal lines. Such a model of Islam and such a view about what a good Muslim should always be striving for sounds rather utopian and unconvincing to contemporary religious sensibilities, no matter what one's religion. In the final analysis, therefore, the de-linking of the church from the state is the most fruitful approach to Islam and other religions, as well, in both homogeneous and heterogeneous societies.

Islamic Liberalism in India: A Brief Overview

It seems (on sociological grounds) that in the long run the majority of Muslims all over the world will turn to some form of Islamic liberalism on the lines of Azad rather than of Iqbal. And (paradoxically) on a dispassionate analysis, Jinnah's basic approach to religion would be seen to be closer to the person whom he bitterly opposed as a *'showboy'* on the chessboard of Indian politics than to the august person whose political dream Jinnah (toward the close of his life) translated into reality without, perhaps, fully realizing the chasm in their respective approaches to Islam.

Explanatory Notes

(1) If the basic doctrines or beliefs of religion could have been amenable to inductive or deductive proof in this life, religious faith, as a basic human attitude toward an essentially inscrutable mystery of 'Being', or of the Universe, would have lost its *raison d'etre*. In other words, the attainment of objective certainty through the possibility of verification or proof destroys the space or soil where any kind of faith could take root and flourish. The very uncertainty (in the objective sense) provides the *ontic* ground or opportunity for certainty (in the existential or subjective sense) that, say, God inspired the Prophet ﷺ, that there is a day of final reckoning; that a moral law operates at the cosmic level.

(2) The rejection of theories of revelation does not amount to the rejection of faith in revelation just as the rejection of an anthropomorphic conception of God or Divine attributes does not amount to rejection of faith in God. No conception of God can be equated with ultimate Reality or God whom man seeks to conceptualize. Every conception is merely an attempt to build a finite conceptual model or picture of Reality. Anyone who equates the model with 'That' of which it is the model or picture commits the fallacy of 'false identification'. This fallacy may well be called 'conceptual idolatry'; a far more serious matter than idol-worship in the traditional sense. The following verses are highly significant in this context:

(16: 74)

So coin not similitudes for Allah. Lo! Allah knoweth; ye know not.

(69:1–3)

The Reality. What is the Reality? Ah, what will convey unto thee what the reality is?

(3) The vowels were super-imposed upon the Qur'anic text sometime during the reign of the *Umayyad Caliph*, Abdul Malik bin Marwan (d. 705), probably at the instance of the administrator, Hajjaj bin Yusuf, that is, some seventy years after the death of the Prophet ﷺ (632) in order to ensure correct reading and pronunciation of the text by Muslims whose mother tongue was not Arabic or the standard Arabic of the Meccan region. Even now printed Qur'an's without the vowels are quite common in the Arabic speaking region. See Qazi Mazharuddin Bilgrami's lucid work, in Urdu, on *Qur'anic Studies*, Aligarh, 1980.

(4) The question arises: How does faith in the revelation of the Qur'an arise? Obviously, faith arises due to cultural conditioning, to begin with. Later on some measure of justification becomes possible for an educated and intelligent person. But it must be conceded that no conclusive justification can ever be provided for this particular or, any other religious, conviction.

Even if it be granted that the Prophet ﷺ was unlettered and that the Qur'an possesses extraordinary literary charm and power, the truth of these claims, severally or jointly, does not amount to the truth of the claim that the Qur'an is revealed in the strict traditional sense. One may well hold that some future Arabic composition might excel the Qur'an. Again, there are quite a few well-established instances of semi-literate persons producing excellent literary work and also instances of poets, musicians, painters, and mathematicians claiming to have been given masterpieces readymade or to have produced them in a flash without effort or labor. The famous English poets: Blake, Wordsworth, Shelley. Keats and the musical genius Mozart, have made such claims. One obscure and moderately educated American woman of the 19th century, called Mrs. Curren, produced a historical novel, *The Sorry Tale*, through extended 'automatic writing'. Her case was thoroughly investigated by, competent and reliable American psychologist, Dr. W. F. Prince, in his work *The Case of Patience Worth*. (The interested reader may profitably consult G. N. M. Tyrell, *The Personality of Man*, Penguin, 1918.

(5) The problem of conscientious objection has been discussed in the last section of this chapter.

Explanatory Notes

(6) The length of the verses themselves also differs enormously. Some verses consist of two words only, while some others run into over two hundred.

(7) Muslim scholars have greatly stressed the importance of knowing the 'context of revelation' (*shan-e-nazul*) for the proper understanding of the Qur'an. They also hold several prima facie factual or descriptive verses to be really metaphorical or allegorical, and also distinguish between literal and non-literal styles of Qur'anic expression.

(8) Consider the following Qur'anic verses:

(66:1)

O Prophet! Why bannest thou that which Allah hath made lawful for thee, seeking to please thy wives? And Allah is Forgiving, Merciful.

(66:3–4)

When the Prophet confided a fact unto one of his wives and when she afterward divulged it and Allah apprised him thereof, he made known (to her) part thereof and passed over part. And when he told it to her she said: Who hath told thee? He said: The Knower, the Aware hath told me. If ye twain turn unto Allah repentant, (ye have cause to do so) for your hearts desired (the ban); and if ye aid one another against him (Muhammad) then lo! Allah, even He, is his protecting Friend, and Gabriel and the righteous among the believers; and furthermore the angels are his helpers.

(24:27)

O Ye who believe! Enter not houses other than your own without first announcing your presence and invoking peace upon the folk thereof. That is better for you that ye may be heedful.

(9) *Consider the following verses:*

(111:1–5)

The power of Abu Lahab will perish, and he will perish. And his wife, the wood carrier will have upon her neck a halter of palm fiber.

(24:6–9)

As for those who accuse their wives but have no witnesses except themselves; let the testimony of one of them be four testimonies, (swearing) by Allah that he is of those who speak the truth;

And yet a fifth invoking the curse of Allah on him if he is of those who lie.

And it shall avert the punishment from her if she bear witness before Allah four times that the thing he saith is indeed false. And a fifth (time) that the wrath of Allah be upon her if he speaketh truth.

(33:37)

And when thou saidst unto him on whom Allah hath conferred favor and thou hast conferred favor: Keep thy wife to thyself, and fear Allah and thou didst hide in thy mind that which Allah was to bring to light, and thou didst fear mankind whereas Allah had a better right that thou shouldst fear Him. So when Zayd had performed the necessary formality (of divorce) from her, We gave her unto thee in marriage, so that (henceforth) there may be no sin for believers in respect of wives of their adopted sons, when the latter have performed the necessary formality (of release) from them. The commandment of Allah must be fulfilled.

Explanatory Notes

(10) This feature of the Qur'an seems to suggest that a distinction must be made between verses which embody (a) basic values and directive principles, (b) categorical or fundamental laws, (c) derived laws or ordinances, and (d) rules or regulations. The implication is that literal adherence to the rules and regulations should be subordinate to the promotion of the basic values and implementation of the supreme directive principles of the Islamic or Qur'anic value system.

(11) Sir Syed committed this mistake in his misdirected attempt to defend his view that Islam totally rejects miracles.

(12) Every natural language uses expressions in the literal sense as well as in the non-literal sense found in similies, allegories, metaphors, phrases, idioms, proverbs, anecdotes, parables, and so on. The language of the Qur'an does likewise. Here are some examples of Qur'anic verses, which, obviously, must be understood, in the non-literal sense in order to yield a proper meaning.

(a)   (2:7) *Allah hath sealed their hearing and their hearts, and on their eyes is a covering. Theirs will be an awful doom.*

(2;10)

In their hearts is a disease, and Allah increased their disease. A painful doom is theirs because they lie.

(2:15)

Allah (Himself) doth mock them, leaving them to wander blindly on in their contumacy.

In the above verses if the expression '*Allah increaseth their disease*' be understood literally, this would mean that instead of helping or guiding His creatures, God misleads or harms them. By the very nature of the case this meaning is unacceptable. The additional clause '*because they lie*' confirms what is really the case and that the preceding expression is merely a phrase of the Qur'anic language, rather than a literal truth. Likewise *'Allah (Himself) doth mock them'* is a phrase.

> **(b)** (2:193, 194) *And fight them until persecution is no more, and religion is for Allah. But if they desist, then let there be no hostility except against wrongdoers. The forbidden month for the forbidden month, and forbidden things in retaliation. And one who attacked you; attack him in like manner as he attacked you.*

In the above verses the expression *'attack him in like manner as he attacked you'* cannot be acted upon in the literal sense. If, for instance, the enemy attacks me with a sword, I need not retaliate in the *'like manner'* in the literal sense.

> **(c)** (2:245) *Who is it that will lend unto Allah a goodly loan, so that He may give it increase manifold? Allah straiteneth and enlargeth. Unto Him ye will return.*

In the above verse *'lending a loan'* to Allah is plainly a phrase to be understood in the non-literal sense.

> **(d)** (3:166, 167) *That which befell you, on the day when the two armies met, was by permission of Allah; that he might know the true believers; And that He might know the hypocrites unto whom it was said..*

In the above verses the expression *'that He (God) might know'* cannot be understood in the literal sense of ascertaining something not known before, since God is omniscient. The expression is clearly a Qur'anic phrase just like *'God hath sealed their hearts'*.

> **(e)** (4:88) *What aileth you that ye are become two parties regarding the hypocrites, when Allah cast them back (to disbelief) because of what they earned? Seek ye to guide him whom Allah hath sent astray? He whom Allah sendeth astray, for him thou (O Muhammad) canst not find a road.*

(4:142)

Lo! The hypocrites seek to beguile Allah, but it is Allah who beguileth them. When they stand up to worship they perform it languidly and to be seen of men and are mindful of Allah but little;

In the above verses the expressions *'Allah cast them back to disbelief'*; *'whom Allah hath sent astray'*; and lastly, *'it is Allah who beguileth them'* are also Qur'anic phrases.

Further examples need not be given here due to limitations of space. The issue of non-literal interpretation is crucially important both theoretically and for practical purposes.

(13) Here are some verses, which appear to be vague, metaphorical or allusive:

(17:60)

And (it was a warning) when We told thee: Lo! Thy Lord encompasseth mankind, and We appointed the vision which We showed thee as an ordeal for mankind, and (likewise) the Accursed Tree in the Qur'an. We warn them, but it increaseth them in naught save gross impiety.

(18:9)

Or deemest thou that the People of the Cave and the Inscription are a wonder among Our portents.

(18:83)

They will ask thee of Dhul-Qarneyn. Say: I shall recite unto you a remembrance of him.

(18:94)

They said: O Dhul-Qarneyn. Lo! Gog and Magog are spoiling the land. So may we pay thee tribute on condition that thou set a barrier between us and them?

(37:62)

Is this better as a welcome, or the tree of Zaqqam?

(54:1,2)

The hour drew nigh and the moon was rent in twain. And if they behold a portent they turn away and say: Prolonged illusion.

(14) The literary excellence and spiritual power of the Qur'an is conceded even by non-Muslim Arabic scholars who unanimously hold the Qur'an to be a literary masterpiece with an inimitable style. Palmer, Nicholson, and Arberry, are all of this view.

(15) The popular view of acquiring spiritual gains (*sawab*) through the ritual recitation of the Qur'an without either understanding the contents or bothering to act upon them is a distorted and misleading view of the 'ontogenetic' function of the Qur'an in the life of the authentic believer. As mentioned earlier, the Qur'an helps to purify and build the inner spiritual being or fiber of man even as the brush strokes of the artist go to build the picture he envisions. Unless the inner goodness of being is generated and becomes the spring of good conduct, right actions will remain sporadic and fluctuating impulsive acts. On the other hand, without overt good conduct the sheer goodness of being is a spiritual mirage, which deceives both the person himself and others. This 'ontogenetic' function is performed, principally, by the mystical verses and illustrates the psychological rule that as a man thinks, so he tends to become. It is also indirectly performed by exhortative and prescriptive verses when they are habitually acted upon. This illustrates the principle stressed by William James that, if one acts afraid/confident/lazy, one really becomes so,

(16) Qur'anic texts repeatedly bracket not fasting and prayers (*Roza Namaz*) as popularly believed but faith and righteous action (*Iman wa amale sali'i*) on the one hand, and prayers and wealth-tax (*Salat wa Zakat*) on the other.

(17) The evils of adultery, murder, fraud, adulteration, perjury, misappropriation or theft, persecution of the innocent, breach of promise, legal injustice out of fear or favor; all arise and turn on the deliberate flight from speaking the truth, or facing the truth or its natural consequences squarely and without evasion. The fear of truth is, thus, man's inner Satan (*Shaitan*), while the love of truth is the God within man. This basic truth accounts for the beauty and power of Shakespeare's famous lines, though they come from the lips of a character (Polonius), more worldly-wise than moral:

(*Hamlet*, Act 1,3. 78-80)

".. to thine own self be true, and it must follow, as the night the day, Thou canst not then be false to any man"

(18) On a number of occasions the second *Caliph*, Umar, departed from the acknowledged decisions or actions of the Prophet ﷺ in political, fiscal, administrative and legal matters (though not in transcendental *I-Thou* matters) on the ground that the changed circumstances demanded a fresh approach. Ali, who later became the fourth *Caliph*, and was a young man at the time, favored strict literal adherence to the practices of the Prophet ﷺ, but deferred, in good faith, to the constitutional authority of the then *Caliph*, Umar, for instance, strictly prohibited tillers of conquered lands in Egypt from being dispossessed and their land being taken over by Muslims, while Ali was inclined to do what had been done earlier after the capture of Khyber. For further details, see Shibli's Life of Umar, *Al-Farooq*, in Urdu, or its English translation by Zafar Ali Khan, *Al-Farooq: Umar the Great*, Lahore, 1962.

(19) This theme has been elaborated in the third chapter,

(20) I have not been able to pinpoint the first writer to say that permitting any deviation from the Prophet's ﷺ interpretation of the Qur'anic

text, in any matter whatsoever, reduces the Prophet's ﷺ status to a mere 'postman' or messenger in the literal sense. This expression has, however, been referred to by several writers. According to this line of thinking, the acceptance of the Prophet ﷺ as the recipient of Divine revelation logically implies the acceptance of the Prophet's ﷺ infallibility. This assumption or inference, however, is not self-evident. On the contrary, neither the Prophet ﷺ himself made this claim nor his earliest and closest companions held him in this light, despite their unbounded respect, admiration and devotion to the messenger of God, and despite the Qur'anic verses commanding the Muslims to *'obey God and the Prophet'* or to *'help God and the Prophet'*. There are reasons to hold that the concept of the infallibility of the Prophet ﷺ arose among the Muslims as a natural consequence of the *Shia* belief that the *'imams'*, as the natural successors to the Prophet ﷺ and divinely charged with the mission of completing the Prophetic mission, were innocent and infallible. This logically implies the infallibility of the Prophet ﷺ who has a higher status than the *'imam'*.

(21) This subject has been dealt with in considerable detail in the second chapter.

(22) Suspending one's judgment for a limited time is understandable, but indefinite or permanent suspension becomes impracticable. A choice becomes more or less unavoidable in situations demanding action. Thus, in addition to the first two options, (e) also turns out to be invalid, to my mind. I personally prefer the last response. For further details, please see the second chapter and also my work, *Quest for Islam*, Allied Publishers, New Delhi, 1977.

(23) See the last few pages of the previous chapter for the various alternatives, which are open in such a situation.

(24) Democracy, as a way of life, is not merely a form of government but a pervasive basic pattern of social relationships in general, extending to the family, the school, the workshop, the playground, the club, and, of course, the church. Democracy in this wide sense flows from a definite concept of man; the classic Greek or Renaissance image of man as a creative and noble being, albeit with some mixture of evil, a being who can be trusted to act responsibly and reasonably, provided he is given due respect and love.

Democracy assumes that though men often do go wrong for one reason or other, the majority will not go wrong in the majority of their decisions on the majority of occasions, and, further, that their moral or intellectual lapses would be self-corrected in the course of time. This feature, together with the peaceful method of resolving all issues, including the devolution of power or transfer of authority to the duly elected majority (ever subject to the vigilant eye of the dissenting minority, enjoying the inalienable right to become the ruling majority at the appropriate time), makes democracy the 'least worst' form of government, despite its several limitations.

Generally speaking, Muslims find it very difficult to transcend the Semitic concept of man as the unworthy sinner. This view was considerably modified in Western Europe in the latter part of the 18th century due to the impact of the natural and the social sciences. This theme has been fully elaborated in the next chapter.

(25) The '*existential echo*' means that the command is inwardly accepted (whether spontaneously or reflectively) as valid, just or reasonable and which, therefore, ought to be obeyed for its own sake. The higher inner response of the person thus harmonizes with the evaluation or command given by the Authority.

(26) The Qur'anic provision of separate rules of punishment for slaves confirms that the letter of the Qur'an does not contemplate or imply the abolition of slavery in the future. However, the Qur'an prescribes manumission of slaves as a form of penance or atonement for several sins or lapses. The emancipation of slaves is, thus, indirectly encouraged. Consider the following Qur'anic verses.

(4:25)

And whoso is not able to afford to marry free, believing women, let them marry from the believing maids whom your right hands possess. Allah knoweth best (concerning) your faith. Ye (proceed; one from another; So wed them by permission of their folk, and give unto them their portions in kindness, they being honest, not debauched, nor of loose conduct. And if when they are honorably married they commit lewdness they shall incur half of the punishment (prescribed) for free women (in that case). This is for him among you who feared to commit sin. But to have patience would be better for you. Allah is Forgiving, Merciful.

(58:3)

Those who put away their wives (by saying they are as their mothers) and afterward would go back on that which they have said, (the penalty) in that case (is) the freeing of a slave before they touch one another. Unto this ye are exhorted; and Allah is Informed of what ye do.

(90:12–17)

Ah, what will convey unto thee what the Ascent is, It is to free a slave, And to feed in the day of hunger, An orphan near of kin, Or some poor wretch in misery, And to be of those who believe and exhort one another to perseverance. And exhort one another to pity.

(27) Slavery was a flourishing institution in Arabia in the 1920's, and for several decades thereafter. It was not formally abolished in the Kingdom until 1962. The pilgrimage was the main source. Nigerians and Sudanese would sell their children in Mecca to help pay for their journey home, and the slave trade was one traditional source of the Shareef's wealth.

In Najd every emir and sheikh had at least one black family living in his household, and their children were assigned as playmates to the children in the household of their age and sex, growing up with them and often becoming their close companions in adult life.

"When Prince Faisal ibn Abdul Aziz visited New York in 1944, the management of the Waldorf Astoria were shocked that he brought his slave Merzouk with him. But they were still more horrified when the Prince insisted that his companion should eat, as he always did, at the same table as

Explanatory Notes

his master; for this involved admitting Merzouk to the Wedgwood Room, and no black had ever been allowed in there before."

The above quotation is from Robert Lacey's, *The Kingdom*, Oxford, 1981.

(28) The relevant Qur'anic verse is as follows:

(2:178, 179)

O ye who believe! Retaliation is prescribed for you in the matter of the murdered, the freeman for the freeman and the slave for the slave, and the female for the female. And for him who is forgiven somewhat by his (injured) brother, prosecution according to usage and payment unto him in kindness. This is an alleviation and a mercy from your Lord. He who transgresseth after this will have a painful doom. And there is life for you in retaliation, O men of understanding, that ye may ward off (evil).

(29) Islamic liberals of all hues and shades have adopted precisely this very approach, which continues to flourish in modern Egypt, Turkey, Indonesia, Iraq, Syria and many other parts of the Islamic world and was until recently the official approach in Pakistan and India as well.

(30) See the following verse:

(8:60)

Make ready for them all thou canst of (armed) force and of horses (tethered), that thereby ye may dismay the enemy of Allah and your enemy and others beside them whom ye know not.

(31) The relevant Qur'anic verses are as follows:

(5:38, 39)

As for the thief, both male and female, cut off their hands, this the reward of their own deeds, an exemplary punishment from Allah. Allah is Mighty, Wise. But whoso repenteth after his wrongdoing and amendeth, lo! Allah will relent toward him. Lo! Allah is Forgiving, Merciful.

(32) It should be noted that the traditional Islamic law (*Shariah*) has never followed the Qur'anic command, in the literal sense, free from all qualifications whatsoever. Thus, according to the *Shariah*, the Qur'anic penalty is not attracted by thefts of foodstuff, petty cash, musical instruments, or by culprits who happen to be close relations or servants of the aggrieved person. Perhaps, the basic principle underlying Umar's approach was further developed by Muslim jurists to promote equity rather than literal adherence to the letter of the law. Why, then, should this approach not be extended to other matters mentioned in the Qur'an? See the standard work, *Minhajet Talibin* by An Nawwai (English translation by E.C. Howard), London, 1914, pp. 443-44.

(33) Eric Fromm, *Fear of Freedom*, London, 1960. In what follows, I am greatly indebted to Fromm's analysis.

(34) Karl Jasper's (d. 1969) is one of the most original and influential exponents of the existentialist approach to philosophy. Deeply committed to democratic values, he defied the might of Hitler who terminated his teaching job. The Allied victory in the Second World War led to the restoration of his Professorship. He is as famous as his compatriot, Heidegger, or the French thinker, Sartre.

(35) See Muhammad Iqbal's *Reconstruction of Religious Thoughts in Islam*, Lahore, 1962.

(36) For a remarkably objective and comprehensive history of the social cultural developments in modern Turkey, see Berkes, N. *Development of Secularism in Turkey*, Montreal, 1964.

(37) John Locke (d. 1704) of Oxford, influential British thinker, Immanuel Kant (d. 1804) of Germany, and Voltaire (d. 1778) of France attacked dogmatism

both in philosophy and theology and greatly helped in the flowering of a critical scientific world view, representative democracy, respect for the individual, and tolerance. Among the intellectuals, Marx (d. 1883) enjoys the greatest single influence. Engels (d. 1895) was his intellectual collaborator and friend.

(38) The history of religion clearly explains the root cause of confusion on this score. The view that Islam stands for the organic unity of the church and the state, the sacred and the profane, while Christianity bifurcates life, *'rendering unto Caesar the things which are Caesar's and to God the things which are God's'* is an oversimplified interpretation of the early history of the two religions.

Christianity functioned as a more or less cultural intruder in an alien Roman environment for centuries before becoming the official or established religion of the Holy Roman Empire, under Constantine 1 (d. 337). The bifurcation of life into the sacred and the secular or separation between the church and the state characterized only pre-establishment Christianity which began as a commitment to Christ and a spiritual discipline, just as Islam, six centuries later, began as a commitment to God and his Prophet ﷺ. The period of pre-establishment Islam was brief, while that of Christianity was very long. However, both religions eventually developed into total maps of the good life in all its aspects, Islam very rapidly, indeed, in less than twenty years, while Christianity very slowly, in the course of more than three centuries. Otherwise, medieval Christianity, and Islam cannot be distinguished at all in their 'totalist' approach.

It is important to point out that the Protestantism of Martin Luther (d. 1546) was only a protest against the infallible authority of the Pope, rather than against the totalist character of Christianity.

The same is true of the French reformer, Calvin (d. 1564). It was only in the latter half of the 18th century that the totalist character or all embracing casuistic complexion of Christianity was effectively questioned, thanks to the impact of science and of the liberal thought of philosophers such as Hume (d. 1766) and Kant, and deists such as Lord Herbert, Shaftesbury (d. 1713), Bishop Butler (d. 1752), and William Paley (d. 1805), all of England. I cannot do better than giving a rather lengthy quotation from a well-known British writer of the last century, J.A. Froude, from his work *Short Studies on Great Subjects*, quoted in Bhagwan Das's *The Essential Unity of All Religions*, Benares, 1939, pages 8-9:

Authenticity and Islamic Liberalism

"A religion which holds possession of our lives, which directs us at each step which we take, becomes part of our own souls. Unless, in some shape or other, it prescribes a rule of conduct, it inevitably loses its hold. The Catholic system scarce leaves an hour without its stated duties: such and such forms to be gone through; such and such prayers to be repeated. Calvinism superseded these formal observances by yet more noble practical observances. It was ever present with its behests in fixing the scale of permitted expenditure, in regulating the dress, the enjoyments, the hours of sleep and labor, sternly cutting short all idle pleasures, luxury, sternly insisting on the right performance of all practical work, the trade, the handicraft, or whatever it might be, as something for every thread and fibre of which a man would one day be called to account. Religion is the wholesome ordering of human life: the guide to furnish us with our daily duties in the round of common occupation; the lamp to light us along our road and to show us where to place our steps".

Turning to Hinduism, the following two quotations, one from a Westerner and the other from a well-known Indian, should suffice for the purpose. The excerpts have been taken from Nirad Chaudhuri's *Hinduism*, New Delhi, 1979, page 10, and pages 11-12.

"...with the Hindu, religion is not a thing for times and seasons only, but professes to regulate his life in all its many relations. It regulates the ceremonies attendant on his birth, his early training, his food, and its cooking, his style of dress and its manufacture, his employment, marriage, amusements; his whole life from before his birth, until generation, until generations after his death. Religion seeks to regulate not only the private life of the Hindu, but also his domestic and national relations, and no contingencies are possible for which it has not provided laws". (Wilkin's, W. J., *Modern Hinduism*, 1887)

"With other peoples religion is only a part of life; there are things religious, and there are things lay and secular. To the Hindu, his whole life was religion. To other peoples, their relations to God and to the spiritual world are things sharply distinguished from their relations to man and to the temporal world. To the Hindu, his relations to God and his relations to man, his spiritual life and his temporal life are incapable of being so distinguished. They form one compact and harmonious whole, to separate which into compartments is to break the entire fabric. All life to him was religion, and religion never received a name from him, because it never had for him an existence apart from all that had received a name ....

Explanatory Notes

(Bankim Chandra Chatterji (1838-94). The quotation is from a Bengali essay (1888) expounding the nature of Hinduism.

(39) Herbert Butterfield, noted Cambridge historian is well-known for his work, *Origins of Modern Science*, London, 1957. Robert Briffault's work, *Making of Humanity*, London, 1919, has been much acclaimed, as also A. N. Whitehead's, *Science and the Modem World*, New York, 1954. Whitehead was a noted mathematician and philosopher of Cambridge. Bertrand Russell's works are well-known. See his *Impact of Science on Society*, London, 1952. J. D. Bemal's *Science in History*, London, 1954, is a monumental work.

(40) Systematic study of the reported sayings and doings of the Prophet ﷺ *(hadith)* together with knowledge of the context of the revelation of Qur'anic verses has been deemed to be sufficient historical knowledge for the good Muslim. Some progress in the direction of teaching Islamic history has recently been made in Deoband and Nadwa schools, but the study of world history or the history of ideas is still a far cry. Christian theologians, on the other hand, are well-versed in history and the natural and the social sciences.

(41) Copernicus (d. 1543), Polish astronomer, was the first among the moderns to revive the long forgotten ancient Greek theory that the earth goes round the sun. Descartes (d. 1650), influential French philosopher and mathematician, followed the method of constructive doubt, which is the basis of the critical scientific worldview. Spinoza (d. 1677) of Holland and Leibniz (d. 1716) of Germany greatly stimulated Western thought. Newton (d. 1727) of Cambridge, Galileo (d. 1642) of Italy, Kepler (d. 1630) of Germany, and Maxwell (d. 1879) of Great Britain made extremely fruitful advances in physics and mathematics. See Bernal's work, op cit. Notes 117

(42) Adam Smith (d. 790) of Oxford is the father of Economics.

(43) Positivism, in its broadest sense, is the view that only such truth-claims, as can possibly be verified in the logical or the scientific sense, constitute positive knowledge, while all else is mere opinion, guess, or futile speculation. *Scientism* goes a step further to say that non-scientific truthclaims are not worth serious argument or commitment. *Scientism* is the root cause of the 'nihilistic climate' or indifference to moral and spiritual values in contemporary society. This recognition is, however, helping Western man to recover his lost balance or sense of proportion. The West's search for man's

lost soul is also reflected in its growing interest in the wisdom of the East; Buddhist, Hindu and Islamic, as the case may be.

(44) See Bronowski J. and Mazlish, B., *The Western Intellectual Tradition*, Pelican, 1963.

(45) Goethe (d. 1832) the greatest German poet and a versatile genius, was fascinated by Islamic as well as Sanskrit culture and has greatly enriched liberal humanism. Hegel (d. 1831) influential German philosopher, formulated the dialectical method of grasping and understanding the spirit of ever-developing or dynamic reality, including different forms of society and culture; the state, the church, art, philosophy, morality, and so on. Hegel greatly influenced Marx who accepted the dialectical method but combined it with philosophical materialism.

(46) Herbert Spencer (d. 1903) was a prolific British writer and thinker who viewed evolution as a basic and pervasive feature of reality, as a whole, but whose thought was less speculative and abstruse than that of Hegel, and more idealistic than that of Marx. Darwin's theory of evolution, on the other hand, was a purely scientific hypothesis applicable to biological organisms alone and was supported by empirical data.

(47) Charles Darwin (d. 1882) published his epoch-making work, *On the Origin of Species*, in 1859. After tenaciously resisting what was held to be a most obnoxious atheistic approach, Christian theology came to terms with Darwinism by the end of the century. Bishop Wilberforce, of Oxford, was the arch critic of Darwin, while T. H. Huxley the main defender.

In view of the mass of scientific evidence (in the form of fossils, and minutely measured structures) deemed to verify or render extremely probable the hypothesis of the survival of the fittest through natural selection, scientists were compelled to accept Darwin's theory. Further qualifications and refinements were incorporated later on. Christian theologians, in general were led to assimilate the concept of evolution as a method of Divine creation.

Muslim theologians, on the other hand, still continue to resist the concept on the mistaken assumption that evolution and Divine creation are incompatible. They also misconstrue the neo-evolutionary philosophical theories put forward by the critics of Darwin's original theory, namely, Lloyd Morgan, (d. 1936) and the influential French philosopher, Bergson (d. 1941) as a rebuttal of the basic concept of evolution as such. This inference is totally fallacious.

(48) William James (d. 1910) of Harvard, the greatest American philosopher, rejected abstract metaphysical speculation, and held that meaning and truth must be ascertained on the basis of experience and practical utility. The analytical approach to philosophy practiced by G. E. Moore (d. 1958) and Russell (d. 1969) of Cambridge has radically changed the philosophical temper of the modern British and American mind. Wittgenstein (d. 1951) of Austrian extraction, who settled down and taught at Cambridge gave a new and more fruitful turn to the analytical method by stressing the plural uses of words and expressions of 'ordinary language' instead of trying to analyze meanings in the manner of Moore and Russell. Distinguished British thinkers such as John Wisdom, and Gilbert Ryle have fruitfully applied this method to diverse problems.

(49) Deism is natural or supra-religious theism transcending the dogmas, rituals and particularities of different religions, while Theism is generally associated with a particular religious tradition. However, the expression 'Christian Deism' is not entirely redundant.

Deism holds reason or intuition, rather than any revealed book or person, as the supreme authority and is thus free of all dogmatism. However, it errs in holding that human reason or intuition can prove the basic truths of religion without revelation; God, life after death, moral order in the Divine scheme of things, the Divine spark in man. Religious existentialism does not claim such truths to be rationally demonstrable, and, in the final analysis, this helps rather than harm the cause of genuine religion.

(50) Linguistic analysis clearly exposed the fallacy of the early Positivists who held that religious expressions were devoid of any 'cognitive meaning' and had merely 'emotive meaning'; a blanket term (applied to ethical, aesthetic and all sorts of expressions) which the Positivists used for denigrating religious language vis-a-vis actual or logical statements. The linguistic analysts carefully identified and described, in a neutral fashion, the unique features of religious language (just as the Positivists had earlier done with respect to the language of science and mathematics) without any attempt

to glorify or denigrate religious language. This impartial and accurate type of analysis has helped all to understand the real nature of religious feeling and certainty and also to encourage one to make authentic choice, one way or the other, without the illusion of possessing logical or scientific certainty. In short, the movement of linguistic analysis has helped religion to come of age by shedding the old illusions of dogmatic philosophy and theology.

(51) Kierkegaard (d. 1855), Danish Protestant theologian, is the father of modern Christian existentialism. Not much known during his lifetime, his approach and writings are now of tremendous importance and influence in the Western world. Nietzsche (d. 1900), of Germany, is the father of atheistic existentialism holding the will to self-assertion or power rather than ideas, reason, moral purpose, or Divine providence, as the pervasive and basic feature of reality, as a whole. Mysticism, existentialism and Marxism, despite their differences, agree in dethroning discursive reason from its supreme authority and prestige in the classical Western idealistic tradition from Plato to Hegel.

(52) Thomas Aquinas (d. 1274) of Italy is the greatest Christian theologian of the medieval period. He held that Christian theism was rationally demonstrable, provided one approached it with intellectual humility and understood the nature of analogical language. His influence is still considerable in the Catholic Church.

(53) A few examples out of a vast treasure are the poetry (in Persian) of Jalaluddin Rumi (d. 1273), Fariduddin Attar (d. 1210), Sadi (d. 1291), Khusro (d. 1325), the Urdu poetry of Mir Taqi Mir (d. 1810), Mir Dad (d. 1785), Ghalib (d. 1869), and a goodly portion of the Persian and Urdu poetry of Iqbal (d. 1938),

It seems, the mystical or the existentialist approach, adumbrated in the above literature, would prevail in the Islamic world in the long run despite the current form taken by the movement of Islamic resurgence in Pakistan, Iran, and elsewhere. Likewise, Azad's version of Islamic existentialism is more likely to acquire a universal appeal than Iqbal's stress on the organic unity of the church and the state in Islam. This subject has been fully elaborated in the next chapter. See Azad's monumental commentary on *surah* Fatiha in his *Tarjumanul Qur'an*.

Explanatory Notes

The works of Tagore, Gandhi, Aurobindo, Radhakrishnan, and Nehru are well-known. The following may be mentioned specifically: Tagore, *Religion of Man*, London, 1931; Khwaja, J. and Alvi, Z., *Readings from Gandhi*, Aligarh, 1969, Aurobindo, *On Yoga*, Pondicherry, 1957; Radhakrishnan, *Recovery of Faith*, London, 1963; Nehru. *The Discovery of India*, Calcutta, 1946.

(54) Rudolph Otto (d. 1937), noted German religious thinker, first used the term 'numinous' to identify the differentia of religious experience or response from other forms of experience, the perceptual, logical, ethical, aesthetic, and spiritual. The religious experience, according to Otto, is the experience of communion with an all-powerful and holy Thou. This was also the essential idea of the German thinker, Schleiermacher (d. 1834), and is a form of religious existentialism.

(55) It is a fairly common belief in Islamic quarters that Christianity, or any religion for that matter, which confines itself to individual purification or mystical experience, without any message of social or collective action, is a degenerate religion condemned to eventual extinction. According to this line of thinking, contemporary Christian existentialism is a mere apology for religion since it does not respect the organic unity of man's life. This criticism is invalid since the existentialist approach to religion by no means underestimates the crucial importance of the social good in an exclusive concern for individual salvation. The existentialist approach seeks social good, not through dogmatic or institutional religion, but through collective human wisdom flowing from spiritual renewal consequent upon authentic religious faith or commitment to a value system, with or without faith in God, as the case may be.

(56) The term 'fundamentalism' is commonly used in modern literature and Western media to denote a religious approach characterized (more or less) by any one, some, or all of the following adjectives; closed, defensive, sectarian, over-puritanical, regimented, authoritarian, legalist, theocratic, pre-critical. This usage is highly misleading, since the term 'fundamentalism' tends to suggest commitment to the fundamentals of a religion rather than to its peripheral beliefs and practices. In my view the term, *'Islamic totalism'* best describes the position contrary to *'Islamic liberalism'*. Hence, I have used the expressions *'totalist approach to, or conception, of religion'*, or *'totalist dimension'* of religion in this work and also elsewhere.

Authenticity and Islamic Liberalism

(57) To illustrate this point, both Sir Syed and Badruddin Tyabji stood for Islamic liberalism but their political approaches differed widely. Again, Muhammad Ali Jinnah always was and remained liberal in the religious sense, though his early secular nationalism later on changed into Pakistani Muslim nationalism.

(58) If liberalism be understood in the sense of receptivity of the tradition to general human progress in knowledge, not only Iqbal but also Maududi (who is one of the fathers of contemporary Islamic Resurgence) could be said to be liberal, in relation to Abdul Wahab of the 18th century, the patron saint of modern Saudi Arabia. On the other hand, if the separation between the church and the state be included in the definition of Islamic liberalism (as in the case of Christian and Hindu liberalism); Iqbal would be excluded from the category of Muslim liberals.

(59) Cultural or religious absolutism is, primarily, the product of the ethnocentric condition of man, which was more or less unavoidable until very recent times. Fast global communication and mass media are drastically reducing, if not eliminating, the natural ethnocentricity of human groups.

(60) The concept of exclusive salvation is not only totally disconsonant with the religious temper and spiritual sensibility of the modern mind, but is also not found in the Qur'an which, in the final analysis, is the supreme locus of authority for the Muslim. Belief in exclusive salvation is common to all Semitic religions, as popularly understood, while the Aryan religions view salvation as the release from the cycle of repeated births and deaths in accordance with the impersonal law of karma. This approach de-links salvation from adherence to any particular creed and makes salvation a function of right deeds alone. Different religions are viewed as different paths to the same end. Thus, religious pluralism is native to religions of Indian origin and their adherents do not need any intellectual reorientation to achieve this philosophically mature and socially fruitful approach. Unfortunately, however, Hindu society is bedevilled by the evil of the deep-rooted caste system, which ill accords with humanism.

(61) As a cultural phenomenon religion is an integral part of human society and cannot remain unaffected by changes in the total human condition. Islam cannot claim to be exempt from this basic sociological truth.

Explanatory Notes

The logic of events leading to Christian liberalism in the 18th century, thus, tends to produce more or less similar changes in Islam in the 20th. In view of the fact that each religion is rooted in its own past, we should not expect any mechanical parallelism in the responses of different religions to the human situation. Moreover, history does not represent an uninterrupted unilinear progress toward any goal, even though a broad trend or direction of human affairs may possibly be identified, if we think in terms of the human family as a whole, and take very long periods of time as units for our historical survey. Even so, we come across enormous fluctuations and glaring failures. For instance, periods of intellectual and cultural progress of a nation are followed by cultural decay and barbarism, religious liberalism by brutal repression, democratic rule by dictatorship and vice versa.

As an illustration, the second half of the 19th century was the period of religious liberal reform in the West as well as in Muslim countries, India, and China, while the second half of the present century is witnessing a surge not only of 'Islamic fundamentalism', but also of Christian fundamentalism or neo-orthodoxy in America, and of Hindu and Sikh fundamentalism in India, though, obviously, the concrete nuances and contours of the fundamentalist assertion differ in each religion. The same period is witnessing the partial decline of over-confident and militant communism and its subtle liberalization in Eastern Europe, China, India, and even in the Soviet Union itself.

Fluctuations, cyclical change, linear accelerations/slow-downs or even reversals of ideational-attitudinal currents extending to a couple of decades or even a century or so, however, should not be equated with the broad direction of the 'movement of history' - the story of human society as a whole; provided the direction is empirically ascertainable rather than a mere projection of one's hopes and fears or the product of theoretical philosophical history or dialectics. Again, the 'direction of history' (if any) should not be equated with any 'goal of history' in the religious or philosophical sense, since such a goal can never be established on the basis of empirical history or sociology. However, man lives by hope. And it is perfectly proper to hope that one's own goals rather than of others really coincide with the direction of history' (in other words, that one is on the winning side in the drama of history) provided one has carefully sought illumination from empirical history. Such historical faith sustains man's ceaseless striving for the eventual success of his own ideas and ideals. For a balanced and refreshing analysis of Christian fundamentalism in the United States, see Nathan Glaser's article

'*Pluralism and Fundamentalism*', in *The American Review*, Autumn, 1983, Vol. 28, No.1. For a detailed analysis of the methodology of history and the concepts of 'The movement, direction and goal of history', see my rather lengthy article, '*History: Theory, Philosophy and Wisdom*', in the periodical *Man and Development*, June 1983, Vol. 5, No. 2.

(62) There is no mention in reliable historical accounts of the conversion of the Hindu ruler of the region to Islam during the lifetime of the Prophet ﷺ and of the spread of Islam among a section of the local people, (as is found in folklore or mentioned in much later popular Persian or local narratives of the region).

(63) The approach of the Sultans to the propagation of Islam was remarkably similar to that of the British rulers of India several centuries later. Neither the East India Company nor the British Parliament ever felt called upon to save the souls of the Indian masses. The Christian missionaries did this without any substantial material help from the Christian rulers, and the *Sufi* saints did the same in the medieval period. Among the Sultans, only Feroze Tughlaq (d. 1388), Sikandar Sultan of Kashmir (d. 1410) and Sikandar Lodi (d. 1517) adopted the approach of aggressive proselytism. The most shameful and tragic episode of intolerance is the killing of the Hindu scholar and saint, Buddhan Brahman, during the reign of Sikandar Lodi.

(64) It is crucially important not to confuse the views and attitudes of some theologians or administrators with the actual policies followed by the Sultans, just as it is important to keep apart the views and predilections of different political parties and the press from those of the government itself. Hasty and false generalizations must also be avoided. Before we pass judgments of value the spirit of the times (*zeitgeist*) must be taken into account without, however, explaining away its limitations or adopting a defensive or partisan approach. Keeping the above principles in view, we find that though a number of temples were destroyed by Muslim rulers, the destruction of temples was never wholesale but was confined to a few centrally or strategically located temples and was calculated (according to the then '*zeitgeist*') to symbolize the sovereignty of the victors in battle, (more or less at par with the hoisting of the flag of the victor on the fort or citadel of the captured territory). It would be a fallacy to construe this practice (which civilized humanity has now completely outgrown and which we now would judge as atrocious if it were to be observed in our own time: as a proof of

the intention, or of the act of persecution of non-Muslims or of coercing them to change their faith. In fact, the Muslim rulers were least inclined to do so, as mentioned earlier.

The beliefs and customs of the Hindu masses were left loudly untouched and they enjoyed full freedom to practice their rites and rituals and celebrated their numerous seasonal fairs and festivals. Rather, the Muslims themselves started to participate in them, especially in rural areas, although a section of the puritanical theologians disapproved of the spirit of comradeship. The construction of new temples was generally banned, though the existing ones could be repaired. Later on, in the Mughal period, several temples were given state grants or permanent endowments, even by Aurangzeb. See Pande, B.N., *Reorientation of Study of Medieval Indian History*, Allahabad, 1978.

(65) The most balanced view concerning the socioreligious conditions in medieval India is found, in my opinion, in late M. Habib's penetrating article, *'An Introduction to the Study of Medieval India'*, first published in the *Aligarh Magazine*, and reprinted in Vol. I of Habib's *Collected Works (edited by Prof. K.A. Nizami)*, Aligarh, 1974. The theme is continued (though the excursion into Marxist theory is crude and uncalled for) in Habib's Introduction to the Aligarh edition of Eliot and Dowson's *History of India, Vol. II*, also reprinted in the *Collected Works*, same volume.

Habib's findings (derived from critically ascertained facts derived from original sources) reveal the sense in which medieval society was 'functionally' secular and tolerant, despite the legal fiction about India being a 'land of Islam' (*dar-ul-Islam*) and the sovereign power of the Sultans being, in theory, delegated to them by the Abbasid *Caliphs* of Baghdad till 1258 and hereafter, by the Fatimite *Caliphs* of Cairo. It may be noted that the Mughal emperors did away with this practice and repudiated even the legal fiction as such, assuming the title of King and 'shadow of God' instead of *Sultan* and vicegerent of the *Caliph*.

The Muslim *Sultans* and emperors intuitively demarcated the spheres of state and religion, and held that the ruler was father to all his subjects irrespective of their religion.

(66) The ban on intermarriage and inter-dining certainly prevented the rise of liberal humanism in the contemporary sense. However, mutual tolerance and understanding or 'the agreement to differ', which is the crux

of the matter, did prevail. The view that the entire medieval period of Indian history is the period of Muslim tyranny over helpless Hindu subjects is not only a gross exaggeration but a total distortion of now well-established facts; ascertained through objective investigation (which is a continuing process) independent of any nationalist or Muslim bias.

(67) Al-Beruni is one of the half a dozen geniuses of the Islamic world. Spending several years in India, he mastered the Sanskrit language to make a critical study of Indian thought and culture, with sympathetic objectivity. He declared that Hindus believed in the unity of God, despite their idol worship. Standing for tolerance and pointing out the unity of basic concepts in the diversity of ideas and forms, Al-Beruni deserves to be called the father of Comparative Religion. See his monumental work, in English translation, *India*, N. Y., 1971, from which the following excerpt has been taken, as quoted in, Nirad Chaudhury's *Hinduism*:

"The beliefs of educated and uneducated people differ in every nation; for the former try to conceive abstract ideas and to define general principles, whilst the latter do not pass beyond the apprehension of the senses.... The Hindus believe with regard to God that he is one, eternal, without beginning and end, acting by free will, almighty, all-wise, living, giving life, ruling, preserving; one who in his sovereignty is unique, beyond all likeness and unlikeness and that he does not resemble anything nor does anything resemble him.... This is what educated people believe about God. ... If we now pass from the ideas of educated people among the Hindus to those of common people, we must say that they present a great variety. Some of them are simply abominable".

Al-Beruni's basic approach is reflected in the liberal movements of *Bhakti* and *Sufism* in the medieval period. Ramanand, Kabir, Nanak, Raidas, Dadu, Malukdas, Sundardas, Chaitanya, and Namdev are well-known for their liberal humanitarianism. Says Tara Chand in his *Influence of Islam on Indian Culture*, Allahabad, 1963, p. 165: "Akbar's, *Deen-e-Ilahi* was not an isolated freak of an autocrat who had more power than he knew how to employ, but an inevitable result of the forces which were deeply surging in India's breast, and finding expression in the teachings of men like Kabir."

(68) Historians argue whether *Deen-e-Ilahi* was a new religion or merely a liberal interpretation of Islam. Even if we hold the latter view, it definitely had the air or complexion of a cult or sect and demanded absolute devotion to the royal guru, which facts understandably created apprehensions in orthodox

circles. That the quest for spiritual truth, on the part of Akbar's inner circle, was alloyed with the quest for power or influence cannot be denied. In any case, it must be conceded that the court and the wider social elite throbbed with intellectual and cultural activity, thanks to the brilliance of Shaikh Mubarak, Abul Fazal, Fyzee, Fathullah Shirazi, and some other members.

(69) The character and role of Aurangzeb is perhaps the most emotionally charged controversy of medieval Indian history. Partisan approaches have been very common until very recently, but a balanced and dispassionate assessment has recently emerged, thanks to the continuing research free from political and religious passions and prejudices.

Aurangzeb's policy of territorial expansion and administrative centralism (as distinct from Akbar's federalism) was a matter of politics and not the result of any animus against the Hindus, Sikhs or Mahrattas, or for that matter, the *Shias*. The contemporary Sikh politics of agitation provides a remarkable parallel of the tendency to confuse political issues with religious convictions. Nevertheless, Aurangzeb's banning of music in his court, his discriminatory excise duties on Hindu traders (1665), his destruction of some temples (1669), his imposition of *jizya* (1679) show that his approach to Islam was very different, indeed, from the liberal views of Akbar and Dara Shikoh.

Dara Shikoh was the first to translate into Persian selected *Upanishads* from the original Sanskrit. This was a most laudable and internationally significant event. However, Dara's work on Comparative Religion entitled *Confluence of the Two Oceans* abounds in fanciful and forced similarities between Islam and Hinduism. Such approaches tend to obstruct genuine interaction between different religions or cultural traditions.

(70) See Spear, P. *Twilight of the Moghuls*, Cambridge, 1951, and Bidwell, S. *Swords for Hire*, London, 1971.

(71) Even earlier than Sir Syed, the poet Ghalib (d. 1869), had deciphered the significance of recent events and pleaded for a fresh look at the heritage of Islam and Mughal culture in the light of Western science and technology.

Among the earliest helpers and associates of Sir Syed, mention must be made of Samiullah Khan (d. 1908), whose subsequent differences on policy and some personal matters, has led to ignoring or overlooking his great contribution in the early phase of the *Aligarh movement*. The other person is Mohsinul Mulk (d. 1907), and later on Viqarul Mulk (d. 1917). The literary galaxy around Sir Syed included, apart from Shibli, Zakaullah (d. 1910), Nazir Ahmed (d. 1912), Hali (d. 1914), and Mumtaz Ali.

(72) Deoband has played a glorious role (from the platforms of the *Khilafat* and Congress organizations) in India's freedom struggle, producing such eminent patriots as Mahmudul Hasan (d. 1921), Husain Ahmad Madani (d. 1957), Hifzur Rahman (d. 1962) among several others. However, the basic thrust of the Deoband approach to Islam has totally differed from Islamic liberalism. Obaidullah Sindhi (d. 1944) who collaborated with the legendary freedom fighter and romantic revolutionary, Raja Mahendra Pratap (d. 1979), however, did stand for Islamic liberalism.

The roving romantic champion of pan-Islamism, Jamaluddin Afghani (d. 1897) who had his own brand of Islamic liberalism also attacked Sir Syed's ideas on Islam as also his subservience to the British, thereby indirectly strengthening the conservative opposition. Though Jamaluddin had a violent temper and was disposed to polemics rather than objective analysis, he was a charismatic figure who inspired many all over the Islamic world, including the sober and constructive writer and reformer of Egypt, Muhammad Abduh (d. 1905). See Qazi Abdul Gaffar's *Life of Afghani*, in Urdu, Hyderabad, 1940.

(73) The British rulers indulged the fears and apprehensions of the Muslims, more out of an imperial instinct or calculated self-interest (as the case may be) than out of sympathy or principled support for the idea of separate electorates, totally contrary to British political sensibility and culture in the modern age. Though the record of some British administrators at the district and provincial levels was not beyond reproach, to charge the British rulers for having 'created' communal friction to divide and rule would, in my opinion, amount to an unkind exaggeration or hasty generalization.

(74) The movement of Balkan nationalism was inaugurated by the success of modern Greece in emancipating herself from the Ottoman Empire in the first quarter of the 19th century. Subsequently, the movement spread all over Eastern Europe, and, by the end of the last century, Istanbul and its adjoining territories were left as the only European constituent of the once mighty and far-flung Ottoman Empire. Arab nationalism also

Explanatory Notes

emerged soon after the Greek, chiefly in Iraq and Lebanon, and the Allies actively supported the challengers to the Ottoman power. Sir Syed had been inclined to view Turkey's conflicts and difficulties as a regional political conflict rather than a religious conflict between Islam and Christianity. The *Khilafat* movement, on the other hand, gave a religious color to the entire issue.

(75) Shibli's monumental biography of the second *Caliph*, Umar, is one of the most illuminating and permanently relevant books on Islam. The insight and balanced judgment displayed in this work remain unsurpassed even today. After a distinguished teaching career at the M. A. O. College, Aligarh; Shibli helped to found the Nadwa seminary in Lucknow in 1894, but finding the atmosphere too restrictive for his liberal and rationalistic approach to Islam, shifted to Azamgarh. The Nadwa School has now become an internationally known center under the guidance of the reputed scholar, Abdul Hasan Ali. A person of great integrity and learning though he in his approach to Islam lacks the philosophical penetration, sharp clarity and liberal dimension characteristic of Shibli.

(76) It is significant that, in the name of *Shariah*, Muhammad Ali opposed the application to Muslims of the *Sharda Bill* seeking to prevent child marriage. However, it would be most unfair to ignore or minimize his immense contribution to the freedom struggle because of a few lapses on his part. Perhaps, his temperamental traits rather than his Islamic approach were more responsible for his errors of judgment.

(77) One may well disapprove of some of the policies and actions of Kamal Ataturk, but his genius is unquestionable. History has vindicated his realistic vision, clarity and courage, though not some of his naive and unhappy attempts to westernize an entire nation through legislation concerning dress, food, and entertainment, etc.

(78) Nor for that matter did Jinnah ever uphold the concept of an Islamic state, as understood in contemporary Pakistan, which has definitely moved away from the vision of its founder. In fairness to him I cannot help quoting, at some length, from his famous speech before the Constituent Assembly of Pakistan on August 11, 1947, as quoted in M. Munir's *From Jinnah to Zia*, Delhi, 1981.

Authenticity and Islamic Liberalism

"... *If you will work in cooperation forgetting the past, burying the hatchet, you are bound to succeed. If you change your past and work together in a spirit that everyone of you, no matter to what community he belongs, no matter what relations he had with you in the past, no matter what is his color, caste or creed, is first, second, and last a citizen of this state with equal rights, privileges and obligations, there will be no end to the progress you will make*".

"*You are free, you are free to go to your temples, and you are free to go to your mosques or any other place of worship in this state of Pakistan. You may belong to any religion, caste or creed that has nothing to do with the business of the state. We are starting in the days when there is no discrimination, no distinction between one community and another, no discrimination between one caste or creed or another. We are starting with this fundamental principle that we are all citizens and equal citizens of one state. ... Now I think you should keep that in front of us as our ideal, and you will find that in course of time Hindus would cease to be Hindus, Muslims would cease to be Muslims, not in the religious sense, because that is the personal faith of each individual, but in the political sense, as citizens of the state*".

(79) The year 1923 is memorable in the *Jamia's* early history at Aligarh where P.C. Ray, the great scientist, savant and patriot, delivered the Convocation address. This address carries a foreword giving a lucid exposition of Islamic liberalism, by the then Vice-Chancellor, A.M. Khwaja.

(80) Doing full justice in the matter of mentioning specific names here and at other places in this work is almost impossible. Some names are bound to figure in all lists, while others would be included or excluded depending upon different criteria. The criterion I have tried to follow is '*influence of published work with a bearing on Islamic liberalism*', rather than the intellectual caliber, total personality and general contribution to culture or society. I beg the reader's kind indulgence for my acts of commission or omission in this regard. Names, which figure in the main text of the chapter, have been generally excluded in these lists.

Among intellectuals mention may be made of Mohammad Habib (d. 1971), Haroon Khan Sherwani (d. 1980), Shafat Ahmed (d. 1948), K. G. Saiyidain (d. 1969), A. A. Fyzee (d. 1982), S. Abdul Latif (d. 1971), Shaikh Abdullah of Aligarh (d. 1965), S. M. Ikram (d. 1973), Muhammad Ali of Lahore (d. 1951), Abdullah Yusuf Ali (d. 1953), and Khwaja Kamaluddin.

From the fifties onwards, mention may be made of Humayun Kabir (d. 1969), Rafiq Zakaria (d. 2005), Hifzur Rahman (d. 1962), S. A. Akbarabadi, M. M. Shareef (d. 1965), Caliph Abdul Hakim (d. 1959), A. K. Brohi (d. 1987), Fazlur Rahman (d. 1988), Aziz Ahmad (d. 1982), Ahmed Ali, Ghulam Jilani Barq, and Ghulam Ahmad Parvez (d. 1985). The last eight are from Pakistan.

(81) Apart from Hasrat Mohani (d. 1951), who belongs to the earlier generation, the liberal poets include Majaz (d. 1955), Makhdoom (d. 1969), Jazbi, Sardar Jafri (d. 2000), Faiz (d. 1984), and, in the next generation, Khalilur Rahman (d. 1978), and Waheed Akhtar (d. 1996). Among biographers, novelists, critics and other writers mention may be made of Qazi Abdul Ghaffar (d. 1956), Tofail Ahmad (d. 1946), Azim Beg Chughtai (d. 1941), Abdul Qadir of Lahore (d. 1950), Ejaz Husain, Ehtisham Husain (d. 1972), Imtiaz Arshi (d. 1973), Qazi Wadood (d. 1984), Kalimuddin Ahmad (d. 1984), Akhtar Ansari, and Sadat Hasan Manto (d. 1955).

From the fifties onwards, mention may be made of Hayatullah Ansari, Khwaja Ahmad Abbas (d. 1987), Ismat Chughtai (d. 1991), Qurratulain Hyder (d. 2007), Fazlur Rahman. A. A. Suroor, Khursheedul Islam, Masud Husain Khan, Muhammad Hasan, Niaz Fathepuri (d. 1960), Majnoon Gorakhpuri, Sibte Hasan, and Mumtaz Husain. The last four are from Pakistan.

(82) Among Marxists or near Marxists of varying degrees of commitment, mention may be made of K.M. Ashraf (d. 1962), Sajjad Zaheer (d. 1973), Irfan Habib, and Asghar Ali Engineer.

(83) For a detailed criticism of Iqbal's approach the interested reader may consult my work, *Quest for Islam*, op. cit,

(84) The following names spring to my mind out of a much larger list: Ali Yavar Jung (d. 1976), Basher Ahmad Sayeed (d. 1984), Syed Mohammad Tonki (d. 1974), Basheer Husain Zaidi, and Akbar Ali Khan.

(85) Out of a total of 492 Muslim seats in the eleven provincial assemblies of British India the Muslim League won 425 seats (80.6%) in the general elections of 1945-46, held on the basis of the Government of India Act, 1935. Despite the massive victory of the Muslim League, 26.05% of the Muslim votes polled went against the League, that is, against partition and in favor

Authenticity and Islamic Liberalism

of a united secular India with permanent safeguards for the minorities. If we exclude Bengal and confine ourselves to ten provinces only, 32.54% of the Muslim votes went against partition. In Uttar Pradesh, 34.63%, and in Bihar, 26.09% of Muslim votes went against the Muslim League, that is, against partition. The above figures have been taken from *The Indian Annual Register*, January-June, 1946, Vol. I, Calcutta, 1946, pp. 229-31.

In the elections to the Central Assembly, 1945-46, held on the basis of the Constitution of 1919, the Muslim League won 30 out of 30 Muslim seats. However, 13.29% of the Muslim votes went against the League. The relatively lower figure of votes against the League was due to the fact that the franchise for the Central Assembly (according to the 1919 Act) was far more restricted than that for the 1935 Act. For the Central Assembly elections the reader may consult the official Muslim League daily; *Dawn*, dated December 25 and 30, 1945, published from Delhi. Also see Tarachand, *History of the Freedom Movement in India, Vol. IV*, New Delhi, 1972, pp. 460-61.

The figures given in the *Annual Register*, suffer from a minor discrepancy which has been detected in the light of the record maintained in the Parliament Library. This minor discrepancy, however, does not invalidate the basic thesis that a very substantial number of Indian Muslims were opposed to the partition of the country. Indeed, had the general elections been based on adult Muslim franchise even a modest electoral victory of the Muslim League might have become problematic because of its meager hold on the Muslim rural masses who were under the strong influence of the *ulema*, the overwhelming majority of whom stood for a united India.

(86) As regards the most likely outcome in the long run, see the concluding section of this chapter.

(87) Baghdad, the seat of the Caliphate and, possibly, the largest city in the then world, was totally destroyed in 1258 by the Mongol chief, Hulagu Khan. The sweeping military victories of the 'infidel' Mongols had a traumatic effect upon the Muslims who developed an attitude of disillusionment and withdrawal from mundane life.

(88) Recently the history of the *Pious Caliphate* was, reluctantly, included in the syllabus of the Deoband school. The Nadwa at Lucknow has been relatively more liberal in this regard. However, a much more radical change in the syllabus is needed.

Explanatory Notes

(89) The emergence of Bangla Desh in 1971 was the result of a sharp conflict on issues of language, culture, and political and economic interests, having nothing to do with religion. The dominant population in both the eastern and Western wings of Pakistan professed the same religion, and yet the people of the eastern wing demanded separate nationhood, and succeeded in establishing their claim. Thus, the basic premise of the two-nation theory was repudiated. More recently, the tragic conflict between Iran and Iraq and the endemic conflicts between several Arab and Muslim states themselves (including Pakistan and Afghanistan) all expose the fallacy of the view that religion is the only or even the principal bond of unity among men.

(90) The most crucial negative factor is the periodic outbreak of organized violence in our country leading to massive loss of life and property of Muslims. Every *'Bhiwandi'* or *'Moradabad'* sets back the process of emotional integration and the growth of Islamic liberalism through triggering defense mechanisms on overtly communal lines. Riots may not be caused by hatred, but they certainly breed hatred, which in turn, breeds fanaticism and emotional regression of the masses to a condition of savagery and barbarism.

(91) Religious tolerance, in the contemporary sense, is a recent social phenomenon even in Western Europe. Right till the third quarter of the last century the learned fellows of Oxford and Cambridge were obliged to subscribe to the 39 Articles of the Church of England as a precondition for their election. This practice came to an end due to a crisis created by the insistence of the famous Cambridge philosopher, Henry Sidgwick, to resign his fellowship of Trinity College on realizing that he did not inwardly subscribe to some of the thirty-nine Articles. The consequences of Sidgwick's scruples in this regard led to the full maturation of the idea of tolerance which had been put forward by the Oxford philosopher, John Locke, in his famous *Three Letters on Toleration* (1698-92) and which was the guiding principle behind the Glorious Revolution of England in 1688. It is worth recalling that even Locke was not prepared to tolerate atheists.

(92) Even persons of the eminence of Caliph Ali, Ghazali, Ibn-Arabi, Ahmad Sarhandi, and, in recent times, Muhammad Abdullah of Egypt had to face the charges of infidelity or apostasy levelled by their opponents. In fact the Damocles sword of the charge of heresy or apostasy has ever inhibited freethinking, open discussion and public dissemination of liberal ideas in Muslim society. Liberal thinking among Muslims has generally

been confined to drawing rooms and the fear of the consequences of dissent has prevented the bold affirmations of truth, as one sees it, in a spirit of authenticity and humility, as has been the case in Western Europe and America from mid 18th century onwards. The fear of the consequences of dissent has slowed down cultural evolution in the Muslim world as distinct from the superficial Westernization of Muslim societies in matters of dress, entertainment, style of housing, business administration and the trappings of democracy, but without any insight into the concepts and values of modernity. I know several highly reputed Muslim statesmen, lawyers, doctors, scholars, poets and even theologians, who dare not declare in public what they think in private and what they are committed to in the depths of their heart. I lament over what a person of Maududi's stature holds—that any Muslim who loses his faith attracts the death penalty according to the *Shariah*. However, the reputed theologians, Professor Taqi Amini of the Aligarh Muslim University, and Maulana Abul Irfan of Nadwa, do not subscribe to this approach. For Maududi's approach to the issue of apostasy see his brochure, in Urdu, with the title (translated into English): *Punishment for Apostasy in the Islamic Law*, Rampur, 1952.

(93) Sir Syed was charged with expediency apart from being an atheist and heretic. Maulana Azad's credentials to lead *Eid* prayers at Calcutta were questioned in the thirties. In Egypt Muhammad Abduh was the butt of unending criticism and attack because of his liberal measures in *Jamia* Azhar, Cairo, and had eventually to leave the ancient theological university.

(94) Here are some examples of irrational elements which cry out for orthogenetic repudiation:

(a) For all his undoubted intellectual and spiritual attainments Ghazali (d. 1111), perhaps the greatest philosophical theologian of Islam of all time, holds that a true Muslim should, preferably, avoid greeting or having 'dealings' with non-Muslims and also those Muslims who are guilty of innovation (*bidat*) in matters religious. As for friendly and intimate social intercourse with non-Muslims, Ghazali says, that this is *'almost prohibited'* (*haram*) for the true Muslim in the light of Qur'anic texts.

I got the shock of my life in 1982 when I heard the same view from an English Muslim convert. He and his English Muslim circle held a Muslim

Explanatory Notes

of Indian origin to be a leftist, if not a communist, because the Indian had warm and friendly relations with English-Christians. I have discussed this point in the first chapter. For Ghazali's views see his *Ihyoul Ulum* (Urdu translation by Ahsan Siddiqui), Lucknow, 1955, Vol. II, Pt. 5, pp. 212-13.

(b) Ashraf Ali Thanavi (d. 1943) gives a fantastic 'rational explanation' for permitting a Muslim to have four wives at a time. He says that one woman can serve the sexual needs of one man for only three months after pregnancy occurs. The permission of four wives is meant to provide full satisfaction to a married man for a full twelve months, provided he avoids making all the four pregnant at more or less the same time. See his book, in Urdu, whose title (translated into English) is: *The Rational Basis of Islamic Injunctions*. Deoband, (India), 1963.

(c) The very distinguished head of the Deoband seminary, late Qari Tayab, and several other reputed theologians hold that a verse was revealed to the Prophet ﷺ prescribing stoning unto death as a penalty for adultery, but that the verse was abrogated without abrogating the order concerned. To the question whether the Prophet ﷺ could abrogate any verse without the authority of another verse, found in the Qur'anic text, they fail to give any clear answer, without realizing that such authority or power of the Prophet ﷺ would erode the infallible authority of the 'Word of God'. It is significant that many Western scholars (who cannot possibly be charged with being partisans of Islam) have come to the conclusion after careful research that the verse in question was never a part of the Qur'anic text; so the question of its abrogation just did not arise. The theory of abrogation of Qur'anic verses is, however, another matter with which I am not concerned in the present context. See Donaldson, D. M. *Studies in Muslim Ethics*, London, 1953.

(d) There is a report in Bukhari's collection of the sayings and doings of the Prophet ﷺ that when the Prophet ﷺ had the highest degree of communion with God (*meraaj*), He had commanded the Muslims to pray fifty times a day. However, at the advice of Moses (who met the Prophet ﷺ just before and after the supreme event) the Prophet ﷺ requested God to reduce the number from fifty to five. See Bukhari's *Collected Reports (Babul Meraaj)*, English translation by Mohsin Khan, New Delhi, 1984, Vol. V, No. 227. One could go on citing other instances of the same type. The point is that Muslims themselves ought to reject such elements without any qualms of disloyalty to the tradition.

(95) During the course of a discussion between an Arab scholar and a reputed Indian Muslim theologian, in 1965, as to whether the Qur'an supported the heliocentric or the geocentric view, the Arab theologian said that the Qur'an upheld the latter view. When the Indian theologian disputed this claim and asserted that the modern heliocentric view was not incompatible with the Qur'anic text he was told that, despite his sound knowledge of the Arabic language, he did not have the proper credentials for interpreting the real meaning of the Qur'an which could only be grasped by one whose mother tongue was Arabic. The point is that it is essential to distinguish a hidden defense mechanism from a genuine methodological prerequisite.

CONCLUDING DUA

In the name of Allah, Most Beneficent, Most Merciful.

*By the declining day,
Lo! man is in a state of loss,
Save those who believe and do good works, and exhort one another to truth and exhort one another to endurance.*

– Qur'an: Surah Al-Asr (The Time)

Supplemental Essay 1:
Sharing of Religious Life Worlds

Instead of presenting a formal paper I would like to take up some of the questions that were raised by a number of participants here. One observation that was made was that Maulana Azad, Tagore and others were individual humanists and that this was not true of the vast majority of the people or the community as a whole. I would like to say that Maulana Azad of course was a very outstanding person, yet what he said is not entirely new. There are roots in the tradition, which are very old. While the worldview, in Islam, in Christianity or in Hinduism is a unified whole, there are plural versions that may be called layers of different interpretations. There are many mansions in every house. So it is not correct to say that the tradition or the original Qur'an is different and it is only Maulana Azad's genius, which has led him to this position. I would like to share with you two anecdotes that are very well-known among Muslims. One is the anecdote of *Moses and the Shepherd*. It is one of the greatest anecdotal stories in world literature. Dr. Radhakrishnan in his book *Commentary on the Principal Upanishads,* has given such anecdotes from Islam and other religions. Briefly the story is this:

Moses was walking in the foothills in the afternoon and he found a shepherd praying to God, and he was praying to God as if God were a person. The shepherd was saying, '*If I find you I will do this, I will do that, I will massage your body and apply oil,*' etc. When Moses heard this, he said; '*you have committed blasphemy, you have committed idolatry, because God has no body.*' Then God rebuked Moses in the form of *wahy* (revelation), and said, '*I have sent you here not to separate hearts from me. He was in communion with me. After all he was praying to me and do you think that your conception of God is superior to that of the shepherd's? That is not so.*'

Supplemental Essay 1: Sharing of Religious Life Worlds

The other anecdote is to the same effect. When God calls, the person replies 'I am here' and this is called the sound of *Labbaik*. According to one anecdote the sound of *Labbaik* started to come from the heavens, that is, the seat of God (*arsh*). Instead of *Labbaik* emanating from *farsh*, the seat of men. When Gabriel heard *Labbaik* coming from the *arsh*, He was perplexed by the fact that God was saying 'I am *hazir*' or 'I am present'. So the angel Gabriel went to God and asked him what the matter was. God replied that a very good and pious believer was remembering Him and therefore He was responding. So Gabriel came back and started searching the entire world for the believer, but he did not come across any individual who was really praying to God. So he again went back to God and said, 'I am sorry. I searched the entire world but I did not come across any individual who was really praying to God.' So God asked him to go to such and such a place. He went there and found that there was an idol worshipper praying before the idol. So again he went back to God and reported what he had seen. God said, 'Yes he is the Worshipper who is worshipping Me and I am responding to him.'

This sort of an approach is a kind of sharing that may be called sharing of religious life-worlds. This is a tradition and an important part of the tradition of Islam as well as of other religions. So it is not a question of Maulana Azad or, let us say, Humayun Kabir being freaks or complete mutations as it were. It is a long process. But the point is that this is not the dominant tradition. The *Sufi* tradition is not the dominant tradition either. As far as the dominant tradition is concerned I can say that it is the tradition, which creates trouble, and which leads to conflicts. And therefore, the crux of the matter is how one can make the *Sufi* tradition or the tradition, which we think is correct to dominate. That is of course, an educational and cultural matter, and to some extent a political matter, as well.

Another comment made was that the real Islam is the Islam of the Qur'an and not the Islam of humanists like Maulana Azad and others and that real Islam is somehow militant; and it leads to bloodshed, etc. Again I would submit very respectfully, not as an apologist but as a student of Islam, that this is not the case. The real Islam is to be found in the Qur'an and not in subsequent actions or events. This sort of dichotomy exists in all religions, in Christianity also, for example. What is real Christianity? What was the message of Christ? And what was the actual code of conduct or behavior of the Christians, once they acquired political power? So the trouble is

Supplemental Essay 1: Sharing of Religious Life Worlds

that the history of Islam and Christianity in this regard is very different. Islam acquired political power after thirteen years in Mecca and five years in Medina, after roughly eighteen or nineteen years. Then the Prophet ﷺ died ten years after his migration from Mecca. So, let us say, in twenty years Islam became a politically established religion. But Christianity took three centuries to do this. If you compare the behavior of Christianity after its establishment, you find a remarkable similarity in terms of persecutions in the course of the search for power. You find the same thing in the Sikh religion also. But if you want to find out the truth, about the teachings of Islam, the teachings of Christianity and the teachings of *Guru Granth Sahib* then you have to look at the scriptures.

Now I would like to pass on to some general remarks arising out of Dr. Troll's presentation. He posed the question of sharing of alternative life-worlds. I would like to confine myself to this because it is a fundamental question.

My submission is that something more than tolerance is involved in a positive sharing and enjoying of an alternative world-view. It requires a certain conception of religious truth. It requires a whole philosophical, analytical and meta-philosophical background. If you think that religious truths are just like other propositions and are to be viewed in the logic of truth or falsehood, then I don't agree with you. If I think Islam is true in the sense of Aristotelian logic, and Christianity is false, how can I enjoy different world-views? A lot of intellectual preparation has to go into it and that of course is not easy. But those intellectuals, philosophers or musicians, who are capable of doing it, have somehow realized the meaning of 'non-propositional' truth.

Here I would like to remind my friends of a well-known event which happened in 1923 and which may not be known to some of us here. Maulana Mohammad Ali was the Congress President then and Hindu-Muslim unity was at its height. It was just after the *Jallianwalla Bagh* tragedy and when the *Khilafat* issue was at its height. A correspondent wrote to Maulana Mohammad Ali and wanted to know the Islamic position with regards to non-Muslims. Maulana Mohammad Ali said that according to the *Shariah* a non-Muslim, however good he may be, is bound to go to hell, although he may be rewarded for the good works that he had done, he will go to hell nevertheless, and, however superior he may be, morally he is inferior to a

Supplemental Essay 1: Sharing of Religious Life Worlds

Kalmago Musalman because a Muslim who is a *Kalmago*, who is a believer in Islam, is superior. Having said that he stopped. Obviously it was not Maulana Mohammad Ali's own view, because at that time he had publicly declared that he was a lieutenant of Gandhi. He said that Gandhiji was his boss. Later, of course, he repudiated Gandhi, Nehru and others, but at that time he was an established leader of both Hindus and Muslims. In spite of that he gave that traditional view, which was not his own view. As a result of this there was a hue and cry in the Indian press. Imagine Gandhi being regarded as inferior to a very immoral type of Muslim who was a *Kalmago Musalman*.

The Congress session was about to meet after a few weeks, and Mahavir Tyagi told Gandhiji that he would like to move a vote of 'no-confidence' against the Congress President. Gandhiji tried to dissuade Mahavir Tyagi. But Mahavir Tyagi said that he was very indignant and the people were very indignant and they would not rest content without passing a 'no-confidence' motion. Naturally at that time it would have meant a great disturbance and commotion and it would really have made a breach in the platform of Hindu-Muslim unity. So Gandhiji said, 'Tyagi, am I your leader?' Tyagi said, 'Yes, of course'. Gandhiji said, 'I order you not to do this'. And Tyagi withdrew the motion. Gandhiji said that Maulana Mohammad Ali was a friend, and he knew he had committed a mistake but he would like to forgive him. Now this was known to many people close to Gandhiji, but not everyone knew this and some distorted versions appeared in the papers. So it needs a tremendous amount of education, tolerance, and maturity really to share other world-views.

Turning to the question of divine guidance in Islam I must say that this is not restricted to Islam alone. The Qur'an is not the only book. Every country, every nation, and every religion has had its prophets. Secondly, every scripture, and every book has become corrupted, including the Bible, the Torah, and for that matter all scriptures. While details have not been mentioned in the Qur'an it has been repeatedly said that in every age and in every country, the books have been corrupted, but the Qur'an is the only exception. The Qur'an is retained in its pure form; it is infallible; it is perfect and it is the last. This is a very important feature of Islamic consciousness. What happened in Pakistan for example was that the *Ahmadiyas* were declared as non-Muslims. Although Mr. Bhutto, who was the Prime Minister at that time, was personally liberal, he succumbed to political forces and these

Supplemental Essay 1: Sharing of Religious Life Worlds

people were declared non-Muslims. Even the Noble Prize winner Professor Abdus Salam, the great physicist, is regarded as a non-Muslim, although he is a citizen of Pakistan.

The Qur'an is infallible, but it is not possible to understand it unless its abstract teachings are amplified by what the Prophet ﷺ said. The Qur'an is the perfect word of God, uncorrupted, uncontaminated and the Prophet ﷺ is the last messenger of God. He is also perfect, and in some weak sense, he is also infallible. Islamic piety covers the total code of conduct and this means that religion and politics cannot be separated and ought not to be separated. The same sort of outlook is developing among the Sikhs today and there are signs of the same tragedy.

There is also the concept of exclusive salvation, which I have already mentioned in the Gandhian anecdote. These are the features of the dominant view and Maulana Azad, Sir Syed, and many other liberals have repudiated some of them. In my work *Quest for Islam* I have given my own interpretation of Islam. I do not wish to repeat what I have said there.

I now come to the last point. Some of the things in Islam are not acceptable to me at all. For example the unity of the Church and the State is not acceptable to me and the concept of exclusive salvation is also not acceptable to me. But what is to be done? Inside the pale of Islam, either I could repudiate concepts I do not agree with or I could try to re-construct them, and I for one stand for re-construction. This has happened in all religions. Gandhi tried to re-construct Hinduism. The *Brahmo Samaj, Arya Samaj,* and *Prarthana Samaj,* etc. have tried to do the same thing. In Christianity also you have so many great movements. I am also reminded of Russell who always took great pride in not being a Christian. I think what is important is a perfect tolerance for each other as human beings. I know that there are a good number of my Hindu friends who say that they are not Hindus and they tell me that I am not a Muslim. They refuse to label themselves Hindus and they also refuse to label me as a Muslim. I reply that it is up to them to choose their own formulations.

What is the role that a non-Muslim can play here? I think that he can play a very fine and constructive role by trying to be sympathetic and by not trying to criticize from a hostile point of view, but to criticize from a sympathetic point of view.

Supplemental Essay 1: Sharing of Religious Life Worlds

I must confess that the idea of conversion has not appealed to me at all. To think that an entire people could be converted or ought to be converted is a concept of practical invalidity, which has been shown in the course of world history. I get along very well indeed with everyone provided I find that the person, whether he be a missionary, or a scholar or a Marxist, or an economist, is authentic and sincere. I think the concept of interreligious dialogue, is most welcome. We have to look at religions from a functional point of view and not from a dogmatic point of view. From that point of view I think Communism today is functionally a religion.

Schisms, developments in China and India and elsewhere, and the changes that are taking place in Russia, the liberalization and all that have to be included in this exercise of interreligious dialogue. Otherwise, if you speak only in terms of religious people, God's people on the one hand and the Devil's people on the other, that is no dialogue. It is not an interreligious dialogue, because an interreligious dialogue is only possible when we give an extended meaning to the concept of religion. I know this is very difficult but it has to be attempted if man is to survive.

Supplemental Essay 2:
Seven Letters to My RSS Friend

(Letter # 1)

Solan,
August 15, 2002

My Dear Judge *Sahab*,
　Do I need to say how much I cherish our mutual friendship, which sprang up in rather unexpected circumstances? Unneighborly behavior from some quarters (from which it was least expected) had pushed us into litigation. When we stood alone and helpless your spontaneous kindness and sense of fair play moved you to help us, knowing well of the gap between our respective ideological and political orientations.

　Such is my respect for your integrity and love of truth, as you see it, that I feel moved to share with you my sorrow at the recent events in Gujrat, starting from the Godhra incident. I shall avoid all polemics and an adversarial approach, but remain honest to myself and candid with you. A friendly dialogue bears maximum fruit when it flows from a bare minimum of shared basic values and of mutual agreement on recent and some important historical facts. Even such recent events as the burning of the train at Godhra railway station and the subsequent mass killings and loot in Gujrat have lent themselves to several versions or narratives. These differences pertain to facts as well as to values and attitudes. These differences, in turn, are deeply rooted in the way one looks at Indian history and the human situation in

Supplemental Essay 2: Seven Letters to My RSS Friend: Letter #1

general. It will promote better mutual understanding of some recent issues if I share with you my basic worldview and value system and my accepted interpretation of Indian history.

If even highly responsible ministers, administrators and observers differ on the what, why and whither of Gujrat in 2002, how much more difficult, then, must it be to determine the real cause or causes of historical events long past, say, the partition of India in 1947, or of the great upheaval of 1857, or, going back still further, the causes of the defeat of the Indian confederacy in the third battle of Panipat in 1761. Difficult as it is to establish conclusively without any measure of controversy or disagreement the sheer factual course of events in their exact sequence, far more difficult, if not impossible, is the further task of correctly interpreting them or looking at them in the proper perspective. For instance, Muhammad Ghori won the battle of Tarain in 1192, and became the first Sultan of Delhi. But was this victory the victory of Islam over Hinduism? Was Shivaji's defiance of Aurangzeb the struggle of Hinduism against Muslim tyranny? No one answer can be proved true or false in the sense we can prove truthclaims of natural science or mathematics. Yet, we have to take some stand or position on such issues. If we turn to remote or pre-historical events the issues become still more complicated, but we continue to hold beliefs or make judgments with an amazing certainty or emotional conditioning. For instance, were the ancient Aryans native to India or had migrated here from some other region? It is well-known that a century ago, Tilak seriously contested the, then, Western consensus about the origin of the Aryan race in central Eurasia. The growing consensus of informed opinion in the West, now, is that North Africa is the original home of the entire human race. These issues lie in the fields of Anthropology and Evolutionary Biology. In such matters the considered consensus of experts should count more than the views of theologians, politicians or partisan intellectuals.

Let us return to historical times. It is significant that the 'data of history' are not given to the truth seeker as the 'data of nature' are given to the scientific investigator through sense perception or through experiments under controlled conditions of observation. The 'data of history', themselves, are, in part, constructs out of surviving remains of past things or events. Moreover, no two historians select exactly the same set of data out of the total range of data, actually or possibly available. Every historian selects his own unique 'effective' data for a systematic narrative and analysis of the past.

Supplemental Essay 2: Seven Letters to My RSS Friend: Letter #1

Once he fixes his own 'effective' data of history the historian fits them in his favored framework of ideas and values out of several alternatives available. No such framework as such, can, conclusively, be proved true or valid. Yet, one must have some 'basic frame of orientation' (as pointed out by Eric Fromm) in order to understand or existentially respond to the human situation in its totality. Religions and philosophies perform this function. They 'hold' the effective data together and provide one's worldview or total perspective on the human situation as such. Thus, a historian having a *'Hindutva'* frame of orientation would view Sultan Mahmud's destruction of the Somnath temple in the 10/11th century as an Islamic attack against Hindu India. A historian having a humanist-sociological orientation would view the same episode as a medieval Sultan's lust for booty. This admission, however, does not, necessarily, land us into the bog of the un-redeemed relativity of all historical interpretation. Let me explain this point.

A reliable contemporary Persian record states that on his triumphant return to his capital Sultan Mahmud sent valuable gifts to a venerated divine living in Ghazna, Qazi Abul Hasan Baulami. The Qazi returned the royal gifts and severely chastised the Sultan on the ground that Islam did not permit the desecration of any place of worship. Obviously, the honest and bold response of the Qazi had no effect upon the Sultan or on the general course of events in the medieval period marked by religious intolerance or destruction of the places of worship of the 'out-group'. However, in the light of the above authentic story it becomes quite clear that the primary 'leitmotif' of the medieval Sultans was personal aggrandizement and expansion of power, not the promotion or forcible imposition of Islam on infidels. In this sense and to this extent the humanist or secular interpretation of history is more true or valid than the current *'Hindutva'* approach that gives a rather blurred picture of the past. It is worth pointing out that the Talibanist also does the same by glorifying Mahmud's exploits as a Muslim hero or normative figure.

The above remarks apply equally to Nadir Shah's or Ahmad Shah Abdali's role in the 18th century. Their marauding armies killed and looted innocent Indians, Hindus and Muslims alike. This, to my mind, clearly shows the real nature of their motives—lust for booty rather than service of Islam. This also shows that the great Indian Muslim divine of the 18th century, Shah Waliullah of Delhi, was ill advised and grievously mistaken in inviting Abdali to save Islam in India by checking the further rise of Maratha power in the country.

Supplemental Essay 2: Seven Letters to My RSS Friend: Letter #1

Likewise, the *Hindutva* approach avers that the conflict between Shivaji and Aurangzeb was a confrontation between Hindu resurgence and the Islamic establishment. The liberal humanist approach looks upon this chapter of Indian history as a confrontation between a well-established, but declining, imperial Delhi and a rising regional power in the Pune region. The destruction of selected Hindu temples during the medieval period, according to the humanist angle of historical interpretation, was, basically, an exercise to contain political rebellion or defiance rather than an attack on the Hindu faith. Is there any justification for preferring one line of interpretation to the other, or is each interpretation merely arbitrary, so that both are equally right or equally wrong? Well, I submit, valid reasons can be advanced in support of the humanist approach.

For instance, Shivaji had mixed troops or regiments, and respected religious sentiments of all communities or groups. So did Aurangzeb and the Mughal rulers in general. Shivaji did not spare Hindus when he twice attacked and despoiled the wealth of the prosperous citizens of Surat, the, then, principal seaport of India. Again, Aurangzeb endowed several Hindu and Jain temples in different parts of the country, though he did demolish some selected Hindu places of worship that had become centers or rallying points of political defiance. The above facts are well-documented in reliable contemporary sources. Even the Mughal-Sikh relations during Aurangzeb's long reign were far more cordial than gradually came to be believed in later times, primarily due to Abdali's plundering raids and other political developments after the decline of Mughal power. Ranjit Singh, again, inaugurated an era of religious liberalism and tolerance in the kingdom, but his successors failed him woefully. The Muslims of north India lost their self-confidence and élan and withdrew into a fundamentalist shell, under the impact of a steadily growing British domination throughout the land.

This is the right place to refer to the Ayodhya Mandir-Masjid dispute that has become a defining issue for the Indian family. Barely thirty years ago it was a non-issue. So it was for Tulsidas in the time of Akbar and for all the great builders and normative figures of the modern Indian value system and cultural Renaissance inaugurated by Ram Mohan Roy. How come that the Shiv Sena, Vishwa Hindu Parishad, and Bajrang Dal, etc. hit upon the rather sensational discovery that Babar was an Islamic Ravana and the arch villain of Indian history and his legacy of the Babari Masjid was a standing national humiliation, the removal of which was the primary demand of Indian patriotism?

Supplemental Essay 2: Seven Letters to My RSS Friend: Letter #1

The *Ramjanmbhumi* issue had first cropped up in the closing years of the Avadh kingdom under Wajid Ali Shah in the mid 19th century. Local Hindu and Muslim militias had engaged in armed fights over the right of possession or use of ancient sites or buildings and this had resulted in considerable bloodshed. Some Muslim records of the time in Urdu and Persian boast that the Muslim warriors dispatched thousands of Hindu infidels to hell and that God had sent angels to help Muslims against the attacking infidels. Such writings and records betray their utter partiality or lack of objectivity and accuracy of approach.

Whatever the exact nature and course of the dispute might have been, it remains clear that there was no general consensus that Ram was born on the very place where the Babari Masjid had been standing for the last several centuries. All that constituted the popular belief or faith was that the region of Ayodhya was the *janmbhumi* of Ram. There was a plethora of claims about the exact site as such. This disagreement is not at all surprising in the case of a remote supernatural event. The crux of the matter is this: the fabric of the charge that Babar was a Muslim Ravana (who desecrated the birth place of Ram) has been spun out of the deep pre-rational interpretation that the original incursion or advent on Indian soil of Arab, Turkish, or Pathan tribes was an Islamic attack on Hinduism.

Is this interpretation true or valid? I have already said that historical interpretations are organically related to still more basic existential interpretations of the total human situation and such interpretations do not admit of proof in the conclusive scientific or logical sense. It is incontrovertible that the Arab or Turkish tribes who invaded India were Muslim by religion. Therefore, if one insists upon emphasizing the religious identity of the invader, the invasion will always appear as an attack of Islam upon Hinduism. But if one surveys the human situation in general one will realize that dispersal of peoples and races on earth, and the struggle for power and wealth is universal and an integral part of the human story as such. Before Sultan Mahmud and Babar had turned their attention to India they had conquered or tried to conquer lands in central Asia that were inhabited by their own coreligionists. The Aryans and Hindus, in earlier times, had done the same in the vast stretches of the Indian sub-continent. So have all other races and peoples the world over, be they Egyptians, Greeks, Romans, Chinese or Europeans. Now this awareness can and usually does liberate the impartial and careful observer of the human situation from the habit of

Supplemental Essay 2: Seven Letters to My RSS Friend: Letter #1

seeing every person or event under a religious label. The observer becomes open to the concrete quality of life as it flows in history and judges men and matters accordingly. This humanist interpretation of history not only appeals more to several well-informed and noble souls but is more useful for promoting universal peace and harmony.

When one adopts the humanist approach to life the conflicts between different peoples, races, regions and religions in the past do not divide humans into permanently hostile in-groups and out-groups. One starts looking at the conflicts of the past as stages in the slow growth of the human family on a global scale. The victory of an Alexander and the defeat of a Porus, the devastation of a Hulagu or a Nadir Shah, the compassion of an Ashoka, the statesmanship of an Akbar, the aberrations of a Hitler all become achievements or failures of the human family. The true historian, from this angle, does not identify himself or herself with any particular group or adopt a partisan attitude. The rise and fall, achievements and failures, virtues and vices of all peoples and all times become his own. With charity for all and malice toward none he passes judgment on the deed, rather than the doer. His standard remains consistent, but takes into account that human ideas and ideals are subject to the law of evolutionary growth. In short, his range of sympathy gradually becomes universal instead of remaining congealed at a particular parochial level determined by his birth or early conditioning.

Finally, the humanist approach to history and life in general should give due importance to every aspect of human experience. All these aspects or spaces interact and shape the movement of history. Economic historians may not treat cultural historians as a B team, and vice versa. Man does not live by bread alone. But without bread he cannot live at all.

More next time. With kindest regards,

Yours very sincerely,
Jamal Khwaja

Supplemental Essay 2:
Seven Letters to My RSS Friend (Contd.)

(Letter #2)

My Dear Judge *Sahab*,

My first letter dealt with some basic points of Indian historiography. As I did not wish to make the letter longer I did not give my own worldview or basic perspective on the human situation and value system which is the matrix of my interpretation of Indian history. The worldview and value system are the fruit of my own humble search for truth in the broadest sense. However, not being a historian myself, my interpretation of Indian history is based on the work of Indian and foreign historians, internationally renowned and respected, such as Jadunath Sarkar, Moreland, Tarachand, Habib, Pannikar, and Romila Thapar, *et al*. Because of their adopting a critical methodology, and cultivating universal empathy, they avoid (as far as humanly possible) conscious or unconscious bias and defensive reasoning. They follow where the argument leads them, while lesser historians become partial or antipathetic to some person or ideology, as the case may be.

Humans are born as helpless creatures who gradually develop a sense of personal identity or self-image, and acquire a thought and value system reflected in the symbols, rites, rituals, institutions, moral and social codes of a societal unit. This set of ideas, ideals and institutions is transmitted to individuals through cultural conditioning. Every individual, to begin with, accepts them as the natural base for all further growth. Thought systems arise because isolated bits of information never satisfy the human craving for

Supplemental Essay 2: Seven Letters to My RSS Friend: Letter #2

a broad integrated framework of ideas and ideals. The concern for wholeness is the common root of religion, philosophy and science.

Science first describes discrete entities or processes and then seeks their causal or regular interconnections in precise quantitative and verifiable terms. Scientists having creative imagination or intuition project hypothetical natural explanations of these interconnections. When other fellow scientists, on the basis of their own tests, freely confirm previous tests or findings, the hypotheses are accepted as scientific laws, though even then, these laws remain subject to revision in the light of fresh discoveries. This method of scientific investigation is the real strength and glory of science and the essence of the scientific revolution of the modern age as such. It is this method that has enabled man to control and manipulate the external environment as had never happened before in history.

Humankind, however, has other concerns, namely, the creation of beauty, the pursuit of morality and the cultivation of spirituality. Pure science, therefore, is like a banquet at which only a single dish is served. Science, by itself, is unable to guide the human observer how to relate himself to the mystery of the Universe. Even if there be no verifiable or conclusive answer to the riddle of existence and even if all actual or possible attempts at answering the riddle be human projections, the concern for such matters remains irrepressible and also crucially important for balanced inner growth. What is it that constitutes the riddle? Well, it is the universal natural phenomena of biological conception, birth, growth, decay, and death, the ceaseless struggle for survival, the flux of creation and destruction, the regular sequence of events, the power of reason to grasp these interconnections through a mash of imagination and observation, the variety and power of human emotions: hope and joy, pain and despair, suffering and fear, the sexual instinct and mutual attraction of the sexes, the experience of triumph and tragedy, the primary sense of morality and beauty, as distinct from their particular models found at different times and in different places, and finally the enveloping sense of wonder and a sense of mystery or holiness of it all. The above basic features that are invariably and universally present in human life may be said to be the '*ontic dimensions*' of human existence. And what is the right or true interpretation of these dimensions, as a totality without ignoring any single facet as such constitutes the riddle of the Universe.

An abiding depth concern with this mystery or riddle is an integral part of being fully human. Man cannot live by bread alone. Nor can he live by

Supplemental Essay 2: Seven Letters to My RSS Friend: Letter #2

morality, legality, or science alone without giving some central over-arching significance to the cosmos. This can only be done through some existential interpretation, provided by spirituality, religion or philosophy.

Just as the child assimilates the natural language spoken in his milieu, he assimilates the existential interpretation current in his milieu. This interpretation may be called the spiritual language of the spirit, and just as there is a plurality of natural languages, there are plural languages of the spirit. Every such language comprises myths, rites, and rituals to enable the individual to relate himself to the mystery of the Universe, thereby winning solace, courage, guidance and peace in the conduct of life. There is a general tendency to believe that one's own language of the spirit is the sweetest and the best. Moreover, this belief naturally boosts one's group respect or sense of importance or uniqueness in history. One tends to miss the glaring fact that every language of the spirit in instinct with paradox and faith rather than clarity and proof. However, the existence of plural languages of the spirit does not subtract from the beauty and power of any particular language, even as the beauty and power of the great works of, say, Shakespeare do not diminish that of the works of Goethe or Kalidas. If there is no reason why only one language should be spoken by the entire human family, why should it be so terribly important that there should be only one language of the spirit, say, Hinduism, Christianity or Islam? Should not righteous action and authentic commitment, as such, be deemed more important than conversion to any single religious faith? I dare say the concern for doing away with all diversity reflects a concern for power rather than for piety.

I might go even one step further. While pure spirituality (without religious dogma) hugely helps and fortifies man in the midst of the inevitable temptations, failures and tragedies of life, it is not strictly necessary for the pursuit of morality or values in general. Spirituality, like human love cannot be willed or forced through logic. I submit, every interpretation is permissible, but it should not devalue man's existential wonder at the mystery of the Universe. I further submit, this approach is adumbrated in the Gita. The pure Qur'anic approach, without the gloss of traditional views, also converges on this point. Great spiritual humanists hailing from the West also testify to this truth.

I now come to the basic values I have come to accept after an honest and patient search. I will list the following without implying that the list is exhaustive: existential wonder at the mystery of existence, whether or

Supplemental Essay 2: Seven Letters to My RSS Friend: Letter #2

not the sense of wonder and mystery flowers into the idea of the god of religion; clear and honest self-awareness or authenticity; the unconditional will to perform one's duty for its own sake; reverence for all living beings; unconditional respect for the dignity of the individual; the disinterested search for truth; the appreciation and creation of beauty; the pursuit of social justice flowing from active concern for universal welfare; democracy or governance with the consent of the governed; loving tolerance of dissent; universal empathy; universal compassion and kindness; mature heterosexual love with or without physical consummation; and, finally, unconditional inner peace and equanimity.

It must be noted that the above value terms are rather abstract or generalized. Consequently, they all could be variously interpreted by different persons. Here I shall not spell out my own understanding of these terms. I am aware their interpretation is bound to differ in every age due to the ever-changing human situation – the growth in cumulative knowledge, and the tremendously increased communication or dialogue within the human family. Plural interpretations of all basic values are quite natural in human society. The quest for uniformity or sameness in the literal sense is futile and harmful. The *Upanishads* point out that cows may be of different colors, but their milk is the same. In its own idiom the Qur'an also says the same. It is tragic when the quest for power turns this milk into poison, no matter who does this, be they the Taliban destroying the statue of the Buddha or the Bajrang Dal demolishing the Babari Masjid.

The human situation is marked by racial/ethnic and cultural plurality. Every distinct group believes its own 'blood, ideas and ideals' to be superior and tries to get the maximum share of the cake. This triggers the struggle for power both within and between different groups. Aggression and defense may be said to be two sides of the coin of world history. This is punctuated in every age by advances and setbacks depending upon how one looks at the ongoing contest for power and self-assertion.

The players or antagonists in the struggle for power naturally perceive this struggle as a fight between good and evil. This perception gives them inner strength and is also valid at times. But the full truth of the matter is that different individuals and groups reach the peak of their inner energy and vitality at different points of time. Their material interests and cherished ideas and ideals propel a clash between those on the offensive and those on

Supplemental Essay 2: Seven Letters to My RSS Friend: Letter #2

the defensive. Each party emphasizes its concern for ideals, rather than for worldly profit, and the battle is joined. Victory accrues, generally, to those whose ideas and interests harmonize with 'the spirit of the age', as pointed out by the German thinker, Hegel.

Interaction between contending groups goes on in war and peace. Time moves on and fresh ideas and ideals surface. Winners and losers in wars both gain and lose at the cultural level due to the inevitable cross-fertilization of ideas and ideals. This process has been tremendously accelerated by the ongoing communications revolution. Economic as well as cultural 'globalism' is fast emerging in the present age. This has both benefits as well as dangers. Humanity needs friends, not masters. Humanity needs the brotherhood of man, not any lesser one, be it of race, religion, or a nation. Even the brotherhood of man will fail if it ignores the dimension of a higher spirituality. Communism in the form of an aggressive atheistic Humanism has failed. Aggressive religious fundamentalism, be it Islamic, Hindu or Christian will all fail. Loving tolerance and an openness of being is the only valid approach.

Spiritual Humanism will gradually take root through the organized efforts at self-criticism and reform by the humanist vanguard of each religious community. This vanguard will purge the limitations in its own tradition instead of pointing out the flaws of others. Interfaith cooperation will drive out adversarial relationships between different religious traditions. The human family, carried on the wings of science and technology, democracy and spirituality will slowly make Tagore's dream come true when the poet sang:

Where the mind is without fear and the head is held high;

Where knowledge is free;

Where the world is not broken up into fragments by

narrow domestic walls;

Where words come out from the depth of truth;

Where tireless living stretches its arms towards perfection;

Supplemental Essay 2: Seven Letters to My RSS Friend: Letter #2

Where the clear stream of reason has not lost its way into

the dreary desert sand of dead habit;

Where the mind is led forward by Thee into ever widening

thought and action —

Into that heaven of freedom, let my country awake.

Yours very sincerely,
Jamal Khwaja

Supplemental Essay 2:
Seven Letters to My RSS Friend (Contd.)

(Letter #3)

My Dear Judge *Sahab*,

Having outlined my basic world view and value system in the previous letter I shall now briefly indicate the interpretation of medieval Indian history that I accept after having carefully studied eminent humanist historians, Indian and foreign, universally acclaimed for their integrity, objectivity, breadth of scholarship and universal empathy.

The story of India is a chapter of the long and continuing drama of the human struggle for power. New races or ethnic groups have risen from relative obscurity and cultural backwardness to dominate other more cultured and established groups. That Babar was a Muslim does not mean that his attack on India was an Islamic onslaught against Hinduism. After all, Babar had already fought against several Muslim rulers in central Asia before turning his attention to India. In the medieval period one Muslim ruler fought against another Muslim ruler just as in the ancient and medieval eras one Hindu ruler had fought against other Hindu rulers throughout India. Likewise, in the ancient days Greek had fought against Greek no less than against the Roman or Iranian. We see the same happening in the modern age.

The Hindu ethos, in the light of the *Dharmashastras*, prescribes that the cardinal duty of the ruler is to defend and enlarge his dominion. In fact every *raja* aspired to become the '*chakravarti*' ruler or overlord, if he could manage this. It was the duty of the '*praja*' to pursue the four '*pu-

rusharthas' or normal goals of life, unmindful of which *raja* won or lost in the continuing struggle for power. This social ethic was extended to the Muslim rulers when they came on the Indian scene. The legitimacy of the ruler was not made dependent upon his race or religion; his legitimacy flew from victory in battle. Battles and wars did not escalate into extended 'total' wars involving the entire populace. Victory or defeat in battle meant only a change of rulers, within the system prescribed by the *Dharmashastras*, not any enslavement of the population. The erstwhile subjects of the defeated ruler did not feel called upon by duty to overthrow their new ruler.

The above ethos was put in actual practice in medieval India. The Hindu segment, which constituted the overwhelming majority of the population, gave full loyalty to the Muslim rulers. Rebellions and revolts were common, but they cut across the religious divide. In the course of time Muslim rulers who had settled down on Indian soil came to be looked upon as a new warrior caste that had become an integral part of an already mixed population. Muslims also felt the same way. Intermarriage between Muslims and Hindus was ruled out, but so was intercaste marriage within the Hindu fold itself, apart from some exceptions.

As time rolled on the lower castes and weaker sections among the Hindu population felt attracted toward the social egalitarianism and democratic complexion of the Muslim ethos. A considerable section from the lower and backward castes saw the promise of more vertical mobility in the Islamic fold. However, the Muslims themselves were not free from the evil of racial pride and pretensions of superiority. Muslims of Turkish, Persian or Afghan origin did not intermarry with Muslims of Indian origin. The continuing trickle of Muslim immigrants from central Asia never stopped. But the main factor of the growth of the Muslim population in the land was the growing peaceful conversion of the backward and under-privileged Hindu sections and the artisans due to a combination of ideological and economic factors, rather than forcible conversions. These sections saw the promise of greater social equality as Muslims in the new dispensation. As time rolled on a grand composite culture evolved in the form of modern regional languages, architecture, music, amusements, proverbs, and folk religions. In short, the Muslim Sultans acquired political power at the point of the sword (which is the universal pattern of history); but Islam, or rather a particular version of it, spread through an extended peaceful social process.

Supplemental Essay 2: Seven Letters to My RSS Friend: Letter #3

The Hindu populace enjoyed freedom of religious belief and practice, and their personal laws and customs were not interfered with. But there were restrictions on the building of new temples at public places. Hindu princes who accepted the suzerainty of the central power were accorded high status and full honor, retained their throne and exercised vast powers under the feudal system. The revenue, civil, and criminal laws were patterned after the Islamic *Shariah*, but there was no interference with Hindu family laws of marriage, adoption and inheritance, etc.

The Sultans who ruled in the independent kingdoms of Kashmir, Gujrat, Bengal, Golkunda, and Bijapur, etc. before their incorporation into the Mughal Empire were tolerant and just toward all their subjects. Zaynul Abidin (d. 1470) of Kashmir, the most illustrious ruler of the region, was universally loved. He patronized Sanskrit no less than Persian, the saint no less than the *Sufi*. Husayn Shah (d. 1519) of Bengal played a similar role in the eastern region. Later Sher Shah (d. 1545) followed his example and to this day remains a hero to all alike.

In the southern region the Bahmani Sultan, Tajuddin Feroze (d. 1472) gave preference to people from the south (*Dakhnees*) in state employment, irrespective of religion. Mahmud Gawan (d. 1481) the illustrious Prime Minister of the Bahmani kingdom was noted for his functionally secular approach in matters of state. In 1518 the kingdom split into the five sultanates of Golkunda, Bijapur, Bidar, Berar and Ahmadnagar. The Muslim Sultans fought against each other and the great Vijaynagar Empire, still intact, played one Sultan against the other, irrespective of any religious considerations. This *realpolitik* continued until the empire collapsed in 1565. Muslim rulers also liberally rewarded all those who served imperial interests irrespective of religion. Ibrahim Qutub Shah (d. 1580) of Golkunda was a great patron of Telugu, endowed Hindu temples and even discontinued the '*jizya*' despite the provisions of the *Shariah*. Though the *Shariah* extolled religious tolerance and fair play to all subjects it categorized them into two distinct categories —Muslim believers, and the protected people (*dhimmis*) who had to pay '*jizya*' as an additional levy. However, they were not required to pay '*zakat*'.

The fact is that throughout the medieval era the rather pragmatic Muslim rulers and the orthodox Muslim divines and jurists differed on several issues relating to politics and religion. Qazi Mughisuddin of Delhi (during

Supplemental Essay 2: Seven Letters to My RSS Friend: Letter #3

the time of Alauddin Khilji), Mir Hamdani of pre-Mughal Kashmir, Abdul Qadir Badauni (during the reign of Akbar), Shaikh Ahamd Sarhandi (during the time of Jehangir) all stood for the strict application of *Shariah* laws, as interpreted by their own school of jurisprudence. They openly disapproved of the 'functionally secular' approach followed by the vast majority of the Muslim Sultans and the Mughal emperors. The *ulema* passionately proclaimed that the Sultan was bound by the law of the *Shariah* and some even resented the friendly relations between Muslims and nonbelievers and the power and position the latter enjoyed in the royal court and in society. The expression of such views in the writings of the *ulema* has misled some later historians into believing that the views of the *ulema* were actually acted upon in medieval India. But this was far from being the case. These writings merely reveal the mindset of the *ulema* concerned.

It must also be noted that the *ulema* did not agree among themselves and that the *Sufis* had an entirely different approach. And it was the *Sufi* approach of tolerance and universal harmony and human brotherhood that was the guiding star for the rulers. The Indian Muslim sovereigns, in general, sincerely held that religion was a personal matter, and it did not come in the way of complete loyalty to the monarch. The Rajput rulers followed the same approach. While remaining sincerely committed to the essentials or basics of one's own religious faith the Mughals and the Rajputs, from the time of Akbar onwards, stood closer to each other than did Muslims to Muslims or Hindus of one caste to those of another. Coming to more recent times, the great princely states of India, Mysore, Gwalior, Indore, Baroda, Jaipur, Patiala, Kapurthala and many others gave liberal patronage to Muslims who rose to the highest positions in the state.

While the Muslim sovereigns and the nobility in general did not accept, in practice, "the 'fundamentalist' stand of the orthodox *ulema* they yet never presumed to reform or reconstruct the traditional religious thought and value system of Islam. Akbar, and after him, his great grandson, Dara Shikoh (who never became king himself) are the only exceptions who ventured to attempt this task, instead of being content with a mere working secularism. But the results were far from being satisfactory.

It would, therefore, be a blurred rather, distorted, interpretation to view the struggle for power in medieval India as a confrontation between Islam and Hinduism on Indian soil. Sultan Mahmud was certainly a predator,

Supplemental Essay 2: Seven Letters to My RSS Friend: Letter #3

who came, plundered and returned to his own country, but Muhammad Ghori settled down on Indian soil as an Indian ruler who happened to be a Muslim by religion. Thereafter, the players in the game of power became a mixed lot. Babar fought against the combined armies of Ibrahim Lodi and Rana Sanga, Humayun had to struggle against a Muslim rival. The Mughals and Rajputs became firm allies and their adversaries were a mixed lot. The entire artillery of Shivaji was manned by Muslims. Both the rich Hindus and Muslims of Surat were despoiled when Shivaji twice attacked the prosperous Mughal port. Later Nadir Shah and Ahmad Shah Abdali looted Delhi, Lahore and other places without any distinction of Hindu and Muslim.

Shivaji's opposition to Aurangzeb was certainly not directed against Islam or the Muslims. Given the energy, daring and ambition he had, Shivaji would have defied any central authority, Muslim or Hindu. Shivaji's father, a *mansabdar* under the Sultan of Bijapur, was rather unhappy at his brave son's defiant conduct. As an independent ruler, Shivaji was well-disposed to his Muslim subjects. The later struggle between the decaying Mughal power and the Marathas, Jats, Sikhs, and Rohilla Pathans, etc. was, likewise, a struggle for power rather than a religious confrontation.

I would like to round off the above observations on the struggle for power in medieval India by adding a few sociological observations on the quality of social life, as a whole, in that era.

In medieval India Hindus and Muslims, were not two macro groups living in a state of perpetual confrontation. Each group was greatly differentiated into numerous sub-groups that did not think or behave alike. Power was shared by a thin upper crust within each group. The lower sections of each macro group lived the life of honest toil, enjoyed the consolations of its respective faith, shared the common joys and sorrows of life, were loyal to the ruler, irrespective of religion or race, and hoped for ultimate salvation as taught by one's respective belief system or faith.

A thin elite among the Muslims and Hindus constituted the ruling class whose social and cultural life cut across the religious divide. So did the folk culture of the masses, subject to regional variations, inevitable in a country of the size of India. The prince fought, won or lost and wielded power, the

Supplemental Essay 2: Seven Letters to My RSS Friend: Letter #3

warriors shared in his wealth and glory, the *pundits* or the small creative elite enriched culture and received full honors but had little power, the traders ran the economy and amassed wealth but little honor, the artisans produced goods and farmers produced food but were starved of both honor and power, and the rest supported the entire structure with the power, as it were, of their sweat and tears. Each group comprised both Muslims and Hindus. Each group believed (in different ways) that a Supreme Power controlled history according to a plan, not fully transparent to man. This was the inner world of the medieval Indian, be he Hindu or Muslim.

The dark side of the above sketchy portrait of the spirit of the age was the social and administrative wrongs the common man had to suffer due to human lapses and the misdeeds of immediate neighbors or authorities, despite the benevolence of the ruler. He was the father figure to all, but was he, really, accessible to all? Disputes concerning land, money, women, and power, there must have been. Likewise, tension, intrigue, revenge, crime, miscarriages of justice, there must have been. What happened when the traditional institutional structures failed to bring about proper redress, when the *panchayat*, the *qazi*, the *kotwal*, or even the governor, swayed by passion, greed or prejudice, committed a lapse? The only machinery of redress was to have the ear of somebody in the corridors of power, be he Muslim or Hindu. Perhaps, here the Muslim segment stood at a natural advantage in a system that was presided over, at the apex, by a monarch with whom he shared his cherished religious beliefs or faith. This, however, was a bare psychological rather than any concrete advantage of ready access to the father figure as such. Numerous well-placed or well-connected Hindus had more ready access to the ears of royalty or the top nobility than did the average aggrieved Muslim subjects of the empire. Even in the modern democratic system those who vote for the party in power are at a better vantage point than others. In any case, in medieval India not every Muslim was a king, nor every Hindu a pauper. More importantly, kindness and cordiality prevailed between them both as a group and as individuals, and the simple goodness of heart knew no barriers of religion or creed.

Medieval India had seen a rich and magnificent composite culture evolve in the land. The process continued, under the impact of the West, during British rule. A free united India would have led to results even more significant, not only for the people of India but for entire humanity. But this did not happen. It is futile now to lay the blame on this or that quarter. In

Supplemental Essay 2: Seven Letters to My RSS Friend: Letter #3

any case, this is not the place for shedding helpless tears at human folly. The peoples of both India and Pakistan have to make the best of a bad bargain.

Judge *Sahab*, you must be wondering shall I ever come to the subject of Godhra and Gujrat that has prompted me to pour out my heart before you. Well, this I shall do in the letters that follow. Meanwhile do pardon me for a long 'contextual analysis' of a long past. I thought it would be a fruitful preparation for giving a balanced narrative on recent events in Godhra and Gujrat.

Yours very sincerely,
Jamal Khwaja

Supplemental Essay 2:
Seven Letters to My RSS Friend (Contd.)

(Letter # 4)

My Dear Judge *Sahab*,

Having shared with you my basic perspective on the human situation and my interpretation of medieval Indian history it is now time that I share with you my honest response to the incident at the Godhra railway station on February 26, 2002, and the subsequent course of events in Gujrat.

If an ordinary citizen be honestly concerned to know the full truth he will have to turn to such journalists, newspaper editors, and analysts who possess the virtues and practice the method of the good historian. These virtues are universal sympathy, intellectual honesty, impartiality, and access to reliable information on different viewpoints of the concerned parties. These virtues are rather rare in the vast majority of our politicians and a considerable section of the media. However, these virtues do exist in fair abundance in the higher Indian judiciary and the press, at its best. While every political establishment and interest group has its own mouthpiece or compliant medium of publicity, Indian society can rightly be proud of the active functioning of a conscientious apex judiciary and the press. Thus, no matter what ministers, political party chiefs and spokesmen or other apologists might solemnly claim or proclaim the objective truth eventually trickles out despite the quite common practice of concealment or rationalization by interested quarters.

This is true not only in India but also on the international scene. I recall

Supplemental Essay 2: Seven Letters to My RSS Friend: Letter #4

my deep shock and disillusionment several years ago when I first came across the writings of some eminent Western liberal humanists who had 'dutifully exposed' the deeds or misdeeds of their own governments and leaders in, say, Vietnam, Korea, Iraq, Bosnia and other places. I need hardly mention how in the last century Communist and Fascist establishments, with a good conscience, had resorted to deceit and distortion of truth as legitimate tools for promoting their own idea of the just cause.

Coming to Godhra and Gujrat, a large number of eminent persons comprising central Ministers, leaders of all political parties, Indian and foreign journalists, analysts, social activists, members of human rights bodies and of apex statutory commissions have made on the spot investigations in Gujrat. A Niagra of panel discussions on TV and of editorials and articles have flowed. Several world powers have conducted independent investigations to get at the real truth in view of the impact of the Gujrat situation on the global economy and the politics of the entire region. The BBC, widely respected for its tradition of independent judgment and principled neutrality, as well as several other reputable TV channels have given intensive coverage to news and views relating to Gujrat. This vast media environment is marked by a near total discrepancy in the perceptions of the 'sociologically oriented' observers, on the one side and the 'ideologically oriented' (in the present case the *Sangh pariwar*) observers, on the other.

The version of the first side on the Gujrat situation is as follows:

(a) The Godhra incident was bound to trigger off intense rage and feelings of revenge among the majority community; **(b)** the state government should have alerted the districts authorities to the danger, and taken all possible measures to prevent any large scale disturbance of civil peace, **(c)** once large scale violence did break out the administration, for some reason or other, looked the other way round, as if, the horrendous post-Godhra events in several parts of Gujrat were 'a natural reaction' beyond all control, and, in the final analysis, a salutary lesson for the minority community, **(d)** the violent reprisals after the Godhra incident were orchestrated to such an extent that suggests elaborate pre-planning and a well-calculated strategy of destabilizing civil society and destroying the economic backbone of the minority community, **(e)** it was only when

Supplemental Essay 2: Seven Letters to My RSS Friend: Letter #4

the Center deputed the Union Defense Minister to oversee and control an alarming situation that the Chief Minister reluctantly called in the military for restoring civil peace, **(f)** those civil and police authorities who, out of a sense of duty, on their own, had taken prompt and proper action against those engaged in murder, arson and loot, were suddenly shifted to remote areas, for having earned government's displeasure, **(g)** the state government original decision to award a compensation of *two lacs* (about US $4000), each to the victims of the Godhra tragedy while the half of this amount to post-Godhra victims in Gujrat was misconceived and violative of natural justice, **(h)** the conditions at the state relief camps for victims rendered homeless and totally destitute were appalling and shocking, **(i)** there appeared to be little or no cooperation between relief workers/ helping agencies and the police personnel for lodging FIR's (First Information Reports) and rectifying other grievances.

The version of the state government and the *Sangh pariwar* totally differs from the above. The crux of their version is as follows:

The entire press (barring, of course, the organs of the BJP), all private TV channels, social activists, human rights organizations, statutory and voluntary, national and international, the anti-Hindu pseudo-secular opposition parties are all conspiring to falsify or exaggerate the truth. Their sole objective is to spite and malign the efforts of the forces of *Hindutva* and Hindu resurgence, which, after all, means national resurgence. The Muslim minority in Gujrat got what they deserved after Godhra. All the hue and cry in Parliament, the press and the international community that Gujrat was burning was because the enemies of *Hindutva* had and still have a one-point program – destabilizing the forces of Hindu resurgence in Gujrat. In short, there was and is no cause for alarm or any need for intervention by the Center.

I feel deeply concerned at the divergent factual versions as well as interpretations and views aired by top leaders of the *Sangh pariwar*, on the one hand, and other eminent observers and analysts, on the other. What intrigues and pains me, even more than this discrepancy, as such, is the spectacle that the *Sangh pariwar* appears to be totally indifferent to this glaring discrepancy, and unconcerned to discern its reasons and its implications for the nation as a whole. This, I submit, in all humility, is a tragic situation.

Supplemental Essay 2: Seven Letters to My RSS Friend: Letter #4

My concern in this letter is, precisely, to draw the attention of your good self and all true patriots to the above crucial matter, rather than defending, praising or denigrating anybody. It will just not do to blame the media, the opposition parties or the *Sangh pariwar* in a supercilious fashion. Nor will it be wise or patriotic to play political games in an adversarial fashion. True patriotism cries out for sober and honest self-analysis by us all.

I do not know fully the working of the mind of the Gujrat Chief Minister. But I was shocked when, quite early in the crisis period, he announced different scales of compensation to be paid by the state to Hindu and Muslim victims. Subsequently, several other things he has said have shocked me. However, I have always held Advani *Sahab* in considerable regard for his clarity of mind, a *prima facie* clean and consistent political record and a no-nonsense honest approach to men and matters, though, perhaps, lacking in empathy and generosity toward the minorities. I wish he ponders over the intriguing issue of why this enormous discrepancy between the perceptions of the 'humanist family', on the one hand, and the '*Sangh family*', on the other. I am sincerely concerned that all Indians, irrespective of religion or politics, try to determine the real cause of an amazing discrepancy in our perceptions. It would, indeed, be tragic if Advani *Sahab* were to get sucked, without any pangs of intellectual conscience, into the bottomless pit of *realpolitik*. His effusive public praise for Modi *Sahab* intrigues me quite a bit, coming as it does from a person of his intelligence and caliber. Judge *Sahab*, I say this without any grudge or grouse against anybody.

The Prime Minister did exhort the Chief Minister of Gujrat to follow his *'rajdharma'*. But was the exhortation translated into effective action? Poets and sages exhort, ministers act and implement. A Prime Minister may be a poet as well, but action must come first. Despite all the formidable weight of informed analysis in the press and authentic portrayals and panel discussions on TV, national as well as foreign, and its presumable impact on Indian public opinion, the Central government thought it fit to take the least line of resistance and to opt for the strategy of drift and a deaf ear, instead of effectively intervening in order to correct the course of the ship of Gujrat whose captain is a redoubtable *Hindutva* star.

What intrigues and perplexes me most is when some members of the BJP or *Sangh pariwar* allege that the rehabilitation and normalization process in Gujrat has suffered, precisely, because of the activities of the media. Is it

Supplemental Essay 2: Seven Letters to My RSS Friend: Letter #4

not the duty and function of the media to report and inform objectively and impartially what happens in society? I, for my part, stand totally bewildered, when what I deem a virtue appears as a vice in the eyes of the *Sangh pariwar*. When what I deem as the silver lining behind the dark clouds over Gujrat is seen by the *Sangh pariwar* as the source of all evil I begin to doubt whether this glaring discrepancy in perceptions is the result of a political strategy or a deeper crisis of values.

The majority of the allies of the BJP in the NDA coalition at the Center also highlighted the sobering findings of informed and impartial observers. The opposition were, naturally, the most vocal of all in Parliament and the press. Together they gave abundant expression to their anguish at the unwillingness or inability of the Gujrat Chief Minister and his government to restore normalcy in the state as quickly as humanly possible. The country passed through a long period of suspense as to how the highly charged drama of public disagreement between the BJP and its allies will end. Well, it all proved to be a storm in a teacup. The net result, now, is the resignation of the Modi government and a call for midterm polls. There is hardly any doubt in any quarter about the real motives of this denouement.

The Goa Conclave of the BJP held after the Gujrat carnage was a suitable occasion to prove the bona fides of the party and make suitable amends for the mistakes of commission and omission by the ruling party and government in Gujrat. A section of the party (including the Prime Minister himself) was, reportedly, so inclined. According to knowledgeable circles, his maturity and moderation could not match the vigor and ambitions of his younger comrades. Perhaps, the poet in him yielded, once again, to his political flesh. May I, in all humility, point out that the strategy, which emerged after the Goa Conclave had its roots in the short-term goal of retaining power and ignoring ethical considerations? According to Parliamentary ethics, at its best, the Chief Minister should have offered to resign, in earnest, soon after the government's failure to control the drift into anarchy. Either a new leader should have stepped in or Governor's rule should have been proclaimed. What actually happened was that the state, traumatized, as it were, by the 'perceived terrorism' at Godhra overnight regressed into an 'agency of Shiv Sena/Bajrang Dal/Vishwa Hindu Parishad hawks' hell bent on avenging Godhra. The state should have practiced its *'rajdharma'* of initiating effective steps to identify the real culprits and to prosecute them for their crime. Instead, it overlooked, if not abetted, pro-

Supplemental Essay 2: Seven Letters to My RSS Friend: Letter #4

grams of burning revenge and reprisal in the days immediately following the Godhra episode. This seems to be the crux of the matter.

Much worse reprisals and acts of brutality have been committed elsewhere in the course of history. Yet, this is hardly any justification for remaining complacent on the part of the State. I am compelled to say that the Gujrat government's inability or unwillingness to perform its *'rajdharma'* should have had a denouement very different from the strategic and politically motivated dissolution of the Assembly without the government having wiped out the tears and healed the hurts of thousands of innocent victims of the politics of hatred and fanaticism. The allies of the BJP too were more concerned with gaining political mileage and remaining in the good books of their mixed constituency than in honestly serving their proclaimed ideals. The opposition parties desperately tried to wean away some of the BJP allies and create a crisis, but interests prevailed over ideals as usually happens in the game of politics. The Congress and Communist parties have also succumbed, in the past, to the lure of political gains at the expense of principles. However, political adversity and loss of power at the Center has had a salutary effect upon the Congress leadership.

The most blatant exhibition of opportunist politics is, perhaps, the marriage of convenience in the Uttar Pradesh Assembly between *'Manuvadis'* and *'counter-Manuvadis'*. It is yet too early to judge whether it is a marriage, or only an affair to remember. I dare think this union of opposites has created waves of disillusionment in the larger support base of the BJP. Perhaps, due to a variety of reasons a fair chunk of its supporters no longer view it as 'a party with a difference'. A large number of its new adherents and supporters, perhaps, had come to accept its critique of Congress culture on several counts—appeasement of minorities and Dalits, aggressive patronage, overlooking of corruption, judicial delays, and red tape, etc. Such disillusioned sections, after the Bofors uproar, understandably, pinned their hopes on the high sounding rhetoric of the BJP. Perhaps, these very circles stand disillusioned once again on finding that their image of the BJP was just a mirage. I dare say the patently aberrant behavior of the sister organizations of the BJP: the Vishwa Hindu Parishad, Bajrang Dal and the Shiv Sena has greatly tarnished the image of the BJP flagship.

Another crucial factor in the declining fortunes and image of the BJP is the Ram Mandir issue. The romance of Advani *Sahab's Rath Yatra*, floating on the waves of religious sentiments has given way to a pedestrian bus laboring on a rough and bumpy road, greeted by tired and, possibly, hired cheers that lead nowhere. The sober elements in the RSS are none too happy at the clumsy behavior and rather indecent political hunger at the lower rungs of the organization. This political hunger has prompted some youth wings of the RSS in Gujrat to tutor Adivasi quarters to fish in troubled waters and turn against the minorities.

A section of the RSS, BJP and the *Sangh pariwar* honestly thinks that the BJP has lost ground precisely because of the dilution of its core program of Ayodhya, uniform civil code and Kashmir. In all humility, I dare say the real cause lies elsewhere. Before it came to power it cried hoarse against Bofors, but has it not itself spawned several mega Bofors? It had decried pseudo-secularism, but is its nationalism in Gujrat not 'pseudo' itself? Is it not patronizing those who practice 'pseudo' reasoning or 'pseudo' scholarship in the pursuit of truth? How and why alterations have been made in textbooks without informing their authors? If the Communists had done similar things in Bengal earlier; so much the worse for them.

Judge *Sahab*, you must have noticed that I have said almost nothing about the Godhra incident as such. I shall do so in my next letter.

Yours very sincerely,
Jamal Khwaja

Supplemental Essay 2:
Seven Letters to My RSS Friend (Contd.)

(Letter #5)

My Dear Judge *Sahab*,

The Godhra violence was, indeed, a heinous criminal method of settling scores. Human nature being what it is, the brutality and magnitude of the violence was bound to provoke strong revulsion and feelings of revenge, not only against its actual perpetrators, but the entire Muslim community as such. Since rulers, be they elected representatives of the people or hereditary despots, share the same human instincts and feelings, it was also very understandable that the dastardly act infuriated the Gujrat government itself, traumatized, as it were, by the magnitude of the violence. Yet, every sane and balanced judge of human nature in politics would concur that rulers must govern, administrators must administer, and not be swept away by revenge, no matter how intense the raw human response. It is unpardonable for a ruler, administrator or judge to be swept by passion into punishing the innocent for a crime committed by somebody else. Now this is where the state government grievously failed to perform its '*rajdharma*'.

This is, precisely, the charge that was leveled against Rajiv Gandhi's government immediately after Indira Gandhi's assassination. This similarity is, formally, correct but the analogy is, materially, misleading due to the following reason: Modi *Sahab* had long been in power as Chief Minister at the time when innocent persons were made scapegoats by infuriated mobs, while Rajiv Gandhi had just assumed the reins of government in the midst of a terrible national and personal crisis when innocent Sikhs were tortured

Supplemental Essay 2: Seven Letters to My RSS Friend: Letter #5

and killed in sheer reprisal. Moreover, once the state machinery came into action the administrative work of rectifying the wrongs done started in right earnest, even though prosecutions could not be effected due to legal or procedural obstacles.

This is not the place to go into the details of the background or the mechanics of the Godhra incident. Was the burning of the railway coach a deliberate planned exercise by Muslim terrorists, or just a desperate retaliatory act against *'Ramsevaks'* for continually provoking and harassing local Muslim vendors? In any case it was a onetime heinous act of a relatively small group. What happened the next day and days was, however, a total breakdown of all law and order and massive loss of life and property of, palpably, innocent Indian citizens. Here again, more important than the details of the mass revenge is the pattern of revenge and the role of the state in the entire extended period of revenge.

Despite the blood and tears, and a satanic dehumanization in Gujrat it is my honest and firm belief that the Indian people, as a whole, have never accepted, and never will accept the gospel of hate and violence that some sections among both Hindus and Muslims preach and practice. The common Indian, no matter what his or her religion or politics, instinctively realizes that the fire of hatred, if it is allowed to spread, will engulf and destroy the entire nation. The Hindu majority has always been tolerant of religious plurality, though, unfortunately, they have remained trapped in the bog of caste. The Indian people as a whole (including Muslims in undivided India) had also accepted the fact that Indian society, is, essentially, multireligious, and that mutual understanding is the basis of national welfare. The partition was a traumatic experience for Muslims in residual India, whatever fleeting elation and joy it may have brought about for the votaries of political separatism and the surgically delivered nation of Pakistani Muslims.

As is well-known, the political architect and founder of Pakistan, Jinnah, was himself a very modern and Westernized Muslim and he had no sympathy whatsoever with what is termed 'Islamic fundamentalism', in modern parlance. The other Muslim League leaders at the top, and the professional classes, in general, also had a liberal Islamic outlook in varying degrees, though they were highly confused on some basic religious and political concepts of modernity. This conceptual confusion prevails in Pakistan to date. One thing is, however, clear. While religious fundamentalism is an active and highly organized movement possessing considerable money

Supplemental Essay 2: Seven Letters to My RSS Friend: Letter #5

power in Pakistan, the vast majority of the Pakistani Muslims do not care to join or even to follow 'Islamic fundamentalism' in the strict or strong sense advocated by late Maududi, the venerated founder of the well-entrenched *Jamat-e-Islami*. This party is fiercely critical of President Musharraf's liberal Islamic approach that draws inspiration from Jinnah and Kamal Ataturk. The Indian Muslims are even less bothered to listen to the talk of Islamic fundamentalism. Their political common sense has already convinced them that the mixed society of India in which their Hindu brothers form eighty-five percent of the population is ill suited for the politics of religious fundamentalism. The vast majority of Indian Muslims have cast their lot with the direction set by Gandhi, Nehru, and Azad.

Many Indian Muslims do feel inwardly uneasy with the modern idea of de-linking politics with religion because they have been used to the idea that *Shariah* covers every aspect of life. But they have reconciled themselves, in all good faith and sincerity, to make adjustments in the traditional or classical idea of Islam in view of the realities of the Indian situation. I submit that this approach is a halfway house rather than a full or unqualified commitment to spiritual Humanism and secularism. But, then, inner attitudes require centuries to grow and evolve in the minds and hearts of men enjoying security and freedom. Gandhi and Nehru understood the human condition and showed patience and generosity to all. Perhaps, the votaries of *Hindutva* politics today are impatient and their insight into the human condition is blurred, and this makes it hard for them to arrive at a proper and balanced evaluation of the genuine Muslim response to the Indian situation.

The doubts and fears in *Hindutva* quarters arise, more because of Islamic terrorism outside India than because of the religious fundamentalism among Indian Muslims. Since Muslim terrorists in Pakistan, and elsewhere carry on the heinous crime of killing innocents in the name of Islam, non-Muslims are led to accept this claim at its face value. But the truth is entirely different. Religious fundamentalism, as such, springs from cultural isolation and a closed society that hampers free inquiry. Political terrorism, on the other hand, springs from existential anxiety and despair in the face of perceived injustice and the tyranny of the strong over the weak. Moreover, political terrorism cuts across different religions. Here an unexpected parallel exists between Hindu and Muslim perceptions.

Muslims in India may have demanded and loudly cheered the birth of Pakistan, but felt traumatized and suddenly left in the lurch by its creation.

Supplemental Essay 2: Seven Letters to My RSS Friend: Letter #5

They are becoming increasingly insecure in India due to the rising Hindu fascist trends in Indian politics. The Hindus, on the other hand, constitute eighty-five percent of the population and more or less totally control the politics and economics of the land. Yet, they do not feel inwardly secure and in full control of the situation in India. They are scared of the dangers latent in Islamic fundamentalism and terrorism.

The Muslim logic is that Hindus do not behave like a 'big brother', as they should, toward the rather backward small brother. The Hindu logic is that, far from being a younger and weaker brother, the Indian Muslims themselves claim to be and, in fact, are members of a mighty and potentially rich Islamic power bloc stretching from North Africa to South East Asia located right on top of the Indian land mass. In other words, the Hindus do not perceive the Muslims as a weak younger brother but as a potentially larger and more powerful world community. A fear seems to lurk in the depths of the Hindu psyche that neither the Western world, nor the Islamic world wants the peace loving and patient Hindu community to live in peace under their own sky from the Himalayas to the Indian Ocean. And fear is the mother of hate and aggression. In all humility, I submit that this is the root cause of the rising incidents, in recent years, of physical violence against Indian Christians in several parts of the land.

Whatever Christian missionaries may or may not have done in the past to 'save' lost souls in India, the Christian church today has nothing to do with the theory or practice of forcing Christianity on the throats of infidels or of bribing them to join the flock of Christ. The plain truth is that the vast majority of Christian missionaries in India today are models of selfless service, piety and religious scholarship. Even the Pope has accepted plural paths to salvation. The adversarial approach to other religions has undergone an internal revolution in the contemporary Christian value system. On this point all the major religions of the world are fast converging. It is a pity that some *Hindutva* quarters still nurse or air old grievances against Muslims or Christians.

There is no dearth of compassionate and fair-minded Hindus or Muslims in India and Pakistan. They are, in fact, the silent majority. A vocal minority may be said to have hijacked the role of spokesman for Hinduism or Islam, as the case may be. However, it will not be long when the relative supremacy of good over evil in the human heart, armed with the advantages of modern technology, will empower the liberal humanist

Supplemental Essay 2: Seven Letters to My RSS Friend: Letter #5

vanguard within each community to initiate interfaith dialogues. And this is bound to produce very fruitful results in terms of mutual understanding and appreciation of the spiritual wealth found in every religious tradition. This will pave the way for removing ignorance and prejudice in each in-group against out-groups. This will dilute human ethnocentricity that is the natural human condition. This is how modern intellectuals and savants in the West, say, Newton, Gibbon, Goethe, Carlyle, Browne *et al* came to respect and admire *Sufism* and Islamic liberalism, while others, say, Hegel, Schopenhauer, Max Mueller, and Romain Rolland, *et al.* came to respect and admire Vedanta and Yoga. The same was the case with Ram Mohan Roy in the late 18th century and M.N. Roy and Tarachand in the 20th. They all greatly appreciated the historical role of Islam in world history.

The human pursuit of truth, goodness and beauty knows no boundaries of religion or race. This approach is fast spreading in the Western world and America. I, therefore, submit that an inclusive and catholic approach to culture will always score over an exclusive and restrictive approach, be it Hindu, Muslim or Christian. In the final analysis, love for the human and the humane will win over and attract more minds and hearts among good Hindus, Muslims and Christians and Sikhs than love for any limited or exclusivist category, no matter what. This is the destination of man in the modern age of cultural pluralism and global tolerance.

Some in the *Hindutva* quarters (perhaps, with genuine sincerity) say that the Muslims should earn the goodwill of the majority. But goodwill has to be reciprocal. Some voices proclaim that Indian Muslims must prove their loyalty to India. But is or can loyalty be the monopoly of any group? The test is common to all. Is not an unknown lowly paid clerk or school teacher doing an honest job with dedication and efficiency more loyal and a better patriot than those out to amass ill begotten wealth and to misuse power? Where does religion come into the picture? Indeed, those who have nothing else to convince or impress others are tempted to put labels on their ontological shallowness or poverty. There is hardly any need to mention or parade the gods we really love and surrender to, be they Hindu or Muslim. Moreover, the simple goodness of heart and the beauty of the spirit cut across all religious divides. This should suffice to put at rest all mutual fears or doubts in the hearts and minds of all true Hindus and Muslims who really care for patriotism rather than power over others.

Supplemental Essay 2: Seven Letters to My RSS Friend: Letter #5

The letter is getting too long. I shall develop some relevant additional points in my next letter. Meanwhile accept my profound regards and best wishes.

Yours very sincerely,
Jamal Khwaja

Supplemental Essay 2:
Seven Letters to My RSS Friend (Contd.)

(Letter #6)

My Dear Judge *Sahab*,

The founding fathers of the Constitution of free India were inspired by the idea that every citizen of a sovereign state stood equal in regard to basic rights, responsibilities and opportunities, irrespective of religion, caste, region or gender. This approach implied that the state, as such, was not a patron of any one religious creed, and that the Indian republic had no official religion. It will be agreed that this idea was not only laudable but also courageous under the then divisive Hindu-Muslim passions that had been aroused by the politics of partition and the emergence of Pakistan as a Muslim homeland and an Islamic state. I submit, no honest and impartial observer or analyst can over-praise the founding fathers for their wisdom and foresight in framing the Constitution.

Some Hindu quarters have raised voices (perhaps, in all sincerity and good conscience) that the term 'secularism' is an unnecessary borrowing or imitation of Western ideas, under the influence of Nehru, and the secular ideal should be displaced by the ancient Hindu ideal of equal respect for all religions (*sarvadharma sadbhaava*). These quarters argue that the idea of secularism was an understandable response of Western humanitarian reformers to the never ending religious intolerance and conflicts between different religions or sectarian groups in Christian society. Since Hinduism is, intrinsically, free from the virus of intolerance and is committed to the doctrine of free choice of deity (*isht-devata*), free India, having an overwhelmingly Hindu population, should substitute the borrowed Western secular idiom with the ancient traditional idiom of '*sarvadharma sadbhaav*'. These quarters confidently claim that a true Hindu state would guarantee and fully protect all fundamental human rights as the secular dispensation does today. According to these quarters, the stress on secularism not only dilutes national pride, but it also dilutes the distinctive spiritual basis of the Indian value system that has been her glory from time immemorial. Perhaps, these quarters have in mind the example of several Muslim countries, recently liberated from colonial rule, that are Islamic states and yet enjoy the benefits of the modern age and command influence and power in the comity of nations without imitating Western secularism. I submit, this reasoning is sophistry and illusion.

Secularism, in modem parlance, is a clear-cut concept of social and political thought. The definition of Hinduism, or any other religion, for that matter, is, at bottom, a matter of choice and opinion. The basic question, 'what is Hinduism/Islam?' or 'who is a good Hindu/Muslim?' elicits plural answers. Both Gandhiji and Dr. Hedgewar were good Hindus but their idea of Hinduism differed. Gandhiji remarked that if un-touchability were an integral part of Hinduism he was not prepared to call himself a Hindu. He, obviously, believed that un-touchability was not integral to Hinduism. However, I personally know some Hindus who honestly hold that a good Hindu ought to follow Manu's text to the letter. I may add that I honestly respect these Hindu friends for their sincerity and integrity, though I freely express my disagreement with them. The same remarks apply to some Muslim relatives or friends whom I admire for their truthfulness and integrity, without agreeing with their conception or definition of Islam.

Despite the fact that India is a secular state the country has to face serious problems in controlling communal passions and maintaining intergroup harmony. At bottom, these problems arise due to political or economic factors, but interested parties give a religious or communal color to them as a matter of strategy. A secular state, therefore, would always be better placed than a Hindu state to provide an even ground to different players belonging to diverse religions, castes and regions. The same remarks apply to Islamic states having mixed populations.

Supplemental Essay 2: Seven Letters to My RSS Friend: Letter #6

Secularism, as a political concept, flows from a liberal humanist philosophy. This means giving primacy to man's sense of wonder and mystery when he confronts the Universe. Every religion attempts to unravel the mystery of birth and death, good and evil, joy and sorrow, final release from pain and suffering. Answers to such questions can never be proved and different people at different times are bound to give different answers to such existential questions. Such matters should, therefore, not be dealt with by the state and should be left as matters of individual preference or conscience. Secularism holds that the state should not advocate or oppose any attempt at resolving the existential mystery of the Universe. The state should concern itself only with matters of law and order, security, political, economic, educational and administrative arrangements, framing and administering of civil and criminal laws and so on. When secularism is combined with liberal Humanism this adds up to democracy. This implies that the state should perform all the above functions with the consent of all its citizens according to previously agreed procedures so that law becomes the '*ruler*', rather than any person or persons. It is, however, inevitable that law will be interpreted and enforced by the persons concerned.

A serious complication, however, arises in the above definition of secularism if, and when, any organized religion claims that it is more than an existential perspective on the inscrutable mystery of the Universe, and that it is a complete 'blue print of the good life as a whole', and further that it is the religious duty of the believer to live strictly in accordance with the prescribed code as such. Some believers might be convinced that it is also part of their religious duty to convince all others to do the same. Now if the state has a mixed population this approach creates tension and conflict. Even if the citizens belong to one religion only they may well be members of different sects or have diverse views on creedal or social matters. This was the actual situation in medieval Christianity and Islam, and the idea prevailed that the church and state ought to be one.

As we all know, after centuries of doctrinal and also armed conflict the Christians in Western Europe outgrew doctrines that directly or indirectly produce conflict between the church and the state. The *Treaty of Westphalia* in Germany, signed in 1648, was, in essence, the recognition of the principles that **(a)** the church and the state, each have their respective proper jurisdiction and neither should encroach upon the other, **(b)** the state should be neutral and impartial to all its citizens irrespective of the church to which

Supplemental Essay 2: Seven Letters to My RSS Friend: Letter #6

they belong. The *Treaty of Westphalia*, thus initiated the era in which the English philosopher, John Locke, wrote his famous letters on tolerance and the Glorious Revolution took place in Britain in 1688. This was the beginning of the story of religious tolerance in Western Europe, but the story took two centuries to reach a happy ending when Disraeli, Jewish by blood, became Prime Minister of Great Britain.

There are several notable examples of enlightened good Muslims who have authentically accepted the principle of the separation of church and state. However, the great Muslim community the world over has yet to accept this, not merely as a policy for Muslims living in mixed societies, but as an authentic understanding or reinterpretation of Islam in the modern scientific and global age. The Muslim community, as a whole, accepts the idea of the unity of the church and state, and of the *Shariah* as a complete guide to the whole of life. They are not prepared to give up this ideal, but they just cannot resist the pulls and pressures of the modern age. Such Muslims reluctantly, acquiesce to adjustments essential to keep life going. However, there are others who just cannot bring themselves to water down what they term 'true Islam' for the sake of convenience or worldly gains. This approach or position is termed 'Islamic fundamentalism' in modern parlance. I submit the greater Muslim community must engage itself in an honest dialogue to resolve this issue and other connected matters. Other great world religions such as Christianity, Buddhism and Hinduism have already accepted the principle of the separation of church and state.

'Islamic fundamentalism', it should be noted, does not entail the use of terrorist methods against others. Terrorism is a different phenomenon. It is born out of a sense of helpless rage against perceived oppression by super powers who practice double standards and impose their arbitrary decisions on small and weak groups or nations. Suicide missions appear as the only means of expressing their existential anger and frustration against an incurably callous tyranny of the strong over the weak. The perceived oppressors, however, cannot but hit back and contain the attacks on, obviously, innocent people. This is the tragic logic of history. The vicious circle will have to be broken. The United Nations Organization is a great step in this noble direction. But super-powers are ever tempted to turn it into a tool for promoting their own interests. This, again, is quite natural and understandable. It is, therefore, imperative not to lose faith but to persist in doing what is right and avoid what is wrong. And terrorist attacks, suicidal or strategic, against the innocent are definitely wrong. Islam itself strongly prohibits this method of rectifying injustice.

Yours very sincerely,
Jamal Khwaja

Supplemental Essay 2:
Seven Letters to My RSS Friend (contd.)

(Letter #7)

My Dear Judge *Sahab*,

The theory and practice of organized Hinduism does not regulate or control every sphere of human life to the same degree or extent, as does Islam through '*Shariah*'. Hindu society has been rather permissive and tolerant of plural interpretations of both creed and law. In ancient times it accommodated Jain and Buddhist ideas and values within the wider Indian culture. According to judicious historians, due to this conceptual 'openness' of early Brahmanical society Buddhist agnosticism, more or less completely, came to over-shadow Brahmanical orthodoxy in several parts of the land. This lasted till the rise and spread of *Shankaracharya's* revivalist movement in the 9th century. Thereafter both Jainism and Buddhism declined or rather withered away and the contours of Hinduism, as we understand it today, emerged. Scholars have viewed this crucial process differently. Some regard it as the result of persecution of dissent. Others say it happened due to the extreme 'porosity' of Hindu thought and culture. Due to various factors the Hindu population absorbed the conceptual and social innovations of Jain and Buddhist reformers, and, as it were, took the wind out of their sails.

By the 10th century Brahmanical thought became rigid, as Al-Beruni points out in his monumental work on Indian thought and culture. Hindu creativity had become a spent force, as generally happens in the human family. Political infighting between the Hindu rulers and chiefs and a vicious social stratification had resulted in a shocking dehumanization of the lowest class.

Supplemental Essay 2: Seven Letters to My RSS Friend: Letter #7

By the same time the Islamic revolution had grown into a mighty world current. This, rather than the sword of Islam, acted as a catalyst in different parts of the then known world. In India the creative impact of Islam led to the ideas of ethical Theism and *'Bhakti'*. A little later in Western Europe it led to Protestant and Unitarian versions of Christianity.

The Islamic revolution, however, was far from being a finished or perfect product. Its message of social equality was qualified by the idea of the brotherhood and equality of all Muslims, irrespective of race or region, rather than of all men, irrespective of religion or faith. Not only this, this equality and the republican spirit or impulse of Islam remained entangled in the thorns of racial pride and kingly authoritarianism. To make matters even worse, the Sultans in India and the entire nobility could not emancipate themselves from the evil of the vicious caste system in India. Thus, the seeds of early Islamic republicanism and democracy lay fallow and dormant for several centuries before they could flower and flourish in the Western representative democracy of modern times. As we all know, this consummation took place in the Christian rather than in the Muslim world. The scientific and technological revolutions that took place in Western Europe from the end of the 18th century onwards have played a major and crucial role in the full flowering of the seeds of the spiritual Humanism of early Islam. Whether one likes it or not, the West is still at the wheel, and its creativity is intact. However, it has been forced to listen to the wisdom of the East in order to correct several imbalances in the value system of a, hitherto, rather, overconfident and assured modernity.

Western creativity and modernity reached India via Bengal in the late 18th century. Under its impact as well as the earlier influence of Islamic ideas Ram Mohan Roy redefined Hindu spirituality. Almost a century later Sir Syed, leader of the *Aligarh movement* did the same for Islam. The liberal Hindu vanguard retains, till today, the considerable advantage of their early lead. Moreover, the flame that Ram Mohan ignited soon lighted several other lamps in other parts of the great land. The Brahmo movement stirred a new vision before the Hindu psyche leading to the birth of Ramakrishna Mission, Vivekananda, Tagore, Aurobindo, and Krishnamurti, *et al*, and Nehru himself. Sir Syed, on the other hand, to the misfortune of Indian Muslims, in spite of his laudable creative work on Islamic liberalism, merely founded the M.A.O. College that produced good cricketers, Deputy Collectors and lawyers for British India, and, of course, the famous Ali Brothers. But no corresponding rethinking on or redefinition of Islam emerged in

Supplemental Essay 2: Seven Letters to My RSS Friend: Letter #7

a big way from the efforts of Sir Syed. I think, his followers, especially his successors, failed him. He died in 1898, and the partition, fifty years after his death was the nadir of their failure. The responsibility for partition, however, is not theirs alone.

The partition has greatly slowed down the cultural interaction between Islam and Hinduism that had begun in medieval India. However, it is patently clear that the process cannot be arrested, no matter what the political constraints and interests of India, Pakistan and Bangla Desh may demand. None of these independent countries can insulate themselves from the pressures and pulls of cultural modernity, economic interdependence and a growing globalism. They are all faced with problems and challenges from every side, pressure of overpopulation, corrupt politics, misuse of religion or caste for political gains, poor political will and discipline, irresponsible trade unionism and a host of others. Yet, it is a fact that the common man everywhere yearns for mutual understanding and peace and is moved by the simple goodness of the heart, above all talk of religion or politics, in the name of *Jihad, Hindutva* or Western civilization.

I firmly and honestly believe that through trial and error, blood and tears the human family is reaching out for a 'religion of the spirit' without any call for converting to any particular theological creed or tradition. This approach to religion leaves intact the distinctive idiom, and symbols of each historical religion, but unites them all in a common search for values. This is the interfaith approach of all enlightened and noble souls in the world today. Gandhi was the prophet of this religion of the spirit. I cannot help remarking, in all humility, that he remains the most outstanding combination, in modern times, of mass political leadership, conceptual creativity, statesmanship and sainthood. I have no objection if the RSS has different ideas and if its source of inspiration, and light, lies in the life and teachings of Hedgewar, Savarkar or Guru Golwalkar, or if a Bal Thackery looks up to Shivaji, for inspiration and guidance. I respect all sincere devotees and believers, without necessarily agreeing with them. I shall respect all sincere beliefs but I shall remain committed to the truth as I see it. However, I shall protest with all moral force at my command, when the Vishwa Hindu Parishad, Bajrang Dal, Shiv Sena and others resort to violence for achieving their objectives. If militancy or terrorism is evil in the case of *Jihad*, it is also evil in the case of *Hindutva*. There can be no double standards. This is the crux of the matter. I am constrained to express my deep pain and anguish that double standards of behavior have been abundantly displayed in Gujrat

Supplemental Essay 2: Seven Letters to My RSS Friend: Letter #7

at the highest level, notwithstanding the poetic and humanist conscience of the Prime Minister. How and why this happened is a matter I shall not try to judge here. May India prosper and may truth prevail.

With these words, dear Judge *Sahab*, I shall close my correspondence with you on matters of common interest and deep concern.

All the best to you and family and the greater Indian family.

Yours very sincerely,
Jamal Khwaja

Supplemental Essay 3:
Sir Syed, Iqbal and Azad

Six outstanding Muslim religious thinkers and reformers during the last one hundred and fifty years: Sir Syed (d.1898), Mirza Ghulam Ahmad (d. 1908), Shibli Nomani (d. 1914), Amir Ali (d. 1928), Iqbal (d. 1938), and Abul Kalam Azad (d. 1958), shaped the religious sensibility of the Muslims of the Indian sub-continent until roughly the first half of the 20th century. Thereafter, Abul Ala Maududi (d. 1979) deeply influenced the course of Muslim thinking and politics, especially in Pakistan.

When Sir Syed died at the ripe age of eighty-one, Mirza Ghulam Ahmad had already founded the Ahmadi sect in Islam. Iqbal was a young man of immense promise, deeply influenced by Sir Syed's writings and T.W. Arnold's, *The Preaching of Islam*, and Azad, a precocious youth of about fourteen with his remarkably creative mind in ferment due to exposure to diverse streams of influence. Mirza *Sahab*, Iqbal, and Azad, all had come under the spell of Sir Syed, the father of Islamic Liberalism in the sub-continent. I shall briefly state Sir Syed's main theses in order to make it the point of departure for offering some critical comments on the religious thought of Iqbal and Azad. I shall not comment at all on Mirza *Sahab* except to confess that I, for one, feel deeply pained and also ashamed at the intolerance meted to a great Muslim reformer and the entire Ahmadi community. I hold that the Ahmadi movement is entitled to a respectful hearing and full tolerance by all Muslims, no less than by others.

Supplemental Essay 3: Sir Syed, Iqbal and Azad

THE SEARCH FOR THE QUINTESSENCE OF ISLAM:

Every religion has a nuclear core of basic beliefs and values embedded in a wide cultural matrix comprising myths, ancient collective memories, folklore, customs, and stereotyped images, etc. All these elements are enmeshed and the ordinary believer hardly cares to separate the nuclear core from the total cultural matrix of faith and practice. The total cultural tradition is the spiritual atmosphere in which he lives, moves and has his being.

The German Protestant thinker of the 20th century, Bultmann, called the gradual process of distilling the nuclear core of the Christian thought and value system from the cultural matrix of the Christian tradition, the 'demythologization of Christianity. This concept, however, has universal and timeless relevance to all religious traditions. Several creative thinkers and savants of Islam- Al-Beruni (d. app. 1040), Ibn Sina (d. 1037), Ibn Rushd (d. 1198), Al-Ghazali (d. 1111), Ibn Arabi (d.1240), Jalaluddin Rumi (d. 1273), Fariduddin Attar (d. 1229), Ibn Khaldun (d. 1406), Waliullah (d. 1763), and others attempted to grasp the essence of Islam.

Sir Syed also attempted to distill the nuclear essence of Islam in the framework of modern thought, as he understood it. He was not a professionally trained philosopher, social scientist or historian. But his extraordinarily sharp intellect, intuitive insight and common sense, and above all, his intellectual honesty and moral courage enabled him to distill the nuclear core of Islam from its concrete historical forms in space and time. It is instructive to recall that in his earlier pre-critical phase, Sir Syed had adhered to the conventional ideas of his milieu, though even then he had come under the influence of the, relatively, liberal philosophical theology of Shah Waliullah of Delhi. However, soon after the failure of the great Indian rebellion of 1857 against British imperial rule, when Syed Ahmed was roughly forty-five, he outgrew his honestly held ideas and values and became clearly aware of their limitations, without, however, ever rejecting the nuclear core of his Islamic faith. Those who were unable to appreciate the spiritual pilgrimage of the great man and the organic growth of his ideas charged him with having abandoned Islam or distorting the faith for ulterior motives. Half a century later Abul Kalam Azad passed through a similar experience.

Supplemental Essay 3: Sir Syed, Iqbal and Azad

SIR SYED'S ISLAMIC LIBERALISM IN BARE OUTLINE: GOD AND REVELATION

That the Universe is the creation or 'Work of God', and the Qur'an, the 'Word of God', revealed to Muhammad ﷺ, the last and the greatest among the numerous messengers of God, is the kernel of the Islamic faith. Sir Syed thought that this simple faith was rationally demonstrable. He, however, reconstructed the traditional sense or meaning of the attributes of God and of revelation with a view to removing the mythological or anthropomorphic elements deeply embedded in traditional notions.

Sir Syed's critics saw these reconstructive efforts as tantamount to rejecting or repudiating the faith, as such. Thus, for instance, Sir Syed's philosophical understanding of the way in which God creates, maintains and regulates nature or guides the prophets through Divine revelation gave rise to the charge that Sir Syed totally disbelieved in revelation (*wahy*). What Sir Syed had rejected was, not the belief that the Qur'an was the 'Word of God', but the traditional belief concerning the mode of revelation through the agency of an angel. According to Sir Syed, conventional views on this matter reflected the Semitic mode of interpreting or conceptualizing the super-spiritual phenomenon of revelation. Modifying or reconstructing the conventional view in regard to the modus operandi of '*wahy*' is not the same thing as rejecting the faith in revelation, as such.

Sir Syed held that God inspires and guides all creation through an internal mechanism of Divine guidance appropriate to the level of the created being. The terms 'Gabriel' or 'Holy Spirit' do not stand for any external being or agent, but to the Divinely bestowed gift to some especially elected humans among whom Prophet Muhammad ﷺ occupies a unique rank. Sir Syed's views on this crucial matter are, basically, similar to the approach of classical Muslims religious thinkers. The same is true of Azad.

Miracles: Sir Syed also rejected the conventional belief in miracles, though certainly not the belief in Divine omnipotence. He held that the causal uniformity of nature reflected the wisdom and the will of God and also that there was no real conflict between the laws of nature, as taught by science, and Qur'anic reports of miraculous events, which seemingly,

Supplemental Essay 3: Sir Syed, Iqbal and Azad

contradict those laws. Sir Syed removed the seeming contradiction by giving fresh and novel interpretations or meanings of Qur'anic words and expressions. This method was quite successful in several cases, but it did not work in every instance. In any case Sir Syed was perfectly right in questioning traditional interpretations of several Qur'anic verses, and outlining afresh the principles of Qur'anic exegesis based upon Arabic philology and etymology as well as the historical context of revelation.

Spiritualism: In keeping with his scientific and rationalistic approach Sir Syed made a clear distinction between genuine spiritualism (cultivating the ethical and spiritual dimension of the human soul), but doing away with all superstitious beliefs and practices grafted upon the valid elements of Sufi thought and culture. Sir Syed, thus, lauded spiritualism, but decried superstition.

Petitionary Prayer to God: Sir Syed rejected the popular view that God answers the supplications of the faithful by altering the natural course of events without appropriate human actions. However, Sir Syed did accept the efficacy of spiritual prayer as a means of the flow of Divine grace which gives solace to the believer and raises his morale and creativity which, in turn, result in more effective purposeful action.

Status of the Reported sayings of the Prophet *(hadith)*: Sir Syed also questioned the propriety of uncritically accepting '*hadith*' as absolutely binding upon the believer in every walk of life. In the first place, notwithstanding the piety and labors of the esteemed editors of the '*hadith*' its authenticity is not assured like that of the Qur'an. Moreover, it is impossible to treat the Prophet's putative instructions or actions in social, political, economic, administrative, scientific matters on par with Qur'anic injunctions. Now according to Sir Syed, faith in Islam and veneration of the Prophet ﷺ do not impose any religious obligation to do exactly what the Prophet ﷺ did in purely worldly matters. Thus there is nothing 'Islamic' about personal or proper names, dress, food or eating habits, entertainment, style of living, and so on, as long as the believer does not violate any Qur'anic injunction.

Separation of Religion and Politics: Sir Syed redefined the scope of *Shariah* and limited it to the purely religious or spiritual sphere. Indeed, this was the crux of his breakthrough into the spirit of the modern scientific age and its corresponding religious sensibility in general. In the final analysis, Sir Syed stood for the separation of religion and state, even though the

Supplemental Essay 3: Sir Syed, Iqbal and Azad

word 'secularism' may not occur in his writings, and even though he passionately opposed Muslim participation in the Indian National Congress. It is pertinent to point that his unambiguous opposition to the politics of Pan-Islamism earned him bitter criticism from Jamaluddin Afghani, the foremost champion of pan-Islam. Sir Syed consistently held that the violent conflict between Turkey and the predominantly Christian Balkan states was not a holy war between the Crescent and the Cross, but the understandable demand of Balkan nationalism. Sir Syed also did not accept the institution of the Caliphate as an integral part of the Islamic faith, though he fully accepted the idea of Muslim brotherhood.

It would be unfair to maintain that Sir Syed's views on the separation of religion and politics were shaped merely by political exigencies or his desire to be on the right side of the British rulers. Sir Syed was genuinely fascinated by British liberalism, tolerance, fair–play and political institutions, in general, as well as the British contribution to literature, science and technology. In other words, Sir Syed genuinely accepted the liberal thesis of the separation of church and state. Unfortunately, he was not fully aware of the thought and culture of other modern Western nations and of India and China in the ancient period. As a result, Sir Syed could not fully empathize with those Congress leaders who stood for the speedy transplantation of the Westminster pattern of democracy in the extremely heterogeneous Indian society.

IQBAL AND AZAD IN RELATION TO SIR SYED'S DEMYTHOLOGIZATION OF ISLAM:

1. Both, Iqbal and Azad, follow the lead Sir Syed gave in his program of demythologizing Islam and pruning the Islamic nuclear core of all secondary or tertiary accretions, be they of pre-Islamic Arab origin, or later developments in the long career of Islam in history. Iqbal questioned the popular anthropomorphic notions of afterlife, heaven and hell, petitionary prayer, and fate, etc, quite in the manner of Sir Syed. But unlike Sir Syed, Iqbal did not reconstruct these concepts. The same applies to Azad with the exception of the concepts of Divine providence (*Rububiyat*) and Divine revelation (*wahy*). Azad's remarkably suggestive and detailed reinterpretation of these concepts is his lasting contribution to Islamic thought.

2. Theology: Both Iqbal and Azad reject the rationalistic illusions of Sir Syed. They abandoned the claim that reason could prove conclusively

Supplemental Essay 3: Sir Syed, Iqbal and Azad

the existence of God, the revealed character of the Qur'an, and life after death, etc. Sir Syed thought and argued on scholastic lines, while both Iqbal and Azad fully realized the several limitations of pre-Kantian rationalistic theology, Christian, as well as Islamic.

Iqbal's religious approach is existentialist. For him belief in God is not a hypothesis, which explains the features of the Universe, but rather the depth whisper of the soul. The same is the case with Azad. Iqbal, in his poetry, and Azad, in his prose, reach the height of literary beauty and power beyond the reach of Sir Syed. Sir Syed, however, goes into far greater detail and displays far greater candor and moral courage in the course of his restatement of Islam than either Iqbal or Azad.

3. Qur'anic Exegesis: Sir Syed's critical approach to Qur'anic exegesis was vitiated by his far-fetched and twisted interpretations of several Qur'anic texts for the express purpose of proving a particular thesis. The thesis was that miracles never take place, and those Qur'anic texts, which, ostensibly, describe miracles, have been wrongly understood (for various reasons) by Muslim believers and scholars alike. Now, both Iqbal and Azad do not fall into this vicious trap. Nor do they accept as final any particular scientific theory that may have gained currency at the moment. Thus, they do not feel called upon to reconcile any seeming discrepancy between science and scripture by twisting the plain meanings of Qur'anic words or expressions. This was also the approach of Muhammad Abduh, the famed contemporary of Sir Syed in Egypt.

Both Iqbal and Azad had a better understanding of the scientific method and the philosophy of science. They held that natural laws, as revealed by science, were empirical generalizations, rather than logically necessary truths. This approach does not rule out the occurrence of miracles, as logically impossible and leaves the matter open. Conceptual space is thus, provided for a more rational and honest understanding of the scriptures, science and the world in general.

4. The Islamic Nuclear Core: Both Iqbal and Azad were concerned, as was Sir Syed himself, to identify and preserve the Islamic nuclear core rather than conserve every strand – social, cultural, political and economic –constituting the tradition. Sir Syed's Islamic vision was opposed to the idea of Islamization of every detail of life, as if Islam were a total code of

Supplemental Essay 3: Sir Syed, Iqbal and Azad

conduct meant for every conceivable sphere of human activity. Sir Syed's plea to his brother Indian Muslim to keep religion and politics separate was, thus, a matter of principle rather than of sheer expediency. That Sir Syed steadfastly opposed the Congress movement is much too complex an issue to admit of any simple explanation. Both his uncritical admirers and his hostile detractors tend to become one-sided. To trace the ultimate responsibility of the partition of India in 1947 to his shoulders is the height of historical simplism. However, Iqbal, quite clearly, did go back upon Sir Syed's principled separation of religion and politics when he affirmed the organic unity of religion and politics and the all embracing jurisdiction of *Shariah*, even though he did permit, rather encouraged, internal movement of thought within the Muslim community.

Iqbal's view on the organic link between religion and politics, thus, gave intellectual respectability to a version of Islam that Sir Syed had outgrown. Iqbal's concept of the 'organic unity between the church and the state in his famous *Reconstruction of Religious Concepts in Islam*, thus, gave many modern educated Indian Muslims (rather perplexed by Sir Syed's radical interpretation of Islam) a ready excuse for relapsing into the comfort zone of traditional ideas. Azad, on the other hand, not only affirmed the principle of movement within the *Shariah* (as Iqbal also did) but also reaffirmed Sir Syed's approach to the principle of separating religion from politics. It is another matter that their 'contextual politics' was very different. While Sir Syed advocated communitarian politics in his time Azad stood for vigorous nationalist struggle for independence. Both Iqbal and Azad affirm the principle of movement in religious thought and the '*Shariah*'. But they disagree about the jurisdiction of the *Shariah*. Iqbal stuck to the traditional position that it embraced the totality of life; Azad, creatively developed Sir Syed's nascent Islamic liberalism into the modern principle of the separation of church and state. Iqbal's approach is, thus, primarily applicable to purely, or predominantly, Muslim societies; Azad's approach has universal relevance. Iqbal, indirectly, puts the clock back, as it were, in this crucial matter, even though his command over modern Western thought and literature was immensely greater than either Sir Syed's or Azad's. Moreover, he was also far ahead of Sir Syed in his insight into and understanding of the difference between the nature of truth and certainty in the sphere of science and in the sphere of morality, spirituality and art. Sir Syed's scholastic rationalism, on the other hand, was wedded to the illusion that reason can prove the existence of Allah and the revealed status of the Qur'an.

Supplemental Essay 3: Sir Syed, Iqbal and Azad

5. Secularism and Democracy: Azad developed the seed of Sir Syed's nascent secularism into an articulate Islamic Liberalism, which does not fight shy of humanism, nationalism and democracy. While Iqbal, in a sense, regresses from Sir Syed's groping secularism, Azad advances in the direction of modernity in redefining the scope and jurisdiction of the *Shariah*. Azad's position is a creative development of the earlier breakthrough of Sir Syed into religious modernity with regard to three crucial issues, namely, the proper jurisdiction of religion, territorial basis of community and secular democratic basis of governance. Indeed, in some well-known verses he denigrated democracy as a system of government, which counted but did not weigh heads. His fascination for the virtues of the superman and the quest for power (considerably, if not wholly, under the influence of Nietzsche) seems to betray an undercurrent of authoritarian elitism and male chauvinism in his attitudes and outlook.

Iqbal also did not do full justice to the role of nationalism in the modern age. While rightly pointing out the harmful aspects of Western nationalism he ignored or minimized the role of almost all organized world religions in perpetuating divisive tendencies, intolerance, hatred and the suppression of man's freedom and dignity. He also ignored the complications involved in the concept of exclusive salvation and the ideal of one world-one religion. While Iqbal welcomed the federation of Muslim states, Azad stood for religious pluralism based on the interfaith movement. Iqbal's version of Islamic liberalism is well-suited for predominantly Muslim societies; Azad's version of Islamic liberalism has a universal appeal. It may truly be said that notwithstanding the political divide between Sir Syed and Azad, Azad takes over where Sir Syed left in the matter of identifying and refining the nuclear core of universal Islam.

As we all know, Maududi and his school strongly reject the thesis of the separation of religion and politics. Indeed, affirming the organic union of religion and politics is the heart of Islamic fundamentalism in Western terminology. Unfortunately, political passions cloud the accurate understanding of basic concepts. This applies to all of us rather than merely to our out-group whom we too readily perceive as enemies. The real position of one party gets distorted in the other's perception, and this leads to endless controversy. The protagonists of Islamic fundamentalism form a distorted idea of the real position of the believers in secularism whom they regard as the '*wicked enemies of God*'. However, it is patent that those who stand for the principled separation of religion and politics, or those who demarcate their proper spheres are neither against religion, nor wicked. Likewise, those who hold that the *Shariah* is applicable to every sphere of life and that the good Muslim is one who regulates his or her life, up to the minutest details, according to the *sunnah*, are neither terrorists nor knaves. Some who follow this line, obviously, turn into terrorists and become a menace to the human family.

Maududi was a fundamentalist but he never stood for or practiced terrorism. However, he went totally wrong when he projected Islamic liberals, like Sir Syed, Amir Ali, and Azad, *et al* as cosmetic or toothless believers who reduced Islam to merely ritualistic prayers, fasting, *zakat*, and *Hajj*, etc. but gave up the idea that the *Shariah* applied to the totality of life including politics and economics. But this is precisely where Maududi and his school of thought falter. They are unable to see that the 'principled separation of religion from politics' does not mean or imply the banishment of morality from politics, or any devaluation of religion. All that the talk of the separation of religion and politics in modern times means is that citizens of every state should have equal rights and duties and complete equality of status in a democratically governed state run on the basis of an agreed constitution rather than on the basis of any particular religion or creed. It follows that the proper way to achieve the above objective is through free inquiry and democratic discussion, at different levels, rather than conforming to any particular religion or religious authority in the form a person, book or school of thought.

THE PRINCIPLE OF MOVEMENT AS APPLIED TO THE LEGACY OF AZAD:

The human situation is subject to ceaseless change. No thought and value system can claim finality. Azad's contribution, no less than that of Sir Syed or Iqbal, needs to be critically examined and creatively nourished by his admirers. They must follow the spirit of inner freedom (*azadi*) of Azad himself who had won it after a prolonged spiritual struggle. They will be true to Azad only to the extent to which they practice the ethos of inner freedom to choose. Any conviction that does not spring from the soil of inner freedom (without fear of heresy or hope of reward) is liable to be born of cultural conditioning, rather than of authentic faith. Authentic faith is inseparable from inner freedom. What, then, are some of the areas where the legacy of Azad needs creative development by a grateful posterity?

Supplemental Essay 3: Sir Syed, Iqbal and Azad

A) The essential Unity of Religions (*wahdat e deen*) and the idea of tolerance.

Azad questioned the traditional Muslim belief in the exclusive salvation of Muslims. This questioning was based not merely on philosophical grounds, but on an honest and fresh interpretation of relevant Qur'anic texts. However, this interpretation was not entirely novel since Sufi saints and poets have long preached and practiced the tolerance of religious plurality. Some critics of Azad allege that on being sharply criticized in some circles for holding 'un-Islamic' views Azad preferred to beat a hasty retreat by watering down his position or by adopting a studied silence on this crucial issue. My submission is that valid as is Azad 's approach, it must be deepened still further in the light of the study of Comparative Religion and the practice of interfaith dialogue.

The followers of every religious tradition must practice loving tolerance of dissent in the sphere of faith. Intolerance is not an index of the intensity of faith in one's own religion, but rather the absence of true faith. Intolerance inevitably brings about the hardening of one's spiritual arteries and leads to conceit and arrogance. True faith in one's own beliefs and values is quite compatible with genuine appreciation of the elements of value in other faiths. Intolerance of dissent, in the final analysis, results from a compulsive drive to abolish cultural plurality in the human family.

B) Concept of Authenticity:

Azad's view that a common '*deen*' underlies the diversity of religious symbols, rituals, social customs and laws (collectively termed '*Shariah*') is a liberating insight which he shares with Sir Syed and also the Sufis. Islamic liberals in general define '*iman*' as authentic commitment to Islam as a '*deen*'. But what about authentic commitment to '*deen's*' other than the Islamic *deen*, as such? It is impossible to claim that there are no '*deen's*' other than Islam in the face of the obvious plurality of creeds and religious traditions found in the human family. And it is equally obvious that some among the devotees or followers of any particular '*deen*' are truly sincere and also authentic, some are sincere but not authentic in the strict sense of having made an inner free choice, some are 'strategic hypocrites', while some (perhaps the great majority of the followers) are merely products of

Supplemental Essay 3: Sir Syed, Iqbal and Azad

cultural conditioning. It appears to me that Islamic liberals (including Sir Syed, Iqbal and Azad) stop at this point. They do not reach the level of Sufi poets and other mystics who have arrived at the concept of 'pure authenticity' or 'authentic being', in the contemporary existentialist sense. This means that a person begins to hear the depth whispers of his own being in the stillness of his inner freedom and then freely responds, to the inscrutable mystery of 'Being'. Authenticity, in the existentialist sense, is not bound to any particular faith or set of beliefs, just as Kant's 'good will' is not bound to any particular system of morality.

The above existentialist approach accords the highest value or sanctity to the condition of 'pure authenticity' of an inwardly free man quite irrespective of the concrete belief system he may hold. Now, if this approach be accepted, a sincere Muslim believer, without compromising his own Islamic faith, may well venerate an authentic Christian. Likewise, a theist may respect an atheist, provided the latter be authentic, that is, if his atheism is an inwardly free and honest response to the mystery of Being. Both Sir Syed and Iqbal stressed '*iman*' more than '*Shariah*'. But for both of them '*iman*' meant Islamic '*iman*', rather than 'pure authenticity' in the strict contemporary existentialist sense when an inwardly free truth-seeker, in all humility and courage, confronts the mystery of 'Being'. 'Authenticity', in the above sense, eludes the reach of Azad. Neither Sir Syed, nor Azad, embrace it in its full depth, as is done by some contemporary Christian theologians.

Muslim theologians are yet distant from assimilating this liberating concept, though the Sufis did this long ago. The 19th century Urdu poet, Ghalib, celebrates this concept, but then, he had no theological credentials.

C) Religion as a Particular Language of the Spirit:

Leading contemporary analytical and existentialist thinkers hold that every religion is a particular mode of existential response to the mystery of 'Being'. No particular response or existential perspective can be proved in the logical or scientific sense; each response, however, can be of varying degrees of depth commitment. In other words, religious experience is closer to moral or aesthetic awareness, rather than to perceptual or logical cognition. Another way of expressing the same insight is to hold that each religion is a distinct language for expressing man's idea of the Holy and the human sense of reverence and mystery at the contemplation of 'Being', without its having been fractured through perception or conceptualization. Just like natural languages, each language of the spirit has its own distinctive idiom and grammar, or symbols and rites, which perform, basically, the same three functions of self-purification, inner fortification and cosmic integration. Now, in view of the in-built diversities of the human situation the idea of 'one humanity-one language', does not sound feasible, even though this is logically possible. Just as linguistic hegemony is, practically, ruled out in the case of natural languages, it is, also ruled out for the different 'languages of the spirit' spoken by the human family. In other words, the human family requires not one formal religion, or the dominance of any particular religion, but full freedom of growth and loving dialogue between fellow-pilgrims in the quest for values whose horizons ever recede as moves forward.

Azad's liberal views on the unity of faith (*deen*), universal salvation and the separation of politics and religion were steps in the broad direction of religious existentialism and pluralism in the place of the global hegemony of any particular religious tradition.

D) The Principle of Secularism:

Azad's principled separation of politics and religion, in the Indian context, is right. But his writings and public utterances do not make it sufficiently clear what course he proposed for predominantly Muslim societies. It needs pointing out that secularism is right not only in the case of mixed societies but also in the case of predominantly Muslim societies. The rationale behind this approach is that the social customs and the polity (which Muslims inherited from its original Jewish and Arab environment) must be de-linked from the core of the Islamic faith and value system. The primary scope of the *Shariah* ought to be restricted to pure spirituality as the essence of religion (*deen*). Polity, in the modern age, ought to be guided by democratic decision making based on autonomous and informed inquiry, as is being done in the case of natural sciences.

The first to affirm the principled separation of religion from politics were the founding fathers of the American Constitution, although they themselves were deeply committed to the Christian faith and to value based politics. Their reason was that the union of religion and politics, inevitably, makes the established religion intolerant of other religions. This was the precise and precious lesson America had learnt from the experience of the European peoples.

Supplemental Essay 3: Sir Syed, Iqbal and Azad

The principled separation of church and state, however, does not mean or imply that politics has no need to be regulated by moral and spiritual values. I strongly feel that many who strongly oppose secular politics and insist that the lasting strength and beauty of true Islam lies, precisely, in preserving and promoting the *'organic unity of religion and state'*, consciously or subconsciously equate secular politics with immoral or unethical politics. They do so because of their still deeper conviction that morality and spirituality are not possible without belief in a personal God or without following religious laws or prescriptions in every walk of life. I submit that this belief is a half-truth. This is not the place to debate this complex issue. I have fully discussed this issue in my other published works.

About Jamal Khwaja
and His Works

Jamal Khwaja has written seven major books, numerous articles and scholarly essays. Anyone interested in the intersection of Islam and Modernity will find Khwaja to be a reliable guide. Readers of his work will be informed, inspired, and intellectually liberated. Muslim readers will feel emotionally aligned with the Qur'an and find themselves empowered to live as authentic Muslims in the heart of the multicultural global village.

Khwaja's work is the definitive contemporary discussion regarding Islam and Modernity. Explore it. You will be profoundly rewarded.

Some illuminating excerpts from his works are presented below. They will enable readers to see for themselves the clarity, range and depth of his writings.

Jamal Khwaja was born in Delhi in 1928*. His ancestors had been closely connected with the Islamic reform movement, inaugurated by Sir Syed Ahmed Khan, the founder of the famous M.A.O. College, Aligarh in the second half of the 19th century, and the Indian freedom movement under Gandhi's leadership in the first half of the 20th century. After doing his M.A. in Philosophy from the Aligarh Muslim University, India, he obtained an Honors degree from Christ's College Cambridge, UK. Later he spent a year studying the German language and European existentialism at Munster University, Germany. At Cambridge he was deeply influenced

---

*   Jamal Khwaja was born in Delhi on August 12, 1926. However, most official records show 1928 as the year of birth.

Appendix: About Jamal Khwaja and His Works

by the work of C.D. Broad, Wittgenstein and John Wisdom, apart from his college tutor, I.T. Ramsey who later became Professor of Christian Religion at Oxford. It was the latter's influence, which, taught Khwaja to appreciate the inner beauty and power of pure spirituality. Khwaja was thus led to appreciate the value of linguistic analysis as a tool of philosophical inquiry and to combine the quest for clarity with the insights and depth of the existentialist approach to religion and spirituality.

Khwaja was appointed Lecturer in Philosophy at the *Aligarh Muslim University* in 1953. Before he could begin serious academic work in his chosen field, his family tradition of public work pulled him into a brief spell of active politics under the charismatic Jawahar Lal Nehru; the first Prime Minister of India. Nehru was keen to rejuvenate his team of colleagues through inducting fresh blood into the *Indian National Congress*. He included young Khwaja, then freshly returned from Cambridge, along with four or five other young persons. Khwaja thus became one of the youngest entrants into the Indian Parliament as a member of the *Lok Sabha* (Lower House) from 1957 to 1962. While in the corridors of power, he learned to distinguish between ideals and illusions, and finally chose to pursue the path of knowledge, rather than the path of acquiring authority or power. Returning to his *alma mater* in 1962, he resumed teaching and research in the philosophy of religion. Ever since then Khwaja has lived a quiet life in Aligarh. He was Dean of the *Faculty of Arts* and was a member of important committees of the University Grants Commission and the *Indian Council for Philosophical Research* before retiring as Professor and Chairman of the *Department of Philosophy* in 1988. He was a frequent and active participant in national seminars held at the *Indian Institute of Advanced Study* in Shimla.

He was invited to deliver the *Khuda Bakhsh Memorial Lecture* in Patna. He was one of the official Indian delegates at the *World Philosophical Congress, Brighton*, UK, in 1988, also at the *International Islamic Conference Kuala Lumpur*, Malaysia, in 1967, and the *Pakistan International Philosophy Congress, Peshawar*, Pakistan, in 1964. He has visited the USA and several countries in Western Europe. He performed the *Hajj* in 2005.

Appendix: About Jamal Khwaja and His Works

Khwaja's written works include,

1. *Five Approaches To Philosophy: A discerning philosopher philosophizes about the philosophy of philosophy with wisdom and clarity.*

2. *Quest For Islam: A philosophers approach to religion in the age of science and cultural pluralism.*

3. *Authenticity And Islamic Liberalism: A mature vision of Islamic Liberalism grounded in the Qur'an.*

4. *Essays On Cultural Pluralism: A philosophical framework for authentic interfaith dialogue.*

5. *The Call Of Modernity And Islam: A Muslim's journey into the 21st century.*

6. *Living The Qur'an In Our Times: A vision of how Muslims can revitalize their faith, while being faithful to God and His messenger.*

7. *The Vision Of An Unknown Indian Muslim: My journey to interfaith spirituality.*

Please visit
www.JamalKhwaja.com
for more information

Appendix: About Jamal Khwaja and His Works

1. Five Approaches to Philosophy

A Discerning Philosopher Philosophizes About The Philosophy Of Philosophy With Wisdom and Clarity

This monograph attempts to describe the different, approaches to philosophy, their situational and conceptual fields, their interrelations and limitations. The possibility of combining them into a multidimensional approach is also discussed.

The key notion underlying this essay is that the actual doing of philosophy must be rooted in a critical and comparative meta-philosophy. Most philosophers are so busy in establishing truths, or analyzing words and sentences, as the case may be, that they tend to neglect meta-philosophy. This leads to methodological isolationism and a polemical instead of an irenic approach to philosophical problems.

Excerpts

The present human situation is characterized by scientific uniformity and progress in the midst of philosophical controversy and religious and cultural diversity. This is perhaps the most significant feature of the contemporary situation. This generates the basic conceptual field for the critically oriented contemporary philosopher. It may be called the meta-philosophical field. Methodological, questions like the nature of philosophical, metaphysical, ethical and logical statements, the theories of meaning and truth, and the nature and dynamics of philosophical or ethical controversy, etc., arise within this field. Controversy and disagreement in the midst of progressively expanding scientific and technological standardization appear as anachronisms to the contemporary mind. It is impelled to find the causes and the cure of this incongruity. This leads to

Appendix: About Jamal Khwaja and His Works

an unprecedented interest in meta-problems of almost all the branches of knowledge. The value judgment underlying this quest is that avoidable controversy or conflict is bad and must be overcome. The contemporary analytical and meta-philosophical approaches are the new instruments to serve this basic value, even as previous metaphysical systems were the instruments of serving and defending some value system or other, embedded in past cultural traditions. In other words, harmony or agreement is the motif of contemporary meta-philosophy. It may be said that this is the motif of all philosophy and religion as such. This is probably true. But the range of harmony sought by contemporary philosophers is immensely wider than the range previously sought. Moreover, there is a distinction between a democratic harmony among autonomous individuals freely committing themselves to values, and the harmony that ensues as a result of the commitment to an external *Authority*. No doubt the philosophical theologian claims that since his acceptance of the *Authority* is based upon universally valid reasons, the harmony that accrues is rooted in reason rather than a dogmatic or arbitrary surrender to an *Authority*. *(Chapter 1)*

If philosophical theories and systems are conceptual patterns, then how and in what sense can they be true or false? A landscape or a musical composition may be good or bad. But there is no sense in judging them to be true or false. If, however, philosophy claims to be a conceptual picture of the Universe, as a portrait is of an individual, say, Napoleon, then the terms true or false are applicable to philosophy. But in the case of a portrait, we have the original subject as well as the painting, and the two can be compared. Now where is the original subject in the case of the Universe? Surely, the observed features of the Universe are there. But a philosophical theory is not descriptive. Consider the case of a number of architects, each pressing his design for acceptance by the town planners. There is no standard or Platonic design, with reference to which the claims of the architects could be tested and settled. Even if there were such design, but was in principle inaccessible, there would be no point in claiming truth for a particular design. All that legitimately could be claimed by an architect was that his particular design had such & such advantages under specified conditions, apart from aesthetic value. *(Chapter 4)*

The choice of a valid conceptual field on the basis of the criteria suggested is ultimately a function of reflection and not of an investigation of the facts. Thus the possibility of eventual disagreement among philosophers cannot be eliminated, even though the choice is not arbitrary. Two persons may agree to the rules and yet differ in their application. Philosophical disagreement is thus unavoidable. No approach can eliminate disagreement without any remainder. But the type of disagreement that remains on the multidimensional approach would be the unavoidable minimum like the unavoidable minimum friction of a well-constructed and well-oiled machine or moving body. It would be a fraction of the disagreement that results from a non meta-philosophical or a mono-dimensional approach. The disputes about the nature and tasks of philosophy are a function of a one sided fixation upon selective Paradigms of philosophical questions and answers. The monopolistic grip of selective instances of a general concept is a fairly widespread phenomenon. Marx's theory of the determinants of social change, Freud's theory of the determinants of neuroses, and the different theories of truth or of knowledge, the different theories of the nature of ethical judgments, etc., are all reminders of how the fondness for particular instances or paradigms leads to a general theory concerning the subject matter. Rather than accept or reject any particular theory of philosophy, we must try to see how far it is illuminating, and how far misleading. *(Chapter 7)*

2. Quest For Islam
A Philosopher's Approach To Religion In The Age Of Science And Cultural Pluralism

Quest for Islam is a systematic exposition of Islam in the light of contemporary knowledge by a practicing Muslim. A seminal work, it successfully resolves intellectual difficulties created in traditional interpretations by new knowledge. Among other things, it organically integrates core Islamic values with the requirements of plural societies and secular democracies. It thus adds a fresh dimension of value to the Islamic thought-cum-value system. It will appeal greatly to Muslim intellectuals perplexed by the assault of modernity on traditional values and institutions.

Excerpts

The Universe has some basic features which may be said to be its warp and woof, and which remain the same throughout history, e.g., the features of law and order, harmony and beauty of nature, man's moral sense, as distinct from concrete moral codes, the struggle for survival of the species and of individuals, pain and suffering, hope and joy, birth, growth, decay, and death. Natural science does not concern itself with the significance or meaning of these features of the Universe, that is, whether they are just accidental features and could therefore disappear from the cosmic scene, as accidentally as they appeared; or whether they stand rooted in the constitution of the Universe and thus have an *ontic* status or permanent reality. Now the way in which one interprets these features simultaneously influences the personality orientation of the individual, and is in turn, influenced by the original bent of the personality itself.

In other words, there is a dialectical relationship between the existential interpretation and the personality orientation. The interpretation becomes important, since it influences man's inner responses to the Universe in a most subtle manner, though the interpretation has no prima facie bearing upon man's empirical, ethical, or aesthetic response. But the fact is that different existential interpretations constitute different ways of treating the Universe or relating oneself to it, and this inevitably influences the individual's lifestyle and also raises the question as to which particular style is right, and why so. To give an analogy, the practicing scientist does not concern himself with the question whether or why nature behaves uniformly, but takes it for granted, as if it were self-evident or necessarily true, or because it works. But the denial of causal uniformity does not involve any logical contradiction; nor can it be logically proved.

We accept it for two reasons: first, our actual experience suggests as if it were true; and, second, if it were not true, no point would be left in our scientific inquiries, which we deem as valuable and worth pursuing. Likewise, there would be no point left or, to be more accurate, the urge to pursue values would be far less intense, if values were chance and ephemeral products of the blind dance of atoms, without the conservation and growth of values being ontologically guaranteed, despite all seeming obstacles. The concept of God is precisely one particular form of this faith. Belief in God implies that values like truth, goodness, and beauty are neither chance products, nor ultimate and un-derived features of the Universe, but have their source in the ultimate and Supreme Being with whom man could establish an 'I-Thou' dialogue. The existential interpretation is neither a hypothesis, nor a partly justifiable postulate; it is a motivational re-enforcer that integrates the individual's thoughts and feelings into a stable inner way of life or mode of treating the Universe, as distinct from ad hoc and ever variable responses or attitudes. *(Chapter 1)*

If, and when, the interpretation does not harmonize with the scientific conceptual scheme, a revision of its concrete sense may remove the prima facie discord. We may say, for instance, that God's love for His creation is not the same as a mother's love for her child, or that what appears as evil works as an instrumental good in a larger context. This task involves redefining, analyzing, explaining, making distinctions or comparisons either in the spirit of a free exploration of the given data or in the spirit of a defensive reconciliation between theology and science. In the former case, the role of reason is primary, while in the latter, it is secondary. The theologian explores new meanings of traditional concepts in a spirit of defensive reverence to the tradition, while the philosopher freely reflects upon the validity of the religious interpretation. He checks whether the actual data of human experience harmonize with the religious interpretation. This activity, however, does not involve deductive or inductive reasoning but existential elucidation, that is, the illumination of one's hidden depth attitudes, choices, interpretative responses, or images. An existential interpretation, which is chosen by the philosopher, is thus functionally similar to, but genetically or methodologically different from, religious faith. An existential interpretation of some kind or another is unavoidable.

We can only opt for this or that interpretation, but we cannot opt to do away with all interpretation as such. We may claim to avoid all contact with metaphysics or religion, which we may view as the hallmarks of a pre-scientific mentality. Yet the fact is that we cannot live as integrated human beings without some kind of worldview or total perspective on the cosmos. This total perspective, be it religious or philosophical, is at bottom always an existential interpretation of the basic features of human experience cosmic law and order, the mysteries of birth, growth and death, the beauty as well as the fury of nature, good and evil, joy and tragedy. Religious faith is the pre-logical acceptance of an interpretation because of its existential grip over the believer. *(Chapter 1)*

Appendix: About Jamal Khwaja and His Works

3. Authenticity And Islamic Liberalism
A Mature Vision Of Islamic Liberalism Grounded In The Qur'an

"Authenticity and Islamic Liberalism" is a collection of four original and highly stimulating papers on the liberal existentialist approach to religion with special reference to Islam in India. Each paper deals with an independent theme; yet, a consistent analytical existentialist approach makes them a well-orchestrated and balanced exposition of what may best be called "Islamic Liberalism."

Excerpts

Every religion has a nuclear core of basic beliefs and values embedded in a wide cultural matrix comprising myths, ancient collective memories, folklore, customs, and stereotyped images, etc. All these elements are enmeshed and the ordinary believer hardly cares to separate the nuclear core from the total cultural matrix of faith and practice. The total cultural tradition is the spiritual atmosphere in which he lives, moves and has his being. The German religious thinker of the 20th century, Bultmann, called the gradual process of distilling the nuclear core of Christian thought and value system from the cultural matrix of the Christian tradition, the 'demythologization of Christianity. This concept, however, has universal and timeless relevance to all religious traditions. Several creative thinkers and savants of Islam; Al-Beruni (d. app. 1040), Ibn Sina (d. 1037), Ibn Rushd (d. 1198), Al-Ghazzali (d. 1111), Ibn Arabi (d. 1240), Jalaluddin Rumi (d. 1273), Fariduddin Attar (d. 1229), Ibn Khaldun (d. 1406), Shah Wali Ullah (d. 1763) and others attempted to grasp the essence of Islam.

Sir Syed attempted to distill the nuclear essence of Islam in the framework of modern thought, as he understood it. He was not a professionally trained philosopher, social scientist or historian. But his extraordinarily sharp intellect, intuitive insight and common sense, and above all, his intellectual honesty and moral courage enabled him to distill the nuclear core of Islam from its concrete historical forms in space and time. It is instructive to recall that in his earlier pre-critical phase, Sir Syed had adhered to the conventional ideas of his milieu, though even then he had come under the influence of the, relatively, liberal philosophical theology of Shah Wali Ullah, of Delhi. However, soon after the failure of the great Indian rebellion of 1857 against British imperial rule, when Syed Ahmad was roughly forty five, he outgrew his honestly held ideas and values and became clearly aware of their limitations, without, however, ever rejecting the nuclear core of his Islamic faith. Those who were unable to appreciate the spiritual pilgrimage of the great man and the organic growth of his ideas charged him with having abandoned Islam or distorting the faith for ulterior motives. Half a century later Abul Kalam Azad passed through a similar experience. *(Supplemental Essay 3)*

Azad's principled separation of politics and religion, in the Indian context, is right. His writings and public utterances do not make it sufficiently clear what course he proposed for predominantly Muslim societies. It needs pointing out that secularism is right not only in the case of mixed societies but also in the case of predominantly Muslim societies. The rationale behind this approach is that the social customs and the polity (which Muslims inherited from its original Jewish and Arab environment) must be de-linked from the core of the Islamic faith and value system. The primary scope of the *shariah* ought to be restricted to pure spirituality as the essence of religion (*deen*). Polity, in the modern age, ought to be guided by democratic decision making based on autonomous and informed inquiry, as is being done in the case of natural sciences. The first to affirm the principled separation of religion from politics were the founding fathers of the American constitution, although they themselves were deeply committed to the Christian faith and to value based politics. Their reason was that the union of religion and politics, inevitably, makes the established religion intolerant of other religions. This was the precise and precious lesson America had learned from the experience of the European peoples.

The principled separation of church and state, however, does not mean or imply that politics has no need to be regulated by moral and spiritual values. I strongly feel that many who strongly oppose secular politics and insist that the lasting strength and beauty of true Islam lies, precisely, in preserving and promoting the 'organic unity of religion and state', consciously or subconsciously equate secular politics with immoral or unethical politics. They do so because of their still deeper conviction that morality and spirituality are not possible without belief in a personal God or without following religious laws or prescriptions in every walk of life. I submit that this belief is a half-truth. This is not the place to debate this complex issue. I have fully discussed this issue in my other published works. *(Pages 188-189)*

Appendix: About Jamal Khwaja and His Works

4. Essays On Cultural Pluralism

A Philosophical Approach To Interfaith Spirituality In The Age Of Science

Ours are times when religion is systematically being used; unconsciously by some and deliberately by others, in the service of politics and personal gain, rather than spirituality. However, perceptive and honest minds among all religious communities view different religions as diverse "languages of the spirit," each valid and nourishing in its own way.

An impartial study of different religions shows the underlying unity in the diversity of religions. All religions are attempts to satisfy the human sense of wonder and awe at the inscrutable mystery of the Universe. This common function produces the unity while the diverse conditions in which different religions arise and grow produce the diversity.

Excerpts

Now, though Mahavira and Buddha denied *Brahman* and the sanctity and infallibility of the Vedas, they both accepted basic moral and spiritual values and the principle of *karma*. It is, therefore, reasonable to hold that the followers of Mahavira and Buddha, or for that matter, the followers of any other religious tradition (provided they eschew the moral evils or vices mentioned above) do not come under the purview of the above verses of the Gita. In other words, the approach of the Gita is so catholic that notwithstanding its own commitment to *Vaishnavite Anthrotheism* (faith in the divinity of Sri Krishna), it seems to permit the conceptual elimination of even God/Brahman from one's value system for agnostics and others. Possibly, this is the explanation of how and why both Jainism and Buddhism, after an extended period of conflict with Brahmanical orthodoxy, and even a measure of persecution by the custodians of the

Vedic tradition, eventually came to be regarded as unorthodox schools or sects of Hinduism in the larger sense.

Blessed are the good and simple and authentic believers in a caring Personal God. Blessed are they who can plumb the depths of their being and can hear *'the music of the spheres'* and see *'the light of a thousand suns blaze forth all at once'*, and act dutifully without attachment to the fruits. Blessed too are they whose journey in inner space brings them to *'Brahman without attributes'*, and fortifies the *'Atman'*. But what about those whose honest and sustained quest for truth meets with a bewildered inner silence and the darkness of an unending night of the soul, and yet they remain sensitive to truth, goodness and beauty, and go on responding to the call of duty for its own sake? This is the crucial question facing and dividing humanity today. *(Essay 1)*

An impartial study of different religions shows the underlying unity in the diversity of religions. All religions are attempts to satisfy the human sense of wonder and awe at the inscrutable mystery of the Universe. This common function produces the unity while the diverse conditions in which different religions arise and grow produce the diversity. However, the differences in belief, on a deeper analysis, turn out to be merely different ways of performing the same function in the basic economy of human life. In other words, different beliefs turn out to be different versions or species of a more basic generic belief. For instance, the belief that God reveals His will to a human messenger or prophet and the belief that God incarnates Himself in human form are two different versions or species of the more fundamental conviction that God intervenes in history to guide man on the right path. Neither of the two beliefs is fully intelligible or transparent to the human mind and both are full of mystery. Likewise, the basic Aryan belief in repeated rebirths in this world and the basic Semitic belief in one single eschatological rebirth are twin species of the more fundamental conviction that as a man soweth, so shall he reap in one form or the other. Both beliefs posit the continuity of life, either in the 'linear' or the 'cyclical' sense, and both motivate man to the same end. *(Essay 3)*

Appendix: About Jamal Khwaja and His Works

If one looks at history from the humanist perspective the political or religious conflicts of the human family in the past turn into humanity's march (in circuitous and halting stages) towards a global federal unity. The victory of an Alexander and the defeat of a Porus in India, the almost total destruction of Baghdad by a Hulagu and the devastations in north India by a Nadir Shah, the compassion of an Ashoka, the statesmanship of an Akbar, the aberrations of a Hitler, all become the achievements or failures of the human family. With charity for all and malice toward none, the historian passes judgment on the deed, rather than the doer. His standards remain consistent, but he takes into account that human ideas and ideals are subject to the law of evolutionary growth. In short, his range of sympathy gradually becomes universal instead of remaining congealed at a particular parochial level determined by his birth or early conditioning.

It is significant that the data of history are not given to the truth seeker, as are the data of nature to the scientific investigator through sense perception or experiments under controlled conditions of observation. The data of history are themselves, in part, constructs out of surviving remains of past things or events. Moreover, no two historians select exactly the same set of data out of the total range available. Historians select their own unique 'effective' data for a systematic narrative and analysis of the past. The historian fits these data in his favored framework of ideas and values out of several alternatives available. No such framework, as such, can be proved as conclusively true, or valid. Yet, one must have some basic frame of orientation (as pointed out by Erich Fromm) in order to understand or existentially respond to the human situation in totality.

Religions and philosophies, in different ways, perform this function. They hold their effective data together and enable one to arrive at a total perspective on the human situation as such. Thus, a historian having a *Hindutva* frame of orientation would tend to view Sultan Mahmud's destruction of the Somnath temple, Gujarat, in the 10th century as an Islamic attack on Hindu India. A historian with a humanist sociological orientation would view the same episode as a medieval Sultan's lust for booty. This admission, however, does not amount to unrelieved relativity of historical interpretation as such.

Let me explain this point further. A reliable contemporary Persian record of Mahmud's time states that after returning to his capital, covered with glory and laden with booty, the Sultan sent some valuable gifts to a venerated divine of Ghazna; Qazi Abul Hasan Baulami. The Qazi returned the royal gifts and severely chastised the Sultan for violating the *shariah*, which prohibited the desecration of any place of worship. Obviously, the honest and bold response of the Qazi had no effect upon the Sultan and the general course of events in medieval time. However, the above authentic story makes it quite clear that the primary *'leitmotif'* of the medieval Sultans was personal aggrandizement and expansion of power, not the promotion of Islam or forcible conversion. In this sense and to this extent, therefore, the humanist interpretation of history becomes more valid than the *Hindutva* interpretation that rejoices in Muslim baiting and distortion of the past. By the same token those Muslims who glorify Sultan Mahmud as an Islamic hero, misinterpret or distort Islam and also harm Muslims and all of humanity. *(Essay 6)*

Appendix: About Jamal Khwaja and His Works

5. The Call of Modernity And Islam
A Muslim's Journey Into The 21st Century

The Call Of Modernity And Islam is a timely and welcome anthology of ten scholarly essays that focus creatively on the urgent need to re-energize Islamic culture and institutions. The essays span an enormous disciplinary range. Professor Khwaja moves back and forth with consummate ease between religion, science, philosophy, history, and the social sciences to paint a fully integrated, big picture of the encounter between Islam and modernity.

Excerpts

The predicament of Muslims in the modern age is that their religious tradition stands for the unity of religion and state while the modern mind stands for the separation of religion and state. The Islamic tradition is that Islam is not merely a spiritual discipline, but a complete way of life, including a polity (*shariah*). Though not inspired like the Qur'an, the *shariah* is deemed as all embracing and sacrosanct. Only the *ulema* are empowered to modify it according to a definite procedure. But it would be absurd to claim or expect that the *shariah* should be binding on the Parliament of a sovereign secular state. Muslims in general hold that a sovereign secular democratic state is bound to fall headlong into 'Satanic' politics and the amoral pursuit of power. In other words, they equate the separation of religion from politics with immoral politics. They honestly tend to hold that the secular approach to politics destroys or erodes true Islam, which is a seamless and complete map of conduct according to Divine guidance.

This is the spiritual predicament of traditional Muslims all over the world including the followers of Mawdudi's school of Islamic thought that is, relatively, liberal, but falls short of the fully integrated and spiritualized religious sensibility of the modern mind. Western educated Muslims in general, and, particularly, those belonging to plural societies are, increasingly, becoming aware of this predicament. But they lack the moral courage and credentials to question the validity of the time honored traditional approach and the exclusive authority of the *ulema* in such matters. Another reason why the educated Muslim laity is reluctant to assert itself is the lack of proper grounding in religious learning and the Arabic language. These perplexed believers silently wait for the day when the *ulema*, on their own, will take the initiative to revise or redefine the proper scope of the *shariah*. The *ulema*, hardly aware of the complex issues of modernity (understandably) suffer and, unconsciously, go on the defensive when confronted with the immense gap between medieval learning and the much more developed natural and social sciences in the modern age.

I submit, in all humility, they, in the best interests of all concerned, should ponder on the full implications of four basic truths: (a) granted that all Muslim believers must accept the Qur'anic text as infallible, no human interpretation of the text can claim to be infallibly true; (b) interpretation, in some form or other, necessarily, enters into all efforts at understanding the Qur'anic text; c) the proper understanding of any communication involves a frame of reference within which the 'addressee' interprets the words or expressions used in the original communication; (d) the frame of reference as well as the concrete meanings or usages of words, necessarily change in the course of time. These truths apply to all communications or languages including the 'Word of God'. It follows that whosoever interprets the Qur'an, whether one be an Arabic speaking lay person or scholar, necessarily, interprets the Scripture relative to one's own set of Arabic usage and understanding of the context of the communication. *(Essay 2)*

6. Living The Quran In Our Times

A vision of how Muslims can revitalize their faith, while being faithful to God and His messenger

In the past, authentic Muslims, including the closest Companions of the Prophet, often differed sharply in their political and social beliefs. In our times, the challenges posed by modernity have made such differences especially toxic. In this work, the Author clarifies the core teachings of perennial Islam and their continuing relevance to our daily lives.

Excerpts

Perennial Islam, as joyful submission to one Supreme Creator and acceptance of the Qur'an as the *'Word of God'*, revealed to Prophet Muhammad, is one thing; the surrender to a static *shariah* conceived as a perfect and total guide for the believer in every walk of life, is quite another. To remain rooted in the perennial spiritual values of the Qur'an, as exemplified in the life and character of the historical Muhammad, the *'Seal of the Prophets'* is one thing; to hold that this implies that believers should actively strive to become 'carbon copies' of the Prophet's actions and life style is quite another. Rootedness in the basic Qur'anic values does not imply a mechanical and un-reflective adherence to Qur'anic injunctions without making a distinction between 'intrinsic' values and 'instrumental' rules. Likewise, genuine reverence and love for the Prophet does not imply the uncritical acceptance of the many miracles or myths

Appendix: About Jamal Khwaja and His Works

found in the popular versions of the Islamic faith, especially the dramatic detailed events and dialogues mentioned in the stories of the Prophet's journey *(meraj)* to God's Throne. To deny such myths or miracles in no way diminishes his sublime spiritual status and his authentic mystical experiences, or his amazing achievements as a historical figure. Muslims generally believe that Prophet Muhammad must have possessed supernatural powers on the ground that earlier prophets performed miracles. Prophet Muhammad being the greatest, God must have endowed him with similar, if not greater, powers, so it is held to be the case. Muslims commonly cite the Qur'anic verse (54:1) as evidence that Prophet Muhammad performed the miracle of splitting the moon *(shaqq ul Qamar)*. Numerous saints and mystics of Islam are also credited with possessing extra-ordinary powers through Divine grace. Sufi tombs attract numerous devotees (both Muslim and others) who seek the intervention of the saints in securing various material benefits for themselves. However, the Qur'an gives no warrant at all for accepting this traditional image of Prophet Muhammad. Indeed, the Qur'an categorically denies that Prophet Muhammad possessed supernatural powers with the sole exception of the gift of Divine revelation *(wahi)*. In other words, the Qur'an is the only miracle, which Prophet Muhammad claimed to possess. *(Chapter 1)*

Millions and millions of Muslim believers will surely and rightly continue to venerate Prophet Muhammad as the perfect exemplar for humanity. An ever-swelling number of non-Muslims of eminence now also acknowledge the administrative, moral and spiritual genius of Prophet Muhammad as one of the super-architects and shapers of human destiny on the world scale. The crucial question is what should be the concrete form, in the modern age, of a true Muslim's veneration for Prophet Muhammad. In answer to the above crucial question, I submit that true reverence and fidelity to Prophet Muhammad consists in trying to make his basic values and objectives, rather than the details of the Prophet's conduct, the pivot of our own lives and activities.

The promotion of Prophet Muhammad's basic values (even if

this task today requires modifying his instructions given in particular situations) is the real meaning of following his example (*sunnah*) in an ever-changing world. This is, precisely, what Caliph Omar had done. The following considerations should help perplexed Muslim believers to realize this liberating truth. First, development or growth takes place in different fields of human activity despite interruptions, retrogressions and reverses. This applies not only to factual knowledge but also to human ideals, values and institutions. Thus, have arisen fresh interpretations of the good life. Universal human rights, rule by consent, peaceful transfer of power, tolerance of dissent, gender equality, and equality of opportunity, are some of the ideals that are the fresh characteristics of the modern age.

Static norms of perfection cannot but arrest the natural movement of ideas and ideals. No particular stage of development can be said to be perfect. It may be thought that for the committed Muslim, at least, the Qur'an is beyond the shadow of imperfection. The crucial point is that the Qur'an has to be understood by human beings whose conceptual framework is bound to change with the passage of time. This framework will always remain subject to various imperfections or limitations. Thus, even if we concede the Qur'an, as the Word of God, to be perfect, its human understanding will always remain a matter of perfection aspired to rather than perfection achieved. Ceaseless growth towards perfection rather than perfection as such is all that man can hope for. Second, a clear distinction should be made between basic values and instrumental rules. The Muslim segment of the human family will not advance forward, but move in ruts alone, if Muslims do not sift the instrumental prescriptions of the Prophet from his basic goals and objectives. The making of this distinction between basic objectives and the means for realizing them should not be confused with the rather facile view that the end justifies the means.

Third, a clear distinction will also have to be made between matters of personal taste and matters of morality and spirituality. Real and honest commitment to the values of the Prophet does not mean that the individual give up his inclinations and preferences in matters of taste.

Fourth, the reported sayings and doings of the Prophet Muhammad are not sufficiently authentic despite the arduous efforts by dedicated and gifted Muslim researchers to separate the chaff from the grain. Though it is true that several Qur'anic texts are inexplicable or will remain vague unless read in the light of the reported sayings or doings of the Prophet there is no justification for bracketing the Qur'an and the *hadith* as equally authentic, or binding. Respect for the latter does not mean unquestioning acceptance. Keeping the above four considerations in mind should help us to realize that the real meaning of fidelity to Prophet Muhammad is not the literal imitation of his conduct but the honest and intelligent endeavor to translate the basic values of the Qur'an and hence of the Prophet into practice in an ever changing human situation. *(Chapter 1)*

Mere conformity to the instrumental rules without intelligently searching for what exactly right action means in the ever-changing human situation society will yield only marginal benefits. The principled acceptance of the semantic distinction between prescriptive Qur'anic verses referring to basic values and those referring to instrumental rules prepares the ground for the believer's own free commitment to basic values without any loss of spiritual autonomy. This transforms obedience to the 'Word of God' into the enjoyment of inner freedom. The Prophet's character beautifully exemplifies these basic values that can never be exhausted by the instrumental rules of the *shariah*. The character of the historical Muhammad, however, is a perennial source of inspiration to humankind in its ceaseless (but ever incomplete) aspiration for attaining perfection and truth. The authentic and prayerful reflection on the Qur'an touches the deepest chord of the authentic human conscience, which is itself the Divine spark in humanity after the individual learns to deconstruct his or her natural ethnocentricity. This is, indeed, the miracle of the Qur'an. *(Chapter 3)*

Reading or reciting my favorite Qur'anic *surahs* or verses, in the original Arabic, profoundly moves me and millions of Muslims, and also many others. However, other scriptures can, and do inspire others, in the same way. I accept this fact with a sense of wonder and humility at the power of different 'sources of inspiration and inner light'. Individuals do get inner light and inspiration from a variety of historical sources, but the ultimate or apex Source is one. The crucial question is not where the light comes from; the crucial question is whether there is light in the inner world of the individual. Any deeply committed believer (no matter what his religion) who acts righteously (according to his authentic values), and concedes that his own faith or conceptualization of the Supreme Mystery of Being is not the only window to the inscrutable mystery, is, to my mind, a fellow pilgrim on the journey of the spirit. To give an analogy from the realm of human love, if one truly loves, no matter whom he loves, he/she attains to the highest level of bliss and blessedness. Obviously, in the realm of love every lover has his or her own beloved and this love brings one into the portals of the Divine.

The fruit of spirituality blossoms on different theological creeds. The essence of spirituality or religious faith, at its best, is the realization of the truth of the unity of all existence and the striving to translate this idea into concrete action. I would, therefore, submit that in the modern age the bare minimum connotation or core of the Islamic faith is as follows: all that exists is the creation of one supreme, self-existing being, and the Qur'an is the revealed 'Word of God' to Prophet Muhammad—as the final exemplar and guide for the Muslims in the never ending and ever evolving quest for the good life. This approach, however, does not imply that no other human exemplars and guides perform the same function for other believers. The ideal of spiritual pluralism is embedded in the Qur'an itself when we read it without the gloss of its various interpretations in the course of history, especially when one tries to discover the underlying spirit and thrust of the Qur'an and the authentic life of Prophet Muhammad, without importing myth or miracle, or resorting to the personality cult.

Creeds and dogmas of any historical religion may appeal to one but leave the other indifferent, may fascinate one but amuse the other. However, the divine flame of spiritual wonder, the wordless but prayerful surrender to the cosmic mystery and retreat into inner silence of the spirit (*shoonya*) is, to my mind, the only '*jewel that shines by its own light*'. Once we accept this we begin to see that different creeds, dogmas or thought patterns are, in essence, different languages or alternate linguistic systems for conceptualizing the mystery of the cosmos beyond human comprehension. Keeping alive the sense of wonder and awe while contemplating the totality (viewed as the Supreme Mystery) is, functionally the same as ever living in the presence of the Supreme Creator and ever engaged in 'righteous action'. This approach to Islam and all other religions promotes the good life far more effectively than believing that any one particular creed or dogma is a precondition of salvation. *(Chapter 7)*

7. The Vision of An Unknown Indian Muslim

My Journey To Interfaith Spirituality

"*In this book I have recounted important facets of the story of my inner intellectual and spiritual growth. It is the story of how, a relatively, dogmatic model of Islam developed into the paradigm that I now accept. In one sentence, my journey has taken me from an honest acceptance that Muslims alone will win salvation to an equally honest acceptance of the beauty and validity of interfaith spirituality.*"

Excerpts

What is not generally known or fully appreciated today is the heroic resistance of some Congressmen (especially Muslim Congressmen) to avert partition. When the All India Congress Committee met to ratify the earlier decision of the Working Committee, jointly taken by Sardar Patel, Nehru, and others who had consented to partition, Maulana Hifzur Rahman, one of the most clearheaded intellectuals among the *ulema*, voted against the resolution. The case of Badshah Khan is the most tragic of all those who strongly and honestly resisted the idea of partition, but failed to avert the day when there was '*darkness at noon*' on August fifteenth, 1947. The division of the Indian family must have been an inner torture for all Indian nationalists, but there were some silver linings of subjective satisfaction that their long struggle, appreciated by their own people, had borne some fruit. Gandhi became (very rightly) the father of independent India, Nehru its Prime Minister, Sardar the architect of its consolidation, Rajendra Babu the President of the Union, Azad the conscience keeper of the Party, Rajagopalachari, the wise old pilot of the '*Rath*' of modern India, and so on. However, Badshah Khan, the brave tragic hero, became a villain and a traitor to his own countrymen and was put into prison in his own land by those he had liberated from foreign yoke. A tragedy of this sheer poignant intensity is, perhaps, without parallel in world history.

Little did the architects of a sovereign homeland for Indian Muslims realize that slightly less than half of the total Muslim population of India would be excluded from the proposed 'homeland'. In other words, that almost half the Indian Muslims, even after the creation of the homeland, would still remain at 'the mercy of the Hindus' in independent India. Little did the ardent champions of Pakistan in Uttar Pradesh, Bihar and other areas of Hindu dominance realize that the logic of Pakistan, as a Muslim homeland, would precipitate the parallel idea that India was or ought to be a Hindu homeland. Little did the ardent dreamers of Pakistan belonging to and living in India realize that those who did not go or could not go would have to live under the shadow of a continuing suspicion of divided loyalties. Little did the young hearts and minds of the dreamers understand the logic of politics and human passions. (Chapter 10)

The root limitation of the RSS (*Rashtriya Swayamsevak Sangh*) philosophical vision and interpretation of Indian history is its 'ahistorical' and totally abstract notion of the *'Rashtra'*. From the RSS angle of vision, the *'Rashtra'* is some eternal and pure Aryan collective entity that is the special creation or manifestation of the *Absolute Brahman*, and is thus, something apart from the common rung of humanity. The RSS intellectuals and ideologues hold that the *'Rashtra'* is the pure historical microcosm of the *Brahmanical* macrocosm and *Bharat* is the territorial locus of this historical process. This stand implies that the language, thought, culture, customs, and institutions of the Aryans of *Bharat* during the golden period of its sacred history (before the scourge of foreign invasions and conquests) were all perfect. Muslims and Christians corrupted them and attempted to destroy the soul of *Bharat*. The Muslims and the British eventually conspired to vivisect the body of 'Mother India' before being compelled to vacate the unholy aggression against India down the centuries. The RSS vision goes on to claim that the soul of India is immortal and destined to conquer all opposition. It is for *Bharat* to teach and for all others to learn the infallible wisdom and truth eternally enshrined

Appendix: About Jamal Khwaja and His Works

in the Vedas. The wisdom of the Vedas is complete and needs no further growth through exposure to and dialogue with other thought systems, cultures and religions. In fact, all these are cultural or conceptual aberrations to be swept aside by Vedic wisdom of a resurrected *Bharat*, freshly emancipated from centuries of accursed foreign rule.

The above philosophical and historical vision and interpretation of Indian history is a species of a closed 'ahistorical' pattern of understanding the concrete growth of the Indian people in history. This type of conceptualization of history completely ignores the concrete processes of the growth of nations and the evolution of human ideas and ideals through continual interaction and dialogue. This approach totally brushes aside the mutual give and take between different wings of the human family in both peace and war. It also ignores the fact that the invader or a foreigner of yesterday becomes the son of the soil tomorrow, provided he settles down, works, dies and mingles with the air and dust of his chosen land, just like those who may have arrived earlier on the common soil. *(Chapter 11)*

I foresee that the leaderless Indian Muslims (presently confused, demoralized, in the grip of a besieged mentality) after two or three general elections will join the mainstream of secular Indian politics instead of functioning as vote banks for political managers, be they secular or religious. The bewildered Indian Muslims (including the erstwhile champions of a separate homeland for Muslims) are now realizing the tremendous folly they committed in 1947. They are fast coming round to the view that they should vote for the man who is honest and has the right agenda in view (irrespective of his religion or caste). I am pretty confident that well educated Muslims having a broad humanist outlook and vision will soon emerge on the Indian scene. The same applies to *Dalits* and OBC's (Other Backward Classes). Nitish Kumar of Bihar has already captured the imagination of the people of India, while Narendra Modi of Gujrat is more likely to take on the image of a boss who gets things done rather than of a statesman and democratic leader. It is my faith in the genius of India that the common man is soon going to see through the dirty tricks as well as honest deceptions of our establishment. Young India is developing the clarity, courage and conviction to embrace the politics of integrity without importing religion, region or caste into the game of power.

The persons who win the free and fair vote of the people must honestly view themselves as servant leaders of the great Indian family, rather than the leader of any particular group. The servant leader will be fully alive to the fact that the Indian family, in its own turn, is an arc (a very large one indeed) of the still larger circle of humanity. Accordingly, he will fully understand the limitations of the dictum, *'my country, right or wrong'* and will take the lead in applying the Gandhian-Nehruvian ethical approach to national and international politics. Today several Christians, upper caste Hindus and Muslims who are compassionate humanists stand rather marginalized in the corridors of caste centered Indian politics. This must go and the 'Obama moment' should arrive. Reinhold Niebuhr and Gandhi inspired Martin Luther King. Likewise, Gandhi inspired Nelson Mandela. When will Gandhi inspire another Indian after Jawaharlal? When will it be? Who will it be? Where in India will it be? All I know is that it will be. Much earlier, Rabindra Nath Tagore had described the land of his dreams in his prayer in the *Gitanjali* in these immortal lines:

> *Where the mind is without fear and the head is held high;*
> *Where knowledge is free;*
> *Where the world is not broken up into fragments by narrow domestic walls;*
> *Where words come out from the depth of truth;*
> *Where tireless living stretches its arms towards perfection;*
> *Where the clear stream of reason has not lost its way into the dreary desert sand of dead habit;*
> *Where the mind is led forward by thee into ever widening thought and action:*
> *Into that heaven of freedom, let my country awake.*

And I, as an Indian Muslim, dream of the day when every Indian Muslim heart will resonate with Tagore's prayer and will cease to bother whether the poet was a Muslim or a Hindu. (Chapter 12)

INDEX

A

Abbasid Caliphate, *81, 113*
Abduh, Muhammad, *116, 122, 182*
Abidin Zainul, *66, 147*
Abu Bakr, *4*
Afghani, Jamaluddin, *80, 116, 181*
Afghanistan, *74, 83, 121*
Aggressive nationalism, *63*
Agha Khan, *72*
Ahmad, Mirza Ghulam, *70, 171*
Ahmed, Syed Sir, *48, 49, 54, 62, 69-77, 79-85, 93, 110, 115-117, 122, 131, 174-175, 177-189*
Ajmal Khan, Hakim, *75*
Akbar, *66, 67, 114-115, 136, 138, 148, 205*
Al-Beruni, *66, 114, 173, 178*
Al-Fatiha, *10, 11, 109*
Ali,
- *Abdul Hasan, 117*
- *Abdullah Yusuf, 119*
- *Amir, 70, 177, 185*
- *Chiragh, 70*
- *Hyder, 67*
- *Mohammad, 73-75, 77, 129, 130*
- *Mumtaz, 116*
Aligarh Movement, *48, 73, 116, 174*
Aligarh Muslim University, *82, 122, 191, 192,*
Al-Kitab wal Sunnah, *24*
Allah, *2, 6, 8, 12-16, 20-24, 27, 89, 91-95, 99-102, 113-114, 125, 183*
Alvi, Z, *109*
Amini, Taqi, *122*
Ansari, M.A., *75*
Aquinas, Thomas, *54, 108*
Arabic, language, *4, 11-12, 14, 68, 85, 90, 124, 180*
Aryan cyclical concept, *45, 110*
Asiatic Society of Bengal, *68*
Ataturk, Kamal, *49, 117, 163*
Attar, Fariduddin, *108, 178*
Auliya, Nizamuddin, *65, 68*
Aurangzeb, *67, 83, 113, 115, 134, 136, 149*
Aurobindo, *55, 62, 109, 174*
Authentic,
- *faith, 1, 30, 33, 185*
- *Muslim, 1, 25, 30, 36, 41*
- *responses, 5, 36, 55*
- *signature, 30*
- *translation, 29*
- *will, 30*
Authenticity, *1, 29-37, 41-42, 122, 142, 178, 186-187, 193, 200*
Authority, *33-37, 40-42, 48, 50, 57, 97, 99, 103, 107, 108, 110, 123, 149, 178, 185, 192*
Azad, MaulanaAbulKalam, *55, 73-75, 78, 81-84 , 87, 108, 122, 127-128, 131, 163, 177-189*

B

Backbiting, evil inherent, *20, 21*
Bangla Desh, *82, 121, 175*
Barelvi, Saiyid Ahmad, *69*
Bedil, *68, 220*
Bernal, *50, 105*
Bharati Sanskriti, *64*

Index

Bilgrami, Qazi Mazharuddin, *90*
Bilgrami, Syed Husain, *72*
Biographical verses, *18*
Brahman, Buddham, *64, 112*
Brahmo Samaj, *69, 71-72, 131, 174*
Bronowski, J., *106*
Butler, Bishop, *103*
Butterfield, *50, 105*

C

Caliph, *4-5, 26, 40, 74, 90, 97, 113*
Calvin, *103, 104*
Chand, Tara *114, 120, 139, 165*
Chatterji, Bankim Chandra, *105*
Chaudhuri, Nirad, *104, 114*
China, *12, 111, 132, 181*
Chishti, Moinuddin, *65*
Christian,
- *existentialism, 108-109*
- *fundamentalism, 111*
- *Reformation, 49*

Christianity, *25, 50-51, 53, 56, 61, 69, 71, 103, 109, 117, 127-131, 141, 164, 169-170, 174, 178*
Communist society, *48, 55*
Conceptual idolatry, *89*
Copernicus, *51, 105*
Creative fidelity, *24, 38*
Cultural,
- *creativity, Muslim, 50*
- *history, 48, 53, 57, 80*

D

Darwin, Charles, *52, 106-107*
Darwinism, *52, 106*
Dayananda, *69*

Democracy, *29, 33, 49, 71-72, 98-99, 103, 122, 142-143, 169, 174, 181, 184*
Deoband, *71, 82, 105, 116, 120, 123*
Deoband, Muslim divines of, *72, 74, 79*
Descartes, *51, 54, 67, 105*
Dialectical Materialist, *33*
Dimensional growth, *38*
Deen-e-Ilahi, 114
Divine,
- *messages, 4*
- *presence, 1*
- *revelation, 1, 2, 26, 35, 37, 60, 98, 179, 181*
- *spark, 32-33, 42, 63, 107*
- *will, 51*

Donaldson, D.M., *123*

E

Egypt, *80, 97, 101, 116, 121-122, 137, 182*
Eliot, T.S., *113*
Engels, Friedrich, *49, 103*
European Renaissance, *48, 98*
Exhortative verses, *18-19*
Existential echo, *34, 38, 99*

F

Fanaticism, *32, 43, 121, 158*
Farid, Baba, *65*
Fazal, Abul, *115*
Fear of freedom, *41-42, 102*
Freud, *28, 31, 32*
Freedom of choice, *36*
Fromm, Eric, *41-42, 102, 135*
Functional genesis, *11*

Fyzee, A.A., *115*

G

Gabriel, *2, 4, 91, 128, 179*
Galileo, *105*
Gandhi, *55, 62, 69, 73-75, 109, 130-131, 161, 163, 168, 175, 191, 215, 218*
Ghaffar, Qazi, Abdul, *119*
Ghalib, *108, 115, 187*
Ghazali, *121-123, 178*
Ghori, Muhammad, *63, 134, 149*
Glaser, Nathan, *111*
Glorious Revolution, *84, 121, 170*
Goethe, *52, 106, 141, 165*

H

Habib, Mohammed, *113, 118, 139*
Halaku, *121, 138*
Hali, *116*
Hasan, Mahmudul, *74, 116*
Hegel, *52, 106, 143, 165*
Hinduism, *50, 55, 62, 64, 66, 104-105, 114, 115, 127, 131, 134, 137, 141, 145, 148, 164, 167-168, 170, 173, 175*
Hindu-Muslim Unity, *73, 129-130*
Hira, Cave of, *2*
Historical revolution, *52, 55-56*
Holy Spirit, *2, 179*
Howard, E.C., *102*
Human situation, *19, 37-38, 44, 47-48, 50, 56, 62, 66, 77-78, 81, 85, 111, 133, 135, 137-139, 142, 153, 185, 188, 194, 205, 212*
Hume, A.O., *72, 103*
Husain, Abid, *75*

Husain, Zakir, *75, 82*
Huxley, T.H., *106*

I

Ibadat, obligations to God, *20*
Ibn-Arabi, *121, 178*
'id', Freud's conception of, *31-32*
Iman bil ghaib, *10*
Iman, life blood of faith, *1, 14, 186-187*
Indian National Congress, *72-73, 181, 192*
Indian Nationalism, *74-76*
Indian society, *64-65, 67-68, 72, 74, 153, 162, 181*
Infallibility of the Qur'an, *26, 35-37, 40*
Interfaith, *143, 165, 175, 184, 186, 193, 203, 215*
Iqbal, Muhammad, *48, 54, 77-80, 84, 86-87, 102, 108, 110, 117-189*
Irfan, MaulanaAbul, *122*
Isht devata, *64, 168*
Islam,
- *approach to, 25, 65, 67, 73-74, 77-80, 82, 86, 115, 116, 117, 214*
- *commitment to, 78, 186*
- *Interpretations, 4, 9, 11-13, 22, 26-27, 37, 41, 48, 70, 80, 84, 97, 114, 131, 170, 180-183, 186*
- *mystery of, 1-4*
- *politics in, 67, 70, 73-75, 81, 147, 163, 167, 175, 177, 180-185, 188-189*
- *religion of, 65, 74-75, 103, 109*
- *structure of, 48*
Islamic,

Index

- *concept and values*, 26, 35, 40, 48, 65, 71, 85, 130, 192
- *existentialism*, 76-77, 108
- *faith*, 1, 4-5, 63, 74, 178-181, 187-188
- *fundamentalism*, 59, 62, 67, 72, 78-79, 111, 162-164, 170, 184
- *law (Shariah)*, 11, 25, 34-35, 47-50, 63, 70-71, 77, 80, 86, 102, 117, 122, 129, 147-148, 163, 170, 173, 180, 183-188
- *liberalism*, 59-62, 67, 70-79, 82-87, 109-110, 116-118, 121, 165, 174, 179, 183-184
- *reinterpretation*, 48, 170, 181
- *resurgence*, 56, 81, 108-110
- *tradition*, 1, 13, 35-41, 47, 69-73, 79, 82, 84-86, 90, 100, 102, 127-128, 141, 148, 163, 179-183, 186

Islamization, program of, 86, 182

J

Jairajpuri, Aslam, 75
James, William, 53, 96, 107
Jamia Millia, 74-75, 82
Janan, Mazhar Jane, 68
Jasper's, Karl, 44, 102
Jinnah, Muhammad Ali, 74-75, 78-81, 87, 110, 117, 162-163
Judaism, 71
Jung I, Salar, 70
Jung, Ali Yavar, 119
Jurisdiction of, 62, 77-78, 80, 183

K

Kabir, Humayun, 119, 128
Kamal, Mustafa, 74, 78
Kant, I., 49, 54, 68, 102-103

Kepler, 51, 105
Khan, Akbar Ali, 119
Khilafat, 73-78, 81, 116-117, 129
Khuda Bakhsh, 70, 192
Khusro, Amir, 66
Khwaja,
- *Abdul Majid,* 75, 82, 118
- *Kamaluddin,* 118
- *Mir Dard,* 68

Kidwai, Rafi Ahmad, 82
Kierkegaard, 54, 108

L

Lacey, Robert, 101
Latif, Abdul, 70, 118
Leibniz, 51, 67, 105
Liberalism, 59-62, 66, 68, 70-79, 82-87, 109-111, 116, 118, 121, 136, 165, 175, 177, 183, 184
Linguistic analysis, 53, 107-108, 192
Locke, John, 49, 54, 102, 121, 170
Lodi, Sikandar, 64, 112-113, 149

M

Madani, Husaini Ahmad, 116
Mahmud, Syed, 75, 82
Marx, 49, 52, 103, 106
Marxism, 52, 76, 108, 114, 132
Maulana Maududi, 78-80, 110, 122
Maxwell, 51, 105-106
Mecca, 2, 13-14, 17, 73, 90, 100, 129
Medina, 2, 14, 17, 73, 129
Marwan, Abdul Malik bin, 90
Mir, Mian, 67
Mir, Taqi Mir, 68, 109
Moore, G.E., 3, 53, 107
Morgan, Llyod, 107

Index

Mubarak, Shaikh, *115*
Mughisuddin, Qazi, *64, 147*
Muhammad, Prophet, *1-5, 11-12, 17, 20-21, 24, 26-27, 34-35, 37, 39-41, 60, 68, 70, 89-91, 97-98, 103, 105, 112, 123, 129, 131, 175, 179, 180, 204, 209-213*
Mujib, M., *75*
Mulk, Mohsinul, *116*
Mulk, Viqarul, *116*
Muqataat, **Mystic prefixes,** *9*
Muslim League, *72, 78-79, 119-120*

N

Nadwa, Islamic learning, *82, 105, 117-118, 120, 122*
Nanak, Guru, *65-66, 114*
Nehru, Jawaharlal, *55, 82, 109, 130, 163, 167, 174, 192*
Newton, *51, 67, 105, 165*
Nietzsche, existentialism, *54-55, 108, 184*
Nizami, K.A., *113*

O

Ontogenetic function, *17, 41, 96-97*
Ontogenetic power, *9, 11, 38*
Original manuscript, *29*
Otto, Rudolph, *56, 109*

P

Pakistan, *56, 59, 74, 78-82, 86, 101, 108-110, 117-122, 130-131, 151, 162-164, 167, 175, 177*
Paley, William, *103*
Pande, B.N., *113*

Permissiveness, *45, 47, 55*
Philosophical positivism, *51*
Pragmatism, emergence of, *53*
Pratap, Raja Mahendra, *116*
Prescriptive contents, *7*

Q

Qur'an, *1-28, 34-41, 60-61, 68, 70, 78-79, 84-85, 90-102, 105, 110, 123-131, 141-142, 179-183, 191, 193*
Qur'anic,
- *molecule, 37-41*
- *nucleus, 37*
- *principles, 39, 60-61, 93, 180*

Qarneyn, Dhul, *95-96*

R

Radhakrishnan, *55, 62, 109, 127*
Rahman, Hifzur, *116, 119*
Ranjit Singh, *69, 136*
Religion,
- *Function of, 44, 47-48, 50, 55-57, 59-61, 77*
- *Jurisdiction of, 62, 77-78, 80, 184*
- *Sociology of, 77*
- *degeneration of, 56*

Religious,
- *existentialism, 43, 47, 56-57, 76, 107, 109, 188*
- *faith, 6, 44-45, 54, 57, 60, 77, 89, 109, 141, 148*
- *law, adjustments, 80*
- *Liberalism, 60, 66, 68, 71, 73, 76, 77, 111, 136*
- *Rationalism, 43, 49, 77*
- *Regression, 73*
- *Revolution, 47, 56, 68*

Index

Resurrection, day of, *12*
Revelation, *1-5, 8, 10-11, 13-15, 17-18, 22-23, 26-29, 35, 37, 41, 60, 70, 89-91, 98, 105, 107, 127, 179-181, 210*
Roy, Rammohun, *62*
Rumi, Jalaluddin, *108, 178*
Russell, *48, 50, 53, 105, 107, 131*
Ryle, Gilbert, *107*

S

Saiyidain, K.G., *118*
Sami-ullah, *115*
Sarhandi, Shaikh Ahmad, *67, 121, 148*
Sarmad, *67*
Satan's handiwork, *21*
Sayeed, Basher Ahmad, *119*
Schleiermacher, *109*
Scientific revolution, *48, 52, 55-56, 140*
Secular humanist, *48*
Self-alienated ego, *42*
Shafiqur Rahman, *75*
Shah, Mohibullah, *67*
Shah, Quli Qutab, *66*
Sharda Act, *74*
Shareef, M.M., *119*
Shariah, *11, 25, 34-35, 47-50, 63, 70-71, 77, 80, 86, 102, 117, 122, 129, 147-148, 163, 170, 173, 180, 183-188*
Sherwani, Haroon Khan, *118*
Shibli, Zakaullah, *116*
Shikoh, Dara, *67, 115, 148*
Shirazi, Fathullah, *115*
Sidgwick, Henry, *121*
Smith, Adam, *51, 67, 105*

Social alienation, *43*
Spencer, Herbert, *52, 106*
Spiritual,
- arrogance, *32*
- power, *38, 96*
Sufi, *68, 81, 84, 112, 128, 130, 147, 163, 165, 180, 186, 187, 196, 210, 203, 226*
Sultans, *63-66, 112-114, 134-135, 146-148, 174, 205-206*
Surah, *4-5, 8-11, 18, 108, 125, 212*
Syed, Mahmud, *75, 82*

T

Tablighi Jamat, *81*
Tagore, Rabindranath, *55, 69, 109, 127, 143, 174, 218*
Tayabji, Badruddin, *70*
Thailand, *86*
Telos, *36-38*
Thanavi, Ashraf Ali, *123*
Theologians, Muslim, *48, 50, 64-68, 80, 106, 112-113, 122-124, 134, 187*
Tipu Sultan, *67-69*
Tonki, Syed Mohammad, *119*
Transcendental, 'I-Thou', *20, 24, 44, 60, 76, 97*
Tughlaq, Feroze, *112*
Turkey, *49, 73, 80, 85, 101, 102, 117, 181*
Turkish revolution, *78*
Tyrell, G.N.M., *90*

U

Umar, Caliph, *4, 6, 26, 40, 97-98, 102, 117*
Uthman, Caliph, *5*

V

Vacuity, *3*
Value system, *20, 33, 38, 49, 55, 62, 80, 93, 109, 134, 136, 139, 145, 148, 164, 168, 174, 178, 185, 188, 195, 197, 200, 201, 203*
Victorian liberalism, *70-72*
Vivekananda, *62, 69, 174*
Voltaire, *49, 68, 102*

W

Waliullah, Shah, *67-69, 71, 135, 178*
Western society, *47, 225*
Whitehead, A.N., *50, 105*
Wisdom, John, *107, 192*
Wittgenstein, *53, 107, 192*

Y

Yusuf, Hajjaj bin, *90*

Z

Zaidi, Basheer, *82, 119*
Zafar, Ali, *97*
Zainul Abidin, *66, 147*

More information about the author
and his various works can be found at the author's website

www.JamalKhwaja.com
Get FREE Downloads of Essays & Articles by the Author

Or, visit
www.AlhamdPublishers.com

www.ingramcontent.com/pod-product-compliance
Lightning Source LLC
Chambersburg PA
CBHW021143080526
44588CB00008B/196